GREAT RELIGIONS
of the World

NATIONAL
GEOGRAPHIC
SOCIETY

GREAT
RELIGIONS
of the World

A VOLUME IN THE STORY OF MAN LIBRARY
PREPARED BY
NATIONAL GEOGRAPHIC BOOK SERVICE
MERLE SEVERY, Chief
RUSSELL BOURNE, Associate Chief
PUBLISHED BY THE NATIONAL GEOGRAPHIC SOCIETY
MELVIN M. PAYNE, President
MELVILLE BELL GROSVENOR, Editor-in-Chief
GILBERT M. GROSVENOR, Editor
FRANC SHOR, Executive Editor for this series

Foreword by
KRISTER STENDAHL
Dean, and John Lord O'Brian Professor of Divinity, Harvard Divinity School; editor of the Harvard Theological Review

Chapters by
ROBERT McAFEE BROWN
Professor of Religion, Stanford University; former Professor of Systematic Theology, Union Theological Seminary; author of The Bible Speaks to You, The Significance of the Church, The Spirit of Protestantism, Observer in Rome, The Ecumenical Revolution; *editor of* The Layman's Theological Library

AMIYA CHAKRAVARTY
University Professor, State University College of New York; former professor at Calcutta University, Madras University, the Punjabi University, Boston University; author of The Saint at Work *(Gandhi),* The Indian Testimony; *editor of* A Tagore Reader

WING-TSIT CHAN
Professor Emeritus of Chinese Culture and Philosophy, Dartmouth College; Gillespie Professor of Philosophy, Chatham College; author of A Source Book in Chinese Philosophy, The Way of Lao Tzu, Religious Trends in Modern China; *co-editor of* The Great Asian Religions

W. D. DAVIES
George Washington Ivey Professor of Research in Christian Origins, Duke University; former professor at Princeton University, Columbia University, Union Theological Seminary; author of Invitation to the New Testament, The Setting of the Sermon on the Mount, Christian Origins and Judaism

HANS J. HILLERBRAND
Professor of History, the City University of New York; former Professor of Modern Church History, Duke University; author of The Reformation: A Narrative History, Ideas and Men in the Sixteenth Century, Christendom Divided; *editor of* Erasmus and His Age, The Protestant Reformation

EDWARD J. JURJI
Professor, History of Religions, Princeton Theological Seminary; author of Illumination in Islamic Mysticism, The Middle East: Its Religion and Culture, Religious Pluralism and World Community, The Phenomenology of Religion; *editor of* The Great Religions of the Modern World

JOSEPH M. KITAGAWA
Dean of Divinity School and Professor, History of Religions, University of Chicago; President, American Society for the Study of Religions; author of Religions of the East, Religion in Japanese History; *editor of* Modern Trends in World Religions; *co-editor of* The Great Asian Religions

HUSTON SMITH
Professor of Philosophy, Massachusetts Institute of Technology; author of The Religions of Man, The Purposes of Higher Education, The Search for America, Condemned to Meaning

OLIVER STATLER
Author of Japanese Inn, Shimoda Story, Modern Japanese Prints: An Art Reborn

HERBERT WEINER
Rabbi, Temple Israel, South Orange (N.J.); former administrator, Hebrew Union College, Jerusalem; author of 9½ Mystics: The Kabbala Today, The Wild Goats of Ein Gedi: A Journal of Religious Encounters in the Holy Land

JOHN P. WHALEN
Former Acting Rector, The Catholic University of America, and Associate Professor of Theology, School of Sacred Theology; managing editor of New Catholic Encyclopedia; *co-editor of* Theological Resources

ELIE WIESEL
Author of A Beggar in Jerusalem, Night, The Jews of Silence, One Generation After

MICHAEL KUH, TED SPIEGEL; *and*
JOHN J. PUTMAN, DAVID F. ROBINSON, *and*
THOMAS J. ABERCROMBIE
of the National Geographic Staff

Editorial Consultants

EMILY BINNS, *Assistant Professor of Religious Education, The Catholic University of America;*
GEORGES FLOROVSKY, *Professor Emeritus of Eastern Church History, Harvard Divinity School, and visiting Professor of Religion and Slavics, Princeton University;*
ABRAHAM J. HESCHEL, *Professor of Jewish Ethics and Mysticism, The Jewish Theological Seminary of America;*
ROBERT C. LESTER, *Professor of Philosophy, University of Colorado;* **JAMES C. LOGAN,** *Professor of Systematic Theology, Wesley Theological Seminary;*
MUHAMMAD ABDUL RAUF, *Director, The Islamic Center, Washington;* **W. A. VISSER 't HOOFT,** *former General Secretary, World Council of Churches, Geneva*

Staff for this Book

MERLE SEVERY
Editor

SEYMOUR L. FISHBEIN
Associate Editor

RUSSELL BOURNE
Project Editor

CHARLES O. HYMAN
Art Director

ANNE DIRKES KOBOR
Illustrations Editor

**ROSS BENNETT,
JULES B. BILLARD,
EDWARD LANOUETTE,
JOHN J. PUTMAN,
DAVID F. ROBINSON,
VERLA LEE SMITH**
Editor-Writers

WILHELM R. SAAKE
Production Manager

**JOHN R. METCALFE,
WILLIAM W. SMITH**
Engraving and Printing

**MARY SWAIN HOOVER,
DIANE S. MARTON,
PAMELA ROWE PEABODY,
SHIRLEY L. SCOTT,
HARRIET WATKINS**
Editorial Research

CONNIE BROWN, *Design*
KAREN EDWARDS, *Production*
BARBARA G. STEWART, *Illustrations*
MARYLINN TAYLOR, *Assistant*
JOHN D. GARST, VIRGINIA L. BAZA, *Maps*
WERNER JANNEY, *Style*
ANNE K. McCAIN, BRIT PETERSON, *Index*
W. E. ROSCHER, JACQUES OSTIER
European Representatives

Photographs by
THOMAS J. ABERCROMBIE,
GORDON W. GAHAN, MICHAEL KUH,
RAGHUBIR SINGH, TED SPIEGEL, *and others*

370 illustrations, 350 in full color, 6 maps

*Greeting dawn with a prayer, a Hindu pilgrim
cleanses sins at "the Gate of Heaven," at Puri
on the Bay of Bengal; photographed by National
Geographic's James P. Blair. In Jerusalem, altar of
three faiths (preceding pages), the Russian Orthodox
church of St. Mary Magdalena, on the Mount of Olives,
looks across the Valley of Kidron to Islam's Dome of
the Rock, gleaming above the site of Solomon's and
Herod's Temples; Ted Spiegel, Rapho Guillumette*

To see the earth as it truly is, small and blue

and beautiful in that eternal silence where it floats,

is to see ourselves as riders on the earth together,

brothers on that bright loveliness in the eternal cold —

brothers who know now they are truly brothers.

ARCHIBALD MacLEISH

FOREWORD

In pictures from space, we can see our world in one glance. By Telstar, we can circle it for instant communication. On a shrinking planet we are bound together in a way that hardly needs theological emphasis: humankind is one family. But if we are truly brothers, and if we feel safe in that knowledge, then we can afford to be different. Indeed, our differences become increasingly important lest our identity be swallowed up.

Given the global oneness, our pluralism is not a liability but an asset. God may be one, but religions are many. They center their power where the culture is most distinct—places like Banaras, Mecca, Rome, Jerusalem.

This book is an invitation to marvel at, learn from, and feel the strangeness and attraction of the great religions of the world. As I turn its pages, I recall a basic rule for any study of religion: We must learn to compare equal to equal. For centuries we have suffered under the habit of comparing our own religion in its ideal form with the actual manifestations of other religions. Sophisticated American tourists still are prone to judge other lands' religions on the basis of hasty impressions of popular piety—a safe way to maintain a sense of superiority, but an unsound method of comparing religions. In truth, the nature and structure of what we call religion differs dramatically from culture to culture.

Some Christians ask, "Is Buddhism, which doesn't recognize God, really a religion?" The very question seeks to impose our Western concepts of creation, being, and significance upon a drastically different theology that begins and ends with a deep, inspired understanding of "nothingness," nirvana.

We must also learn not to compare our own faith today with ancient religious practices. Religions develop and change. Marked differences exist between the religious views expressed by Abraham the patriarch and by Abraham Heschel the theologian, yet both are rightly called Jewish. Or between the evangelist John and Pope John XXIII, between Martin Luther and Martin Luther King. We must compare contemporary with contemporary.

In this book, vivid pictures and text help us see and feel how faith expresses itself in different cultures. Religion speaks to most believers through symbols and ritual acts—rich and suggestive, rarely precise. For it would be a small god indeed who could be caught in the net of precise philosophical language.

As we enter another man's world to study his faith, we should seek to see how it looks from within—and not treat his convictions as artifacts, his temple as a museum. I do not have the right to visit his holy of holies insulated by the rubber soles of my globetrotter shoes. His and ours are vital religions, with the power to cross all frontiers. Buddha will have his witnesses in the West as Christ will have his in the East.

This is a serious book. It could strengthen religious vitality. Let us open our hearts and minds to what each of these great religions has to offer.

KRISTER STENDAHL

CONTENTS

CLOCKWISE FROM UPPER LEFT: TED SPIEGEL,
RAPHO GUILLUMETTE; MICHAEL KUH; JOHN LAUNOIS,
BLACK STAR; BRIAN BRAKE, RAPHO GUILLUMETTE;
THOMAS J. ABERCROMBIE, NATIONAL GEOGRAPHIC STAFF

*Faces fervent and serene mirror
man's eternal quest for truth.
Emotion fierce as pain grips
a Jew praying in Jerusalem
(upper left); meditation enfolds
a Buddhist monk in Thailand
(upper right). In morning sun
a Moslem in Yemen chants
from the Koran (lower left)
and a Hindu woman begins
her day in India with ablution
and prayer (lower right).
Beneath the cross of Jesus
(above) a German bows his
head to commune with God.*

Huston Smith

"LET THERE BE LIGHT"

*T*he vacant lot beside our house in the Chinese town where my parents served as missionaries held a special fascination for me. On the day of a funeral, wealthy families would build on it an elaborate, full-scale paper house, fill it with paper furniture, paper effigies of servants, and piles of paper "ghost money." Sometimes there would even be a paper Ford motorcar on the street out front. Later, straw was heaped against the house. Then, as monks circled it, chanting and playing cymbals and flutes, a torch was applied. In an instant the flames destroyed the paper symbols, making the amenities they represented available to the departed in his new life.

Not far away stood a large building I called the "hotel for the dead," a mausoleum in which the bodies of the wealthier deceased lay for several years before burial. Here people came regularly to pay homage to their ancestors. How spectral that dark hall seemed, with its racks of tightly sealed wooden coffins. Some of its occupants may have arrived sooner than expected as a result of having purchased from Taoist alchemists elixirs to prolong life. These costly and secret brews could achieve the opposite of their intended effect, for they frequently contained dangerous doses of arsenic and mercury.

Folk superstitions mingled freely with Taoist precepts. The streets of our town curved for no apparent reason; I was told this was to thwart demons, who could move only in straight lines. The parents of my friends took their problems to wizened priests with musty books whose logic defied my young mind. They also consulted fortune-tellers who threw sticks to divine the future.

I liked, respected, even loved the people of my town, but I could not understand their beliefs. When I left China to attend college in the United States, they slipped from my mind. I was busy learning American ways. But as the years passed and I devoted my life to the study of philosophy and religion, I remembered my Chinese friends with new understanding. Their rituals and beliefs — however distant from our own — dealt, after all, with matters that concern us all: awe of death and what lies beyond, the need to cope with life's hazards, and the need to know who we are, why we are here, and where we are going.

Amid the dazzling variety of rituals and creeds that distinguish religions, these three themes recur again and again. Man feels the burden of time acutely; we grieve to see the flowers wilt and the leaves fall, for in our hearts we know that we too are transient and will soon disappear. "Time, like an ever-rolling stream, bears all its sons away" — when we hymn such lines we don't simply philosophize, we raise our voices in a human obsession.

It was recognition of the inevitability of death that led a pampered Indian prince to renounce his throne and become Buddha — the Enlightened One. Tradition says he was shielded from all unpleasantness until he accidentally glimpsed three men, one aged, another diseased, a third dead. "Where is the realm of life in which there is neither age nor death?" he cried. His quest for an answer led to the founding of one of the world's great religions.

Endlessly vulnerable to illness, accident, and heartbreak, man feels at times — in Job's telling image — as if even a moth could crush him. We smile today at Pueblo Indian rain dances; our granary is constant, we doubt the efficacy of

OVERLEAF: CHRISTIAN FAITH RISES AFRESH WITH THE EASTER SUN AT THE PARK OF THE RED ROCKS IN DENVER, COLORADO; LOWELL GEORGIA

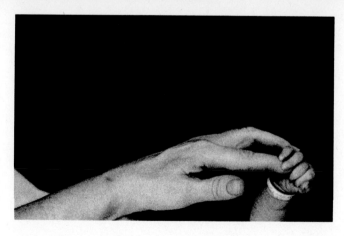

*What shaped this tiny ear?
Those fragile fingers? In the
wonder of an infant we seek
the force that sculptures each
unique form. And in the miracle
of birth—as life, born of love,
begins anew—we sense the
greater miracle of creation.*

And God said unto them, Be fruitful, and multiply

GENESIS 1:28

*A*s they chart a new course together, men
and women the world over acknowledge at
the helm a hand stronger than their own.
In the rites of Montana's Hutterites (above)
the groom takes his bride as "a gift from God."
A Venetian couple exchange vows in church
in front of a priest and witnesses, then run
through a symbolic harvest of rice (right).
Devotees of today's youth culture (top) may
spurn traditional rites, but at ceremony's end
lift voices in an old hymn, "Amazing Grace."

And the two shall become one

their rites. But what do we do when we are desperate? Fume impotently? Rage against the dying of the light? Orate about being masters of our fate? On the two occasions when my life was shattered by the anguish of personal crisis, I did as those Indians did—I prayed for help.

Prayer, of course, is more than petition; there are, besides, prayers of adoration and prayers of meditation. Yet prayer remains in part petition, wherein it is joined by sacrifice. Sacrifices seek results, but they are not simply payment to the gods for favors requested. The will to give is as deep in man as the will to receive —or the need to feel worthy. When the Brahmins of early India offered libations for rain, they were not just bargaining; they were demonstrating their control of the elements. Their rites and formulas kept the monsoons on schedule.

Without a sense of right direction, man feels disoriented and confused. His life lacks meaning and wholeness. Sin pulls against right direction and the wholeness

15

it affords, while atonement brings at-one-ment. One of the reasons for the phenomenal spread of Islam, youngest of the great religions, lies in its answers to these questions. The Koran tells man he is the servant of his creator, then delineates the path he should walk in detail sufficient to help in every human endeavor. The very word "Islam" connotes the "peace that comes when one's life is surrendered to God."

Man seems to have wrestled with these concerns as long as he has been on earth, for anthropologists have found no culture without religion. Primitive man sought his answers in ritual and myth. By participating in ritual actions which imitated the original creative acts of the gods—such as the "First Planting" or "First Mating"—he sought to partake of the timelessness of the gods themselves. Myths developed to embellish these rituals and enrich their meaning.

In time man developed the idea of a soul; he saw it as separable from, yet

dependent on, the body. This is why pharaohs built pyramids—to protect their bodies and the possessions on which their souls depended. Scholars see a connection between the idea of a soul and dreams—in which a person can "travel" without his body leaving the room.

Primitive man also shared with modern man the concept of "sacred space." Such a fragile thing, man's hold on the sacred! It can announce itself with power, only to withdraw in the face of all protestations. "Why hidest thou thy face from me?" sang the Psalmist. To induce the sacred to linger, man has built habitats for it, trying to make a home for it in this bent and broken world. Caves, grottoes, and mountains served originally. Then buildings arose, crude and simple at first, later gathering glory into a Chartres, a Lingaraja, an Isfahan. Each summons the sacred with symbols: spires that aspire to heaven, stained-glass windows and mosaics that stun the senses, the play of light and darkness that speaks eloquently

To every thing
there is a season....
A time to be born,
and a time to die

ECCLESIASTES 3:1, 2

Religions give hope even at life's end. Aran Islanders bury a friend's body, pray for his soul. A gravestone in Bennington, Vermont (below, center), attests belief in the hereafter: "What tho, in solemn silence I within this tomb awhile must lie, Yet hark the trumpets.... Arise ye just, to judgment come."

TOMAS SENNETT. LEFT: JAMES A. SUGAR

MAEKAWA MIKI, SHINTO PROPHETESS

of mystery to the human soul. Temples also served another purpose; they joined heaven to earth. The central, towering pyramid of the temple at Cambodia's Angkor Wat was conceived as a magic mountain that ran through both heaven and earth and—as cosmic axis—held the world stable and in place. Its design repeated heaven: Its moat mirrored the heavenly ocean, its surrounding rock wall the heavenly chain of mountains that held the ocean at bay. As pilgrims crossed the temple's rainbow bridge (rainbows often symbolized the arch from heaven to earth) they believed they were stepping into heaven on earth. They felt they were likely to find gods there too, for gods would feel at home in a place so closely patterned after their own abode.

To archaic man, sacred places were awesome; they were places of power. Facing the burning bush, Moses was enjoined, "Do not come near; put off your shoes from your feet, for the place on which you are standing is holy ground." Sacred places had also to be guarded against pollution. If a woman chanced into the "dream spot" where Australian aborigines gathered to commune with their ancestors, she was immediately killed. Women were denied the appropriate purification rites and were thus regarded as profane—that which must be left in front of *(pro)* the temple *(fane)*.

Sacred time complemented sacred space. We look on Mardi Gras and New Year's Eve as times to let ourselves go. But behind our guarded release, our lowered inhibitions, move shapes dark and old: the orgies through which primitive man re-enacted the primordial chaos that reigned before the gods established order and decorum. New Year's resolutions echo dimly man's determination to mirror this cosmic change by tidying up his own life.

*I*n the period from around 800 B.C. to A.D. 650—a brief span in the life of mankind—religion took a giant swing. Then arose the geniuses who molded the great faiths we follow today: the prophets of Israel, Zoroaster in Persia, Buddha and the Upanishadic seers in India, Confucius and Lao Tzu in China, Jesus in Palestine, and Mohammed in Arabia.

This phenomenal outpouring of religious creativity across the globe coincided with changes in man's secular history. Improved agricultural techniques had led to increased populations, expanded trade, and the accelerated growth of cities. As man found himself dealing more and more with strangers, the old tribal codes, the immemorial rituals and myths no longer sufficed. He had to learn how to behave toward people he did not know.

The faiths taught by these great leaders introduced ethical systems that helped man answer this need. Each one had its Golden Rule: Christianity's "Do unto others..."; Judaism's "What the Lord doth require of thee: Only to do justly, and to love mercy, and to walk humbly with thy God..."; Islam's man who gives his substance "to kinsmen, and orphans, the needy, the traveller, beggars..."; Buddhism's "boundless heart toward all beings"; Hinduism's highest yogi who judges pleasure or pain everywhere by "looking on his neighbor as himself"; Confucianism's "Do not do to others what you would not want others to do to you." These faiths offered common features: sacred scriptures, a systematized

*H*oly places focus men's faith. "Lord Fuji" dwarfs Buddhist monks; on its summit, some Japanese believe, dwell the shades of ancestors. Yearly thousands of pilgrims climb it to strengthen soul and body.

How excellent are thy designs,
O lord of eternity EGYPTIAN HYMN TO THE SUN

theology to relate these teachings to man's life, a priesthood or ministry, rituals and prayer techniques, symbols, and pilgrimages. But profound differences also marked these faiths, especially those of East and West. The stark monotheism of Judaism confronts the 33 million gods in the traditional Hindu pantheon; the Christian envisions a personal God who knows and loves each one of us, while the Buddhist may adhere to an impersonal god who remains aloof from human scramblings. The Western believer may cherish an individual soul that will endure for all eternity; the Easterner may see his soul merging ultimately with a single universal soul, as "the dewdrop slips into the shining Sea."

These fundamental differences in the way man looks at his God and at himself lie rooted in the origins of the various faiths. Hinduism, for instance, evolved slowly through the millenniums, absorbing the beliefs and practices of many peoples. The morning prayers to the sun voiced by millions in India today echo the nature worship brought there 40 centuries ago by Aryan invaders. No act of the gods has ever disturbed the immemorial rhythms of the cosmos. But in the development of Judaism, Christianity, and Islam, God intervenes personally

*M*onuments to once-cherished beliefs bestrew the paths where man has sought the meaning of his universe. Life was eternal, pharaohs divine, said ancient Egyptians whose muscle and crude tools reared Houses of Eternity (right) for their mummified monarchs. A tight-lipped titan of remote Easter Island (above) in the Pacific keeps scholars guessing at its role; perhaps it guarded the dead in some forgotten faith.

and dramatically in human events: Yahweh reaches down to rescue a band of Hebrew slaves from Pharaoh's bondage; God sends his only begotten son to earth to atone for the sins of mankind; Allah speaks through the angel Gabriel in a dark cave to bid Mohammed become his prophet.

Scripture develops these differences. In the Bible, God yearns over his children like a compassionate father: "It was I who taught Ephraim to walk, I took them [the children of Israel] up in my arms. . . ." How different the Supreme Being in the Hindu Rig Veda: "Who knows . . . whence [this world's creation] first came into being? He . . . in highest heaven . . . knows it, or perhaps he knows not."

These various outlooks have profoundly influenced the cultures and ways of life of the peoples who embraced them. The Book of Genesis gives Western man a buoyant optimism in his attempts to change the world. "In the beginning God created the heaven and the earth. . . . And, behold, it was very good." Man was commissioned to "have dominion . . . over every living thing." The Eastern outlook is voiced in the Chinese classic, *Tao Te Ching:* "Those who would take over the earth and shape it to their will, never, I notice, succeed."

PYRAMIDS AT GIZA, JONATHAN S. BLAIR. OPPOSITE: MONDADORI PRESS, PICTORIAL PARADE

Great Father....Send rain on the mountains

SHOSHONI INDIAN CHANT

Modern technology flourished in the West, while China strove to teach men how to live together in harmony and good order.

Sometimes these differences seem to defy rational understanding. Entering the world of Zen Buddhism, for instance, is like stepping through Alice's looking glass. One finds oneself in a topsy-turvy wonderland in which everything seems rather mad. It is a world of bewildering dialogues, riddles, paradoxes, and abrupt non sequiturs, all carried off in the most cheerful and urbane style. One Zen master, when asked the meaning of Zen, lifted a finger. That was his entire answer. Another kicked a ball. Still another slapped the inquirer's face.

Is such a religion playing jokes? Not at all. Zen carries further than other faiths the recognition of the limitations of words and logic. At their best, words provide only a distorted reflection of reality. The highest modes of experience, Zen claims, transcend the reach of words entirely.

On a simpler level, the differences between East and West can be observed in their rituals. The Westerner usually worships congregationally; the Easterner traditionally goes to his temple alone or with his family. The Westerner closes his eyes in prayer to shut out external distractions; some Japanese, fearing internal as well as external distractions, meditate with eyes half-closed.

*I*n the centuries since their founding, the great religions have shaped empires and nations. The fervor of Islam inspired the Arab conquerors to win a realm stretching from Spain to India—a realm which transmitted classical learning during Europe's Dark Ages and displayed a tolerance not always matched by other faiths. The thrust of Christendom sent Crusaders for two centuries to battle in the Holy Land and molded chivalric codes of warfare.

Religion permeates the story of our own nation: Its impulse sent Puritans to settle in Massachusetts, Quakers to Pennsylvania, Catholics to Maryland. "One Nation under God" declares the Pledge of Allegiance; our President takes his oath of office with a hand on the Bible; "In God We Trust" announce the coins in our pockets. Religion has inspired the greatest art: the Parthenon of Greece, the cathedrals of Europe, Dante's *Divine Comedy*, Michelangelo's Sistine Chapel ceiling; the paintings of Raphael, El Greco, Dürer, Rembrandt; the music of Palestrina, Bach, Beethoven, Handel.

More importantly, religion has answered affirmatively the Biblical question, "Am I my brother's keeper?" We see the response in hospitals, orphanages, schools, and social service organizations around the world. We see the same response in the lives of men like Mahatma Gandhi, Albert Schweitzer, Pope John XXIII, and countless others whose names are not matters of history.

Of course the record of the great religions has not been one of blessings only: Institutions are guided by men, so we see wars, persecution, and intolerance. But the great faiths have always stood ready to help man in his common quest to reach out beyond the confines of human experience with all its imperfections and limitations, to seek the fearful glory that contrasts with the banality and fragmentation that mark so much of life. Were we to observe only the seekers we might be tempted to side with the skeptics who see religion as wishful thinking,

*B*ells ajingle, a Pueblo honors the lordly eagle. In prayer to the Great Father or to his couriers the birds, Indians enlisted the divine in the battle for survival—as have men through the ages.

ADAM WOOLFITT

Those who have riches build temples for Thee

12TH-CENTURY HINDU PSALM

*A*ngkor Wat, famed "City Temple" of Cambodia, *lifted its lotus-bud towers in the 12th century. Khmers, blending Buddhist and Hindu themes, built the wonder in a single generation; 18,000 scenes in a sculptured frieze nearly half a mile long mirror their life and faith. Here a Buddhist priest washes a robe at the shrine reclaimed only a century ago from the jungles of Southeast Asia.*

In outpourings of art, each age creates its shrines. Oldest known are caves of France and Spain, painted by hunters 30,000 years ago.

ERNST HAAS. RIGHT: THOMAS J. ABERCROMBIE, NATIONAL GEOGRAPHIC STAFF

My son, attend
unto my wisdom,
and bow thine ear
to my understanding

PROVERBS 5:1

*In holy writ, men of faith inscribed
a vision of their God and themselves and
recorded the precepts that guided their lives.
An American father (above) shares a Bible
story with his children; an Afghan (upper)
instructs his son in the Koran; a Thai
monk (right) teaches Buddha's way to a
tribesman's child. So God's word and man's
wisdom endure from generation to generation.*

26

an effort to compensate for real lacks through imagined substitutes, "pie in the sky by and by." But some men and women have not only groped for the light; they have found it. I think of Isaiah glimpsing the Lord "high and lifted up"; the universe exploding in a bouquet of flowers for Buddha beneath the bo tree; John reporting, "I . . . was in the isle that is called Patmos. . . . I was in the Spirit on the Lord's day. . . ." For St. Augustine it was the voice of a child saying, "Take up and read"; for St. Francis a voice from a crucifix. It is as if these saints had wider windows to see through. The reports they flash back to us affirm our faith. If the doors of our perception were cleansed of self-centeredness and opened to the whole, we would be both astonished and pleased.

Today the great religions stand in a new human era—the age of technology. More and more, science dominates areas once reserved for priests: The psychiatrist replaces the minister for the troubled soul, the economist replaces the bishop as adviser to the head of state. The rural and small-town church, with its stability and familiarity, yields its members to the anonymity of great urban centers. Jet planes and television shrink our world to a "global village," while the hydrogen bomb threatens to destroy God's own creation.

In times like these, today's prophets insist, the Golden Rule is not enough. Now that society as well as nature seems subject to human control, we are responsible for "cruelty systems"—war, prejudice, unfair tax laws—that may have found their way into our political and social order. Others attack aspects

MICHAEL KUH. OPPOSITE, LEFT: WILLIAM J. GAGE; RIGHT: EVE ARNOLD, MAGNUM

Love thy neighbour as thyself

of religions as outmoded: the shepherd imagery of the Bible, the dietary laws of Hinduism, the sharp prohibitions surrounding the Orthodox Jewish Sabbath.

This discontent flourishes not just in the West: One can see it among the young people in India, Burma, Egypt, and in Japan—where the rise of 250 new sects since World War II reveals both a disaffection with the old faiths and a yearning for something to replace them.

Many ancient religions have died, but the great religions described in this book have endured—often by adapting themselves to changed circumstances. Buddhism was attacked as a religion for monks only; in time the Mahayana

Circle of caring joins Jewish youngsters in Seattle's Temple de Hirsch Sinai. Every great faith proclaim

school arose to offer salvation and greater participation to laymen. In the Second Vatican Council we see the Roman Catholic church struggling to meet modern needs without injuring basic creed or structure. The struggle is as old as religion: conservatives seeking to keep hard-won values at hand, radical prophets trying to break through what they see as encrusted tradition.

From time to time we hear a call for a single world religion; after all, we are told, are not all religions the same in all important aspects; do they not all lead ultimately to the same place, like so many rivers pouring into the sea? It is an appealing doctrine, and at least one faith, Baha'i, attempts to institutionalize it.

a Golden Rule, an invitation to brotherhood among strangers yearning to share their planet in peace.

Praise him, all creatures here below

MORNING AND EVENING HYMN

Oft-sung stanzas roll in majestic cadence of a Sunday morn at Hillcrest Heights, Maryland (opposite). In mighty temples or in the whitewashed simplicity of a church at Manchester, Vermont (left); in countless tongues and myriad rituals; in throngs or in solitude man renews his ancient dialogue with the infinite. "Father of all!" hymned the poet Alexander Pope, "in every age, in every clime adored, by saint, by savage, and by sage, Jehovah, Jove, or Lord!"

JOHN LAUNOIS, BLACK STAR. OPPOSITE: GORDON W. GAHAN

But we have seen profound differences that may be impossible to reconcile. Amalgamation holds its own perils. Jawaharlal Nehru, who absorbed so much Western culture, warned against the man who becomes "a queer mixture of East and West, out of place everywhere, at home nowhere." Among my richest memories are scenes of men at worship in their own special way:

Yemenite Jews in a Jerusalem synagogue, dark-skinned men, shoeless, sitting cross-legged and wrapped in the prayer shawls their ancestors wore in the desert, swaying backward and forward as they recited the Torah.

Dai Jo and Lai San, Zen monks, sitting cross-legged and immovable from 3 a.m. to 11 p.m. as they plumbed the Buddha-nature at the center of their beings.

Coptic Christians who, when we took off from Cairo bound for Holy Week observances in Jerusalem, emitted such an eerie and spine-tingling cry of fervor that I wondered if our plane was crashing.

What a strange and wondrous fellowship the God-seekers of every clime, how rich the chorus of their voices. While remaining true to our own faith, we should listen to these other voices, for by listening we may come to understand our fellowman, and understanding leads to love — a concept hallowed by every faith.

There is another gain in exploring man's religions. Every rain dance incarnates some yearning in our own hearts; each altar is laid, each statue shaped by hopes and fears that crouch in some unexplored corner of our own psyches. In this human sense the world's religions, however distant in miles or creed, are all "closer than breathing, nearer than hands and feet." As they lead the mind's eye outward they bend the soul's eye — the Third Eye as Tibetans call it — inward. In seeking to understand man's religions, we explore not only our world but our deepest selves.

HINDUISM

Richly carved temple at Konarak, India, a vision in stone of the sun god Surya's chariot, exalts every "desire of loveliness"; James P. Blair, National Geographic photographer

QUEST FOR THE UNIVERSAL ONE

Amiya Chakravarty

*T*hey came in waves, a pastoral people of Aryan stock from a homeland near
the Caspian Sea. From about 1500 B.C. they threaded the passes of the
Hindu Kush, spreading onto the vast wedge of earth fenced by the seas and
massive walls of ice and rock. As they wandered their new domain, mingling
their own and native beliefs, they hymned the sun which gave them primal fire
and light, praised the breath of life-giving air, wondered at blue space, greeted
the earth under their feet and the waters of life. Their sacred lore, or Vedas,
extolled the gifts of nature as gods, yet asked, "To which god shall we dedicate
our offerings?" The many could not exist without the One.

"I have seen him . . . beyond the darkness, the sun-colored," exclaimed a Vedic
bard. It was a revelation of radiance which reached the source:

> *In the beginning there was neither naught nor aught:*
> *Then there was neither sky nor atmosphere above . . .*
> *Then was there neither day, nor night, nor light, nor darkness,*
> *Only the Existent One breathed calmly, self-contained.*

Thus, from India's ancient Sanskrit chants emerged the central idea of Hinduism: the concept of Brahman, the Supreme Being, the God above all gods, the
source of universal life. The worshiper might seek a particular boon from any of
a multitude of deities; each god in the crowded pantheon was but an aspect
of all-embracing "thousand-headed" Brahman. "Truth is One," the Vedas
proclaimed. "They call him by different names."

34

With no founder or uniform dogma, what generally is regarded as man's oldest living religion started itself; its very name Hinduism derives not from doctrine but geography—the Sanskrit word *Sindhu* or *Indus*, ocean or river. Over four millenniums new cults and philosophies have enriched it, waves of reform have challenged it. Other religions have brought their witness to India—and strengthened rather than weakened this tolerant, marvelously diverse faith. Today it is shared by some 450 million people, most of them in India and nearby lands, some dwelling on Pacific islands, in Africa, and in the New World.

The Vedas themselves are filled with richness and variety—magic and melody, myth, legend, parable, tenderness, and humor. We find a villager, bereaved by the death of a friend, imploring Mother Earth to enfold her son in her mantle of gentle soil; we see feasting and less-than-divine drunkenness on Soma, plant juice worshiped as a god. Preserved orally for centuries, the Vedas were committed to writing along with ritual texts, commentaries, and the philosophical discourses called the Upanishads to form the sacred scriptures of Hinduism.

From the scriptures and the inspiration of later seers the Hindu learns that
all creatures are in a process of spiritual evolution extending through limitless
cycles of time. A man's lifetime is like a bead on a necklace whose other beads
represent past and future lifetimes. Each soul, or *atman*, strives through succes-
sive rebirths to ascend the scale of merit until—after a life of rectitude, self-
control, nonviolence, charity, reverence for all living creatures, and devotion to
ritual—it wins liberation from worldly existence to achieve union with Brahman.
The path toward spiritual ascent is the way of *dharma*; a man must live righteously
according to his station in life, or caste, and he must be faithful to his inner self.
Just as it is the dharma of wind and tide, water and light to maintain their inherent nature, so it is the dharma of man to be human.

Hindu religion reached its height in the Upanishads, a source of strength and
inspiration for the faithful for some 3,000 years. The word means "to sit down
near"—referring to the time when the sages no longer wandered but gathered
their pupils at their feet to share a life of work and meditation in religious communities, or *ashrams*. With profound allegory, ethical precept, and a lofty moral
vision, the Upanishads extend an invitation to all to share in the glory and
adventure of man's journey.

According to Hindu scriptures, a normal, harmonious life consists of four
stages. In youth the initiate, assuming full religious duties as he receives the
"sacred thread," begins a course of study and service in an ashram, guided by a
guru, or spiritual preceptor. Next come the many years of marriage and duty
to family and community. When a Hindu's spiritual growth reaches the third
stage, he detaches himself from materialistic and family obligations to direct his
concern to the wider humanity. In the final phase he prepares himself for the
passage to the unknown reality beyond the borders of this life.

BRONZE SHIVA, 12TH–13TH CENTURIES; NELSON GALLERY-ATKINS MUSEUM, KANSAS CITY. OPPOSITE: RAGHUBIR SINGH

What lies beyond depends upon *karma*, the chain that binds action and the fruits of action. A life well lived brings rewards in the next incarnation. Being born of low degree, to suffering, poverty, and discrimination, supposedly is due to sins committed in previous lives. Hindu folklore abounds in legends about the workings of karma. In one group of morality tales, for example, a foolish man is reborn as a monkey, a cunning one as a jackal, a greedy one as a crow. A tribal myth of Orissa tells of a woman burning with jealousy who is reborn as a chili plant, destined to burn all its life. Conversely, an animal may rise to human status, in stages or all at once if it has done the right deeds, particularly to a personage of high caste.

Yet there is another aspect of karma, easier to understand. Within a single lifetime, what one does today shapes his tomorrow; we reap what we sow. For Hinduism, karma makes clear the logic of morality.

*B*y popular account the Hindu pantheon numbers some 33 million gods. Overarching all, and interpenetrating all existence, is Brahman. Next in importance comes the trinity of Brahma the creator, Vishnu the preserver, and Shiva the destroyer. Brahma is held above popular rites, but Vishnu and

*K*eeping the cadence of the cosmos,
Shiva in the form of the dancing god
Nataraja whirls with the powers
that make him worshiped by millions.
As he tramples the dwarf of sin,
his upper hands bear the flame of
destruction and the throbbing drum
of creation. Thus he embraces death
and renewal, spinning out the endless
cycle of existence. Compassion marks
his rounds: An unencumbered hand,
fingers upraised, says "Fear not,"
while another points to the lifted foot,
a symbolic offer of bliss to believers.

Religion and art, music and drama
merge inseparably in Hindu life,
making vivid the themes of the sacred
writings and the epics of India's
antiquity. By the holy Ganges a
priest (right) recites daily from the
Mahabharata, *a treasured epic some*
eight times longer than the Iliad *and*
Odyssey *combined. Its 90,000 stanzas*
record war, greed, and cunning—
but also sublime and timeless wisdom:
"This is the sum of all . . . righteousness—
In causing pleasure or in giving pain,
In doing good or injury to others . . .
A man obtains a proper rule of action
By looking at his neighbor as himself."

*H*onoring a deadly cobra, a woman of Madras tenders it rice and coconut.
Mystical potency of this "good snake" of Hindu folklore engenders fertility;
its hood, spreading like an umbrella, shielded heroes of ancient legend.

HARRY MILLER

Shiva are venerated in hundreds of guises, colored with legend and folk custom.
Vishnu, beloved protector of the world, has ten chief *avatars,* or forms in which
he descends to earth. Among them are Rama and Krishna, heroes of India's
two great epics, the *Ramayana* and the *Mahabharata.* Other avatars include the
historical Buddha and Kalkin, a savior yet to come. The devotee usually chooses
one aspect of the deity, represented by an image kept in the home.

Shiva, god of destruction, "haunter of the Burning-ground," is also the restor-
er of life and lord of the cosmic dance of creation. As the creation principle he is
widely worshiped in the form of *lingam,* the stylized phallus; fresh flowers, sacred
water, fruit, and rice are profusely poured on the symbolic stone pillars. In
popular imagination Shiva often rides about the countryside on his white bull
Nandi, behaving riotously. The destroyer can be loving—he drinks the full cup
of man's sins to save him, hence Shiva's throat is blue. Again, he has the third
eye of higher consciousness or wisdom, and his forehead shines with divine light.
His most persistent aspect, perhaps, finds him locked in trance on the high, white
Himalayas. In spring his frozen locks melt, freeing the goddess Ganges to
descend with her purifying waters.

Shiva's consort commands a large sect of her own. As Parvati, goddess of the
mountain, she awakens Shiva from his trance—she brings his power to life, for
in her nature resides the feminine creative spark, Shakti. At a great fall festival
in West Bengal she is honored as Durga, the divine mother who brings cool
breezes and flowers, reunites families, and destroys evil. In yet another role, that
of the goddess Kali, she exults in animal sacrifice, still a practice in Bengal but
uncommon in other parts of India today.

*T*he Vedas tell us that ancient Indian society was divided into *varnas,* or
colors, to distinguish the light-skinned Aryan conquerors from the darker
Dravidian people they dominated. Later the term came to stand for a hierarchical grouping based on vocation: Brahmins were the priests and scholars;
Kshatriyas, the rulers and soldiers; Vaishyas, the merchants and farmers; Sudras,
the peasants and servants. This developed—without basis in Hindu scripture
and in the face of ancient ideals of freedom and openness—into the hereditary
caste system that has stirred reformers from Buddha to Gandhi and remains a
vexing problem in India today.

The four basic groups have evolved into more than 3,000 subcastes. Except
for unusual cases, caste is immutably fixed at birth; it limits a Hindu's choice of
occupation, marriage partner, dress, eating habits, religious practice, and his
freedom to move about. He regards those in castes below him as ritually impure.
In some matters the lower castes have more freedom; a Sudra may eat meat and
his widow may remarry—options forbidden to orthodox Brahmins.

A Brahmin, however thirsty, may not accept a drink of water from a Sudra. He
cannot even dine with his own son until after the child is invested with the sacred
thread; not yet bound by caste rules, the boy might contact impurity, thus taint
his father. (Kshatriyas and Vaishyas are also privileged to receive the sacred
thread of the "twice-born.") In southern India where caste customs remain

*Environmental crisis calls forth
Krishna, hero of the pantheon.
As Vishnu incarnate, man's helpmate,
he conquers Kaliya, hydra-headed king
of serpent spirits whose venom has
made the River Yamuna undrinkable.
In this painting of the famed Rajput
School of northwestern India,
cowherds and milkmaids on the banks
hail their idol while Kaliya's serpent
nymphs plead for pity. Banishment,
not death, Krishna decrees.*

*A god for all seasons, Krishna
is painted, sung, and adored for
his pranks as well as his prowess.
In the branches of a kadamba tree
he once hid with the saris of
16,000 girls he caught bathing.
Here he waited until they emerged,
clad only in blushes.*

*As a youthful cowherd he won
renown in legend as the lover
of Radha and her sister milkmaids.
Krishna and Radha's love, though
sensuous, is also symbolic;
the soft, sweet call of his flute
invites each man or maid to sublimate
human passion into a love divine.*

*As charioteer for the warrior chief
Arjuna in the beautiful poem*
Bhagavad-Gita, *or* Lord's Song,
*Krishna teaches not only an "ethic
for war" but also the way of* bhakti,
*devotional love, leading—with
knowledge and righteous action—
to a harmonious spiritual life.
To alienated man "lost in the maze
of* maya [illusion of reality] *until
the heart is human no longer," the
benevolent god offers a loving refuge.*

43

A mid petals strewn by helicopter Jain pilgrims in Mysore worship at the feet of St. Gomatesvara. Their sec...

strong, mere proximity of lower-caste men is considered defiling. Even into modern times a Tiyan—the caste of toddy tappers—could come no closer to a Brahmin than 36 paces; a peasant of Pulayan rank kept at least 96 paces away.

The worst canker of caste is untouchability, still a social force though illegal today. The untouchables are the "outcastes," the millions excluded from the recognized groups and largely ignored. From of old they were the scavengers, the cleaners of latrines, the handlers of animal carcasses in the making of leather. Considered polluted, they could not use the same wells as caste Hindus, walk the same paths, or frequent the schools and temples.

Over the centuries most members of the elite strata closed their eyes to the problem, citing karma. A good untouchable could look forward to a better life next time. Yet in the eyes of a true sage a human being is not a caste man born and bound; it is the inner quality that counts. Saints and moral leaders in every age have challenged untouchability. In the sixth century B.C. protests within Hinduism—partly against exploitation by the priestly class—resulted in the founding of the monastic religions of Jainism, with its distinctive stress on nonviolence and

57-FOOT STONE COLOSSUS AT THE JAINIST CENTER OF SRAVANA BELGOLA, NEAR HASSAN; RAGHUBIR SINGH

n offshoot of Hinduism, extols self-denial, forbids tilling the soil lest it harm even the tiniest of living things.

asceticism, and of Buddhism with its offer of enlightenment to men of all castes. The teachings of Islam, Sikhism, Christianity, and other minority faiths in India also prompted Hindus to loosen the shackles of caste.

The momentum swept on into the modern era. In the 18th and 19th centuries reformers like Rammohun Roy, who helped put an end to suttee, the immolation of widows on their husbands' funeral pyres, and the saintly Ramakrishna advanced the renaissance of true Hinduism. The missionary society founded by Vivekananda, a disciple of Ramakrishna, insisted that the dharma of man — to be human — was more important than hierarchy, and admitted all castes.

Rabindranath Tagore, world-renowned poet and winner of a Nobel prize in 1913, wrote of the untouchables: "Shunned at the temple-gates by the pious; the outcastes, uninitiates, seek their God beyond the artificial, inwardly, in midnight skies, in forest flowers, in love and separation. . . . I have prayed: Deliver us, O man of men, from the creed which flaunts exclusion. . . ."

And then came Gandhi, revered by his people as Mahatma, the "Great-souled." "To see the universal and all-pervading Spirit of Truth face to face one must

*H*oly words of the Granth, the scriptures of the Sikhs, guide a seeker in the
Golden Temple. Glowing domes of the shrine rise on an isle in the Amrit Saras,
or Pool of Immortality, from which the Sikh center of Amritsar takes its name.
JAMES P. BLAIR, NATIONAL GEOGRAPHIC PHOTOGRAPHER

be able to love the meanest of creation as oneself," he preached, transforming
the Hindu ideal of *ahimsa*, nonviolence to living beings, into a political and social
creed. When he recited the sacred texts and denounced unethical customs,
Hindus by the thousands embraced his message. For him the outcaste millions
were *harijans*, children of God. Thanks to his relentless efforts—fasts, vigils,
marches, boycotts—India's constitution banned untouchability. Jobs, college
grants, and seats in parliament are now allotted to the harijans. Education,
meanwhile, is eroding the myth of caste.

Yet the age-old rankings remain the criterion of privilege and religious practice, especially in the countryside. Many a village Brahmin who defers to the economic power of a merchant or farmer still strives to maintain the ritual purity
prescribed by custom. His days are filled
with prayers and devotion to his deities.

In the morning he goes to a stream,
for an orthodox Hindu must touch the
purifying waters before he worships. He
sits facing east and sprinkles water on
his head. After bathing, he sprinkles
more water on the ground to make it
a "holy seat," then offers food, flowers,
and sandalwood paste to the sun god.
He celebrates the glory of the deity with
a *mantra*, a holy text which is the embodiment of the god in sound:

> Om. bhur bhuvah svah
> tat savitur varenyam bhargo
>   devasya dhimahi
> dhiyo yo nah prachodayat. Om.

This Vedic prayer, called Gayatri—
The Savior of the Singer—invokes the
enlightening power of the god and is
imparted to the initiate during the sacred thread ceremony; worshipers chant

SIKHS BLEND HINDU AND MOSLEM BELIEFS

*Amid the religious upheavals of 15th-century
India the Hindu guru Nanak preached reform.
Upon the Hindu ethical system and world view,
with its doctrine of reincarnation and karma,
he grafted Islam's monotheism, disavowing
image worship and caste strictures.*

*Under succeeding gurus Nanak's Sikhs,
or disciples, built temples and compiled the
Granth from writings of Sikh, Moslem, and
Hindu holy men. In 1699 guru Gobind Singh
decreed that the Granth would henceforth serve
as Sikhism's symbolic guru. He also created
the Khalsa (pure), a militant brotherhood
marked by the five k's:* kes, *long hair;* kangha,
comb; kacha, *short pants;* kara, *iron bracelet;*
kirpan, *sword. Today these hardy folk of
the Punjab, famed for valor and numbering
about nine million, proudly take the surname*
Singh (lion), *though not all Singhs are Sikhs.*

it many times a day. The syllable *om* signifies the rounded wholeness of Brahman.

Returning home, the Brahmin makes his morning *puja*, or act of worship, to
his favored deity. A devotee of Vishnu "awakens" a bronze or stone image of
the deity, washes and dresses it, offers flowers and non-animal food—Vishnu
abhors the sacrifice of a living creature. The family performs puja before
every meal, sanctifying the food. Details of the ritual vary if the Brahmin family
follows the god Shiva. A household that has the means may employ a priest to
officiate at domestic worship.

Before a midday puja the typical Brahmin sees to his sons' course of study
with their guru—indispensable for true guidance, as the Upanishads make clear:
"He who knows has a teacher." Late in the day the believer may visit a temple,

worshiping with others or meditating alone in a corner. He may place some offerings on an altar, touch his forehead to the floor as a sign of respect, then slowly depart, walking backward so as not to offend the temple's reigning deity.

Magnificent temple centers lure pilgrims by the thousands across the length and breadth of India. In the far ends of the land stand the famous four: Badrinath in the Himalayas where Shiva reigns; Dwarka in the west, known as Krishna's kingdom; Jagannath on the eastern shore, dedicated to Vishnu; Rameswaram in the south, associated with Rama. Others of renown include the Golden Temple in Banaras and Srirangam in southern Madras, one of the largest temples in the world. Spread over many acres, the great temples with their tanks for ritual bathing, shrines, halls—even bazaars—are cities in themselves, aswirl with activity in every season.

Here gather *sadhus*, or holy men, attached to monastic orders or simply wanderers engrossed in meditation, drifting from one holy site to the next. Here cluster artists and artisans: weavers, painters, sculptors in wood and stone. Ancient libraries and art collections attract scholars; minstrels and poets seek patronage among the pilgrims. Vendors offer flowers, sandalwood, souvenirs.

Villagers whose local shrines may consist of mud huts stand in awe at the majestic architecture, even at ruins like the temple at Konarak, designed in the 13th century as a colossal 12-wheeled chariot for the sun god (page 32). The pageantry of holidays brings excitement to fever pitch; at the famous Car Festival of Jagannath in Puri, worshipers have been known to lie in the path of a huge chariot bearing a deity's image and let themselves be crushed to death. From Jagannath—an avatar of Vishnu—comes the word "juggernaut."

Temple art like temple life has a panoramic quality. Upon outer walls of the more ornately carved shrines the pilgrim sees reliefs representing the gamut of everyday experience—work in the fields, domestic chores, child-rearing. And, since a candid and unobsessed acceptance of every aspect of human life is part of Hindu tradition, explicit sex motifs have their place. Joy is a fundamental element of creation, say the Vedas.

Inside the temple enclosure, walls depict only the lives of saints, and religious emblems and events. Bare walls surround the third, inmost precinct of the prayer hall where the image of the temple deity is kept.

The devotee finds himself in cool darkness as he penetrates the heart of the temple, his eyes adjusting slowly to the faint illumination at the shrine. In a primal stillness where "only the Existent-One breathes calmly, self-contained," the pilgrim prays silently and meditates. Perhaps oblivious even of the image before him, his consciousness merges with the triune wholeness of Brahma, Vishnu, and Shiva—with Brahman.

Some scholars find in the plan of a great temple a metaphor for the Hindu's spiritual quest through the many-layered distractions of life. Curious, intrigued, delighted, sated—at last he seeks to separate himself from the passing show. From the illusions of the world outside he turns inward, to arrive finally at the hidden balance of truth in the heart. Man, fully human, is near the divine.

John J. Putman

Down the Teeming Ganges, Holy River of India

I drove north into the Himalayan foothills, past crying parrots and troops of pink- and black-faced monkeys that scolded as they scampered from the road. Terraced rice fields spilled down the mountainsides; amid them rose thin blue ribbons of smoke from village cookfires.

The road followed the gorge, twisting, climbing. Rarely did the sun burn through the blanket of mist to reveal the river, a serpent of glittering silver rushing by rock walls and sandbars, questing for the sea. Once, through a cleft in the foothills, I saw the Himalayan peaks, pyramids of ice etched by sun and shadow, the river's source.

At Devaprayag I crossed a cable footbridge, walked past a street of tailor shops and down to the bathing steps, or *ghat*, at the confluence of two mountain torrents that form the Ganges. With holy men and pilgrims in loincloths I stripped to my shorts, grasped chains that keep bathers from being swept away, and stepped into the glacier-cold water.

The river rushed into my ears and pulled at my body; in its chill I lost all feeling. Emerging, I stood wet and shivering in the warm autumn sun. An old *pandit* — religious teacher — with parchment-like skin smeared a red *tilak* on my forehead. The mark, reputed to bring good luck, also signifies participation in a Hindu ceremony.

Pilgrims prayed to the Ganges and to other sacred streams: "O holy Mother Ganges! O Yamuna! O Godavari! Saraswati! O Narmada! Sindhu! Kaveri!

BY THE ICE-BLUE LIGHT *of a Himalayan sunrise a Hindu holy man prepares to bathe in the sacred source of the Ganges — a silvery gurgle from an ice cave called Gaumukh, the Cow's Mouth. He and a handful of other hermits dwell nearby the year round, braving bitter mountain winters to meditate upon the waters that Hindus believe poured out of heaven to wash away sin.*

Descending from Gangotri Glacier, this hallowed headwater, the Bhagirathi River, merges with the Alaknanda to form the mainstream of Mother Ganges.

RAGHUBIR SINGH

51

May you all be pleased to be manifest in these waters with which I shall purify myself!" Onto the Ganges' swift-moving breast they cast rose petals, sweetmeats, rice. They filled brass pots with its waters to take home.

"I have bathed in Mother Ganges and I am very glad," one girl said. Another pilgrim touched my arm: "Mother Ganges is holy and very beautiful and lovely. Do you not feel refreshed?" I had seen the little open channels that carry the town's filth into the river just above the ghat. Yet my answer was truthful:

"Yes, in body and in spirit."

It seemed an auspicious beginning to a journey that would become in its own way a pilgrimage. I had come to India to trace the flow of faith along the Ganges —*Ganga Ma,* "Mother Ganges" to millions of Hindus. Since long before the birth of Christ they have come to worship it, bathe in it, drink it, and cast into it the ashes of their dead. A few drops on a man's tongue at the moment of death cleanse his soul of sin. The river is the heart of India and of Hinduism.

Swami Sharadananda appeared at my doorstep in Devaprayag one morning, a bearded figure swathed in ocher robes. For three days he had walked through

RAGHUBIR SINGH

SMOKE FROM PILGRIM FIRES
*swathes Gangotri and its
torrent-side temple to the goddess
Ganges. Thousands journey upriver
each summer, pausing in prayer
at shrines along the way.
Buses unload a few miles below
Gangotri; then, clutching bundles
and staves (opposite), pilgrims
climb a rugged trail to the respite
of campsite and hostel.
From the far corners of the
vast subcontinent they come;
many have never hiked a mountain
mile. Signs of devotion abound:
With the name of Rama painted on
her face and printed on her sari,
a member of the Namdhari sect
(opposite, upper) from distant
Gujarat State proclaims her
dedication to that Hindu god.
Hardier pilgrims toil another
dozen miles to the Cow's Mouth —
though sickly or wealthy
worshipers can ride the backs
of hired porters. At the source
they bathe, light sticks of incense,
pray to the goddess Ganges,
then take some of the holy water
home for use in family rituals.
Awed by the mountains, cleansed
by the stream, wearied souls
go forth with lightened burdens.*

snow, ridden jolting mountain buses, slept in rest houses. Now he laid down his staff and bundle. "I was reluctant to come," he said, "for I was gathering winter provisions. Then I realized you would have come to me if you could, and so I am here and will remain as long as I can help."

He has lived for 14 years as a hermit near one of the river's sources, above Gangotri. The Indian government, wary of foreigners along its sensitive border with Red China's Tibet, refused permission for me to visit him. And so, through mutual friends, I had written the swami asking him to meet me at Devaprayag.

Then I had rented a bungalow and waited. It was a pleasant house, edged with banana and guava trees, the haunt of crows and cuckoos. I met the local astrologer, an impassive man with a library of celestial computations inscribed on birchbark strips, and helped my neighbors harvest their rice. It was backbreaking toil but I remember only the moist smell of black earth, the rasping of our hook-billed knives, and, always, the murmur of the river below.

PERCHED OVER THE GANGES,
*a devotee of yoga—"yoking of
the mind to God"—holds the
"king of dancers" posture.*

*Rules for the discipline were
set in the second century* B.C.
*by the sage Patanjali. Through
the ascetic living, prolonged
body contortion in fixed positions,
and controlled breathing of* hatha,
*or physical, yoga, the yogi
progresses to the contemplative
exercises of the classic* raja,
*or royal, yoga, concentrating on
an object like the nose, the navel,
or a devotional picture. The yogi
seeks to transcend his body and the
world around him and to merge
with the universal spirit.*

*Training takes years.
Some yogis, especially of the
hatha system, claim the ability
to become invisible or to suspend
themselves in midair.*

*Hindu tradition exalts such
ascetics: Each noon a priest
at a temple in Madras State (above)
feeds a pair of vultures revered
as the spirits of two holy men who
lived on the Ganges at Banaras.*

55

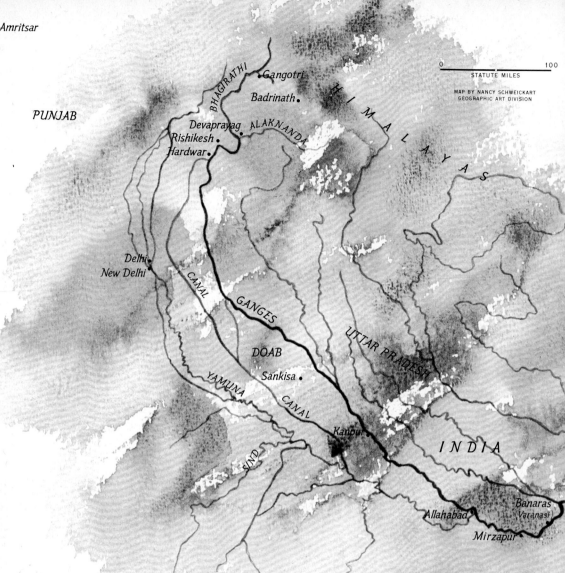

The swami and I sat in the afternoon sun and talked. He told me of summers filled with pilgrims marching to the source, and of winters when he huddled over charcoal embers in his cave and meditated for days while the snow piled six feet deep at the 11,000-foot altitude.

"God wanted me to do this spiritual work," he said, "to meditate and introspect on our scriptures. Why is it written, and what does it mean, that Ganges washes away sin? Can I give any scientific interpretation? Only by committing my own body and mind to this research can I hope to find the answer.

"Often, when I sit by the Ganges," he went on, "I slowly forget my surroundings. A feeling comes into me that I am like a child sitting in my mother's lap with my eyes looking up into her loving face. Then I slowly open my heart and pour out one after another my doubts. Mother Ganges always answers."

One day, after I had bathed in the river with the swami, we walked in the hills above and he told me of his college years, his family's grief at his parting, and of the uncertainty of his quest to reach the universal reality. "If God will reveal himself to me, he will. If not—well, spiritual work is never wasted."

Unlike the learned swami, most sadhus are simple folk who seek spiritual merit through ascetic meandering. Some serve as spiritual counselors. At Rishikesh I consulted a local guru, Mahavir Das. Known as a Jat Wala Baba (Long-haired Man) for his neatly braided toe-length locks, he sat cross-legged in a little shed beside his cave. What is the key to eternal bliss, I asked.

"Control your desires, impose self-discipline." But a young family man should set simple goals until his responsibilities are met. An ancient treatise spells out the time of life for renouncing worldly concerns: "When a householder sees his skin wrinkled, and his hair white, and the sons of his sons, then he may resort to the forest . . . a silent sage subsisting on roots and fruit. . . ."

I thanked the guru for his advice, and he gave me *prasada*, food made holy by being offered to the gods—a banana, a sweetmeat, a spoonful of the Ganges.

I left the foothills at the ancient and holy city of Hardwar, where the

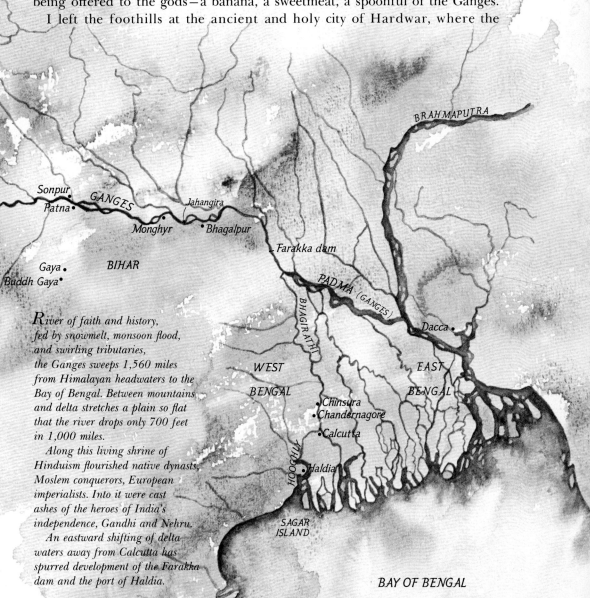

*R*iver of faith and history, fed by snowmelt, monsoon flood, and swirling tributaries, the Ganges sweeps 1,560 miles from Himalayan headwaters to the Bay of Bengal. Between mountains and delta stretches a plain so flat that the river drops only 700 feet in 1,000 miles.

Along this living shrine of Hinduism flourished native dynasts, Moslem conquerors, European imperialists. Into it were cast ashes of the heroes of India's independence, Gandhi and Nehru.

An eastward shifting of delta waters away from Calcutta has spurred development of the Farakka dam and the port of Haldia.

BRAHMAPUTRA

Sonpur
Patna
GANGES
Jahangira
Monghyr
Bhagalpur
Farakka dam
PADMA (GANGES)
Dacca
Gaya
BIHAR
Buddh Gaya
BHAGIRATHI
WEST
BENGAL
EAST
BENGAL
Chinsura
Chandernagore
Calcutta
HOOGHLY
Haldia
SAGAR
ISLAND
BAY OF BENGAL

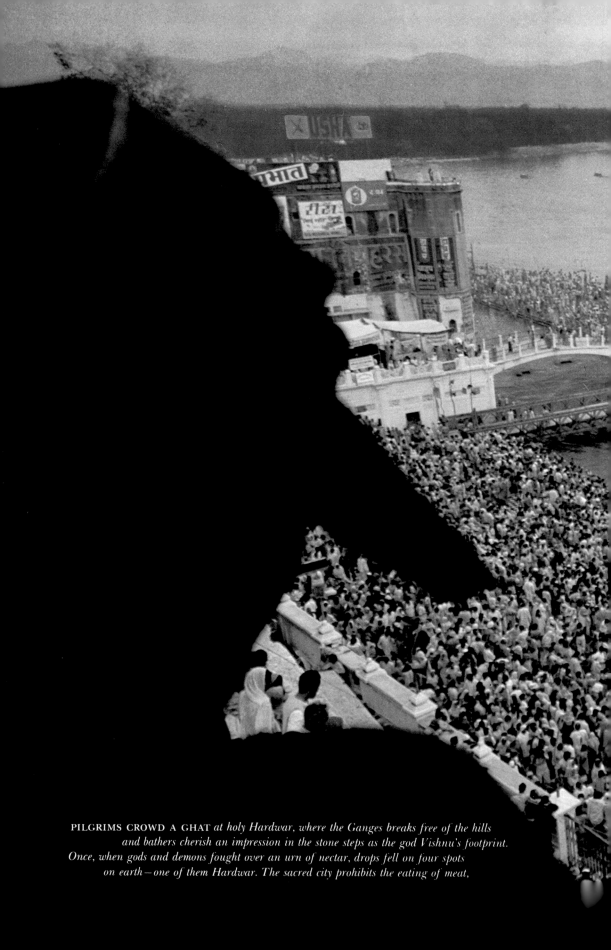

PILGRIMS CROWD A GHAT *at holy Hardwar, where the Ganges breaks free of the hills and bathers cherish an impression in the stone steps as the god Vishnu's footprint. Once, when gods and demons fought over an urn of nectar, drops fell on four spots on earth—one of them Hardwar. The sacred city prohibits the eating of meat,*

"O WATERS! . . . *who are like loving Mothers! Let us resort to you fully for that removal of evil, whereby you gratify us."* Bathers at Banaras (opposite) reflect the fervor of the Vedas; a father teaches his daughter to make her ablutions while a woman murmurs a *mantra, or mystical text. Red tilak on brow may mark her as wed or a participant in Hindu rites. A morning worshiper (above) pours Ganges water to salute "That eye . . . which rises up blazing in the east. . . ."*

river plunges out of its gorge and loops onto the Ganges Plain. Here begins the Ganges canal system that irrigates the vast Doab, the land between the Ganges and Yamuna rivers. Here each year more than two million pilgrims gather to bathe and to gaze on the footprint of the god Vishnu impressed in stone at Hari-ka-charan Ghat.

And here, long ago, dwelt the legendary sage Kapila. Falsely accused by the 60,000 sons of King Sagar of stealing a sacrificial horse, Kapila burned them to ashes. When the king inquired how his sons' wandering spirits might achieve *mukti*, eternal union with the divine, he was told to have the goddess Ganges sent down from heaven to wash their souls. Brahma heard the pleas of the king's family and agreed, but only on condition that the god Shiva break her fall; otherwise her waters might sweep away the whole earth. Shiva caught her in his hair, the Himalayan snow peaks. For many years she wandered in Shiva's hair until, escaping near Gangotri, she began her rush to the sea. In passing she redeemed the 60,000 souls.

I heard the legend many times, each time with variations, for that is the Indian way. The river itself has 108 sacred names, compiled in a little book. My favorite is the 102nd: "Roaming about Rose-apple-tree Island"—Rose-apple-tree Island being an ancient name for India.

*E*very devout Hindu yearns to visit holy Banaras at least once in a lifetime; to die there, many believe, is to be transported immediately to the side of Shiva in his Himalayan paradise.

The city stands midway down the fertile Gangetic plain, one of the world's most densely populated regions where dwell nearly a third of India's 550 millions. Nature sets its rhythms: Blistering April and May, when the temperature climbs to 115° and the parched earth cracks; the monsoon season with its greening gift of rain; winter clear and mild. On the plain I passed village girls, platters of steaming manure on their heads, bound for fields where bullock teams trailing little clouds of dust broke the soil for winter wheat.

Storied cities border the river; busy Kanpur, a

SUPPLICANTS SWARM *to the bank at Banaras, seeking the return of sun and moon, for the demon Rahu, an ancient foe, has darkened the luminary deities—a solar eclipse. Now all things are unclean; the faithful shun food and purify themselves at holy places like Dasashwamedh Ghat (right). One man follows the heavenly drama through circled fingers. When the eclipse ends, then will the leper, the blind man, and the lonely woman again beseech the sun's powers. And on a shining morn the priests again will intone: "Let us adore the light of the Divine Sun. May it enlighten our minds."*

For centuries Hindus have come to die in Banaras, a city sanctified by its site on a northward bend in the Ganges, facing the rising sun. Here a spirit may break the bondage of death and rebirth to win the paradise of eternal repose.

RAGHUBIR SINGH

rail and industrial center; Allahabad, at the confluence of the Yamuna and Ganges, where every 12 years millions gather for Kumbh Mela, the great bathing festival; Mirzapur, famed for its handmade rugs and as a headquarters of the Thugs. Devotees of the goddess Kali, they robbed and strangled victims as sacrifices to her until crushed by the British in the 1830's.

Banaras, established by Aryan settlers, stood as a religious center when Babylon ruled an empire. Around 528 B.C. Buddha came here after his enlightenment and preached his first sermon at nearby Sarnath.

An awareness of death, or rather the transiency of life, pervades Banaras' waterfront. At night water and sky merge in darkness. The temples, houses, and massive embankments rise like ghosts in the mists. And from across the river drifts the soft chant of widows in the Bhajan Ashram, hailing the passionate Krishna and the heroic Rama, incarnations of the god Vishnu: "Hare Krishna, Hare Krishna, Hare Rama, Hare Rama. . . ."

In the charity house, their last home on earth, the widows gave me bits of mint and Ganges water. They believed, they told me, that repetition of the names of revered deities would lead to sanctification—and ultimately to escape from

the cycle of life and death and rebirth to eternal communion with the Supreme Divinity that encompasses all the manifestations of the Hindu gods.

On Manikarnika Ghat the funeral pyres sent reflections dancing over the waters; around the fires tenders performed their weird ballet, stoking, poking with long bamboo poles. A hundred *doms,* members of a subcaste that serve as cremation attendants, man the burning ghats night and day. Their fee: "5 to 100 rupees, depending on the family's wealth," a dom told me as we stood wreathed in the heavy blue smoke.

Male relatives and friends bring the shrouded bodies on bamboo litters, immerse them in the Ganges, then set them on the ghat steps to dry. Placed on cordwood pyres, the bodies are heaped with offerings of sandalwood, camphor, mango leaves, and ghee—clarified butter, which also fuels the fire. Bearing a straw torch, the chief mourner, usually the eldest son, circles the pyre five times and sets it ablaze. Collected in urns, the ashes are cast into the Ganges.

There is little sense of mourning around the burning ghat, for who that is born does not die? Boys bustle by with cordwood, dogs scratch and skirmish, funeral parties await their turn. An old man from the country told me he and 22 others had come to Banaras by boat to bring an uncle's body. "We could have burned him at our village, but here is more sanctity," he said. About 30,000 bodies are cremated here each year.

The scene brought to mind a passage from the *Bhagavad-Gita* in which Lord Krishna consoles the warrior chief Arjuna on the eve of a slaughter:

Worn-out garments are shed by the body:
Worn-out bodies are shed by the dweller within....
New bodies are donned by the dweller, like garments.

But in Banaras there is the exultation of life too: in the cry of the curd seller as he wanders the narrow, crooked streets with his pots on a shoulder pole; in the bedlam of itinerant musicians who show up as if by magic at any house when a son is born; in the jangling of hundreds of bicycle-rickshaw bells; and in the prayers of the devout who crowd the temples, or circle the sacred mint plants, or adorn with flowers and Ganges water the uncounted lingams, short stone monuments representing the god Shiva and the generative force of life.

Because of the prestige of his family and of the sacred origin of kingship, people of Banaras look

RAGHUBIR SINGH

"LET YOUR EYE *go to the sun;*
your life to the wind ... go to
heaven, and then to earth again."
To the sound of somber prayers
kinsmen commit their dead to the
pyres of Manikarnika Ghat (left)
at Banaras. Shrouded corpses
receive a ritual dip, then await
the flames, while a cow forages
for marigolds that garland the biers.
Ashes go into the Ganges,
souls to heaven to await rebirth.

During the holy month of Kartik
"skylamps" over Panchganga Ghat
(above) light up the celestial
abode of ancestral spirits.

ENTHRONED ON HIS HOWDAH,
*the maharaja of Banaras arrives
by elephant for a re-enactment
of the* Ramayana *at the
autumn festival of Dusserah.
Onlookers never tire of the
valorous monkey cohorts (below)
who help Prince Rama rescue his
beloved Sita from the demon king
of Ceylon. Hindus view the epic
couple as models for perfect men
and women, and their triumph
over evil sets the festival theme.*

*Sword at his hand, priests at
his sides, the bejeweled maharaja
sits in state (opposite);
behind him a servant stands
guard with rifle and fly whisk.
Hindu tradition ascribes divine
origin to royalty; in ancient
times the king alone could
perform the greatest of rituals,
the sacrifice of a horse.*

*Modern India has stripped its
princelings of vast land holdings
and political power, but the aura
of sanctity remains to clothe
the maharaja of Banaras as
brightly as his regal raiment.*

RAGHUBIR SINGH

66

to their maharaja, Vibhuti Narain Singh, for religious guidance. Some regard him as a god. If sages disagree on the most auspicious date for a festival, they may seek his help. And no important festivity is complete without his presence on the royal reviewing stand, on one of his elephants, or on the royal lotus barge. Conscious of his responsibilities, he observes a strict personal regimen.

"I drink only Ganges water," he told me as we talked in his office in the palace overlooking the river. "It is holy and very healthful. You know of course that it can keep the longest without spoiling. The last Mogul emperor drank no water but that of the Ganges, and carried it with him in camp always. And he was not a Hindu like me, but a Moslem!"

I noted that the women of his family observe *purdah*, living their lives screened from profane gazes. A covered way leads from their quarters down to the Ganges and the barge with the trapdoor through which they bathe.

"Hindus always showed restraint in exhibiting their women," His Highness said. "But the system became more rigid after the Moslem invasions. Hindus had to protect their women from the conquerors to preserve their way of life."

When the maharaja bade me goodbye in the palace compound, a bearer appeared with an umbrella to shield him from the sun. From the gatehouse came a shouted order; the small military guard, provided by the Indian government, snapped to attention with a rattle of rifles. As I left the city, it was

MISTY MORN *finds elephants awash in a Ganges tributary at the Sonpur fair, where hundreds go up for sale each year. Indians prize the beasts for heavy field work and logging, honor them as legendary rainmakers, worship elephant-headed Ganesha, god of prosperity. But no good times can come without the fierce monsoon rains (opposite) that slake the parched earth from June to September; in dry years crops wither and starvation stalks the land.*

preparing for Divali, the festival of lights which greets the new moon in the holy month of Kartik. I had chosen to observe Divali in a Ganges-side village, for in such humble communities live the majority of India's people.

Mukh Ram is a slight, dark man, 33 years old, a fisherman on the Ganges. His village, Chandrauti, sits on a bluff encircling the ruins of a fort so ancient the villagers know only that one of the kings named their village for his daughter. Its 600 houses shelter some 4,000 people, their lives still marked by the millenniums-old caste system, despite India's land and social reforms.

Here dwell Brahmins, or priests; members of the Kshatriya, the old warrior caste; fishermen and farmers; blacksmiths and sheepherders; weavers and tailors; and 200 families of harijans, the untouchables who mainly work in the fields. Today the untouchables may own land but they still live outside the village in their own compound.

In most households young men follow the trades of their fathers. For the farmers it had been a good year—enough rain, no pests, no crop diseases, and the millet stood high in the fields. Yet the land, carved into tiny holdings, did not produce enough to feed the villagers. They lined up weekly at the government station for wheat and rice rations.

I went fishing with Mukh Ram and his brother. Before boarding the slender, double-ended *nauka*, they prayed: "O Ganga, O Krishna, give us fish and fill our stomachs." As we poled upstream the sun went down, swiftly, a small flaming ball in some distant corner of the sky. To ease the long night ahead, the brothers passed a clay pipe filled with *ganja*—a narcotic—between them. Soon we let out a long net suspended from tin cans and gourds and waited. An hour later we retrieved the net. It yielded two catfish and three smaller fish, worth about five rupees—65 cents—in the market. Back went the net.

Amid the occasional rumble of collapsing mudbanks and the howl of jackals, we chatted. Within the past year three children of the brothers had died. The fathers had consulted a guru, who advised them to pray to the Ganges and their

"SACRED" COWS *bask by the Ganges as pilgrims row out to holy Jahangira,*
its topmost temple dedicated to Shiva. Embodiment of the gods, giver of food and fuel,
the cow has enjoyed veneration since ancient times; a dose of its "five products"—milk, curd,
butter, urine, and dung—purifies body and soul, says Hindu lore. Killing of cows can kindle
rioting in India, where millions roam freely, protected by devotees and some state laws.

RAGHUBIR SINGH

family god, and to place offerings of limes and other fruits in a sacred tank at Banaras. Now, Mukh Ram told me, his brother's wife had noticed that her arm was withering. The two men felt they had been lax in their prayers and that the spirits of the dead children were troubled. They would go to the guru again.

The next day was Divali. The womenfolk mixed fresh batches of manure and mud to patch the walls of monsoon-pitted houses; men gathered under a pipal tree to gamble, casting cowrie shells; the fishermen and I went down at dusk to scrub the boats and set little clay lamps adrift.

When we climbed back up the bluff we found the village transformed into a vision of beauty. At windows, doors, and the corners of houses flickered hundreds of ghee lamps, emplaced by the women.

In the ruin of a room reduced to knee-high walls by the monsoon rains, Mukh Ram knelt before two small images. One depicted Lakshmi, goddess of wealth; the other Ganesha, the elephant-headed god. Mukh Ram lit lamps and garlanded the images with marigolds: "O Lakshmi! O Ganesha! Rid us of our troubles and raise the walls of our house which have fallen." Next door his brother struck his head against the earth: "May our problems cease!"

Some 100 miles below Banaras the river, having coursed the length of Uttar Pradesh, enters the state of Bihar. Here I visited Patna, the capital; Sonpur, where thousands come to bathe and attend an annual fair at which elephants are bought and sold; and the sacred rock of Jahangira, crowned by a cloud of white temples. For a time I traveled by country boat—a bluff-bowed *bufa* with a high stern and a huge triangular rudder. Since we rode the current the two crewmen rarely manned the bamboo oars at the bow, and we often drifted sideways or stern first. We cooked our food and brewed tea on a dung fire in the bow. By day we rigged shelters against the scorching sun; at night, anchored by an island or sandbar, we shivered in the bitter cold.

But I forgot the discomforts in the fascination of life along the river. Wedges of geese honked overhead, pelicans and egrets patrolled the mudflats. Vultures glided down to gather hungrily around a cadaver washed up by the stream.

Inside West Bengal the river splits into two main branches. The larger, the Padma, courses eastward into East Pakistan; the Bhagirathi branch continues southward, eventually becoming the Hooghly River—still Mother Ganges to Hindus. The vast sweep of purple-brown fields gives way to jungle, tasselled stands of jute and sugarcane, and gleaming rice fields. In palm-shaded villages families share ponds edged with lotus or water hyacinth to draw water or raise fish, a staple here.

It was along this stretch that Europeans established their first trading posts on the Ganges. What the Portuguese began here in 1537 did not end until 1951

SWAYING CENSERS *perfume the air to honor Durga on her annual rampage against evil.*
Priests of the Ramakrishna Mission in Banaras dance to a drumbeat as the festival
to the ten-armed goddess swells to its climax: the immersion of her image in the Ganges.
Another form of Shiva's lovely consort Parvati, Durga won fame as a bane of demons.   73

RAGHUBIR SINGH

when France, the last of the colonial powers, left the river. Mementos remain: *"Liberté, Egalité, Fraternité,"* proclaim the city gates of Chandernagore; the Dutch-built church at Chinsura serves as a Hooghly College classroom; and in Christian cemeteries monuments and plaques tersely tell of European wives and children who joined their menfolk in an alien land, only to die far from home.

The Ganges led now to Calcutta, India's largest city and a leading port, an intellectual and artistic center, home of seven million people. On my first visit to the city I had arrived with the goddess Durga, who comes every autumn, weapons in each of her ten hands, to slay the demon Asura.

In Calcutta she finds ample evils to attack. Scenes of poverty and overcrowding assail the senses: streetcars with passengers hanging from doors and windows; sidewalk standpipes where naked children bathe; shrouded forms of thousands asleep on sidewalk and stairway; lepers and cripples begging from passing cars. Scenes of piety and political turmoil add to the hubbub: the Kali temple where priests sacrifice goats on two-pronged altars while barren women tie stones to a spiny tree in quest of fruitfulness; the portraits of Red China's Mao Tse-tung; striking marchers under red banners; and armed constabulary.

During the Durga puja, the festival that honors the goddess, the city seeks to forget its problems. Families put aside grudges, blossom out in new clothes, meet

RAGHUBIR SINGH

CARRIERS *of the world's goods tie up at Calcutta's Kidderpore docks; cookstove smoke swirls from barges, homes to the men who crew them, while dockers swarm across a lowered drawspan.*

The British East India Company founded the city amid jungle and elephant grass in 1690, absorbing three villages. One may have given the settlement its name—Kalikata, honoring the goddess Kali. Once India's capital, its wealth built from the jute trade, Calcutta still ranks as the nation's greatest commercial center and most populous city.

A boatman (above right) poles along a glassy channel of the Hooghly River, Calcutta's link to the sea and, to Hindus, the sacred outlet of Mother Ganges.

old friends in the *pandals*—shrines set up under canopies especially for the festival throughout the city. Each day priests come with cymbals and clouds of incense to awaken the images within; they offer Durga food and precious silks, and in the evening lull her to sleep with soft chants and the rhythmic swish of lion's-tail fans.

I was welcomed everywhere, and received many invitations to participate in the climactic ritual, the immersion of Durga in the river on the final night. When that evening arrived I drove north to a neighborhood by the Circular Canal where mud-brick houses merge into a score of similar communities—the slums where so many of Calcutta's people live.

Pools of dark water splotched the black mud lane. Pigs rooted amid coconut husks and garbage. Children swarmed, the infants without diapers and the girls beautiful with gilded studs in their noses.

"Welcome," said a young man as I entered a

courtyard where stood an altar to the smallpox goddess, an ancient pipal tree, and a pandal. My host was T. R. Das, a leader in the neighborhood fraternity. He and most of his friends were jobless, but they had determined to make this a memorable puja. They had sold subscriptions far and wide, enough to buy an image of the goddess and rent equipment to show a popular Durga film.

The film began as darkness fell. Durga appeared on a lion and moved jerkily toward the Asura demon. She vanished, then appeared as Kali, goddess of death. From the third eye in her forehead a trident-shaped beam shot forth to sever the demon's head. We watched it again and again, until the crowd got restless. Finally Das apologized. The cost of the film had left no money to pay for musicians and a lorry to transport the image. There would be no immersion. As I left, the goddess Durga again rode across the screen to slay evil.

From nearby neighborhoods I could hear the roar of engines, the beat of drums, and the cries of celebrants. Suddenly two trucks swung down the road. In one a huge Durga swayed against her lashings; in the other stood the lesser images of Lakshmi, Ganesha, Hanuman the monkey god, and Saraswati, goddess of wisdom. When the director of the group, a portly magistrate in a white dhoti, invited me aboard for the immersion, I quickly accepted.

After an hour's wait behind a long line of trucks we moved onto the jammed Nimtala Ghat. I went with the smaller images down the steps and aboard a slender nauka hired to take us out. But when Durga came into view, the captain balked; she was too heavy and might sink him. Durga would have to be immersed from the bank. The nauka slipped out into the dark river and we slid the smaller images over the side. Other boats ghosted past. "Ganga Ma! Ganga Ma!" their occupants cried. Scores of images bobbed and drifted slowly downstream, like so many corpses. Tomorrow Calcutta would turn back to her problems.

*O*ne evening a village boat put me ashore on the tip of Sagar Island, where the river meets the sea 80 miles below Calcutta. The little temple of Gangasagar seemed deserted; then I heard the ringing of cymbals for evening worship. The three priests welcomed me, marked my head with the tilak, gave me prasada, and told me again the story of the Ganges.

Early next morning I walked the beach alone. Along it, brought down by the river or washed up by the tide, lay fragments of pottery: mementos of cookfires and puja lamps and granary pots. Among the sherds gleamed seashells from the Bay of Bengal. Their conical shapes reminded me of Hindu temples; their dusky stripes seemed to evoke the very soil of the gentle, troubled land through which I had journeyed. I took the finest of the shells and hurled it far out into the mingling waters of sea and river. "Mother Ganges," I whispered, "take care of your Rose-apple-tree Island." Only the wind and the sea replied.

BURIED TO HIS NECK, *head smeared with ashes, his brow marked with the sign of Shiva, a holy man meditates on Sagar Island in the delta. For him mortification of the flesh intensifies the spiritual quest. Coins tossed on the cloth before him gain spiritual merit for pilgrims who come to bathe where their beloved Ganges yields her waters to the sea.*

RAGHUBIR SINGH

K et-jak. Ket-jak. Menacing, monkeylike sounds quicken the umber dusk. In a palm-flanked templeyard 150 bronze torsos ripple and writhe—a fantasy of flesh and shadow in the flickering light.

Ketjak. Ketjakajak. The chorus shrills to a sinister pitch. Suddenly, sound and undulations cease. The squatting dancers tense. Then, like the tentacles of some incredible sea monster, their arms reach out toward two central figures.

Under attack in the ketjak dance of Bali is the demon Ravana, abductor of Princess Sita in the Hindu epic, the *Ramayana.*

The dance drama of the triumphant monkey army, its movements and staging a delight to visitors, reflects the Balinese love of festivity and the intense concern with religion at the core of their culture. Art, music, dancing—nearly every pursuit of life—has spiritual significance on this Indonesian isle where the gods can belch disaster hot from a volcano's crater or touch terraced earth with a green ballet of growing rice.

The island teems with temples, from hundred-towered Besakih on the wrinkled slopes of Mount Agung to tiny shrines set in shimmering paddies or tucked among clutching roots of sacred *waringin* trees— giant banyans that harbor potent spirits.

Grotesque, often ribald carvings ornament the temples; wind and rain easily erode the soft native sandstone, creating a constant demand for the skills of Bali's master carvers. At these gay, open-air shrines villagers gather for magnificent festivals in which artists in cookery and decor, as well as musicians and dancers, play parts they have practiced since childhood.

Night and day an endless dialogue with deities unfolds in the Balinese blend of Hinduism, ancestor worship, and animism. The family gods are especially close; at the ancestral shrine of his village compound a troubled man may find peace of mind, even solutions to his problems, in a talk with his departed kinfolk.

Brahma in Bali

R eliving a Hindu saga under Bali's balmy skies, dancers at Pliatan's temple mimic monkeys who killed a giant to free Prince Rama's stolen bride.

Indian priests brought the Ramayana *epic, with its heroic monkey general Hanuman (above), to the Indonesian island nine centuries ago. In time Bali embraced the Hindu faith, producing an awesome pantheon of local and imported gods who still guard the garden isle.*

TEMPLE CARVING, 12TH CENTURY, IN BELUR, INDIA; DEAN BROWN FROM NANCY PALMER AGENCY. OPPOSITE: GILBERT M. GROSVENOR, NATIONAL GEOGRAPHIC STAFF

Breath of Brahma wreathes Agung, highest and holiest of Bali's volcanic peaks. When the 10,308-foot-high "navel of the world" erupted in 1963, killing 1,600, god-fearing folk saw the disaster as punishment for their sins. The governor banned entry to Besakih, mother temple on angry Agung's flank; he would go alone to pray for all. Heedless, worshipers by the hundreds braved raining ash to pay homage at the home of their Hindu gods.

Planting every suitable puddle on the 90-mile-long island, farmers harvest rice enough for all two million Balinese. Five times each season the rice goddess Dewi Sri receives tribute of eggs, fronds, and flowers (opposite). For though the soil is rich and the land knows no winter, without her smiles no crop will thrive.

Animism honors the spirits of all things in nature—trees, rocks, rivers, mountains. A trucker nearing a dilapidated bridge pauses to invoke the deity of iron who protects all vehicles. Should a mishap befall, it would be blamed on evil forces or witches—the source of all ill fortune. The driver's accident report might read: "A huge black cat jumped on the hood. His furry paws reached toward me through the window. I lost control. . . ."

On Bali, high is holy. To Mount Agung, where Brahma, Vishnu, Shiva, and all the other gods reside, the souls of the deceased ascend. Relatives loft the dead as near to the gods as gravity and the budget allow. Biers may tower 40 feet. In life, a high-caste Brahmin commands the tallest chair; dead, he merits a high-rise funeral. Shouting to frighten away evil spirits, bearers careen with the corpse on its tower to the

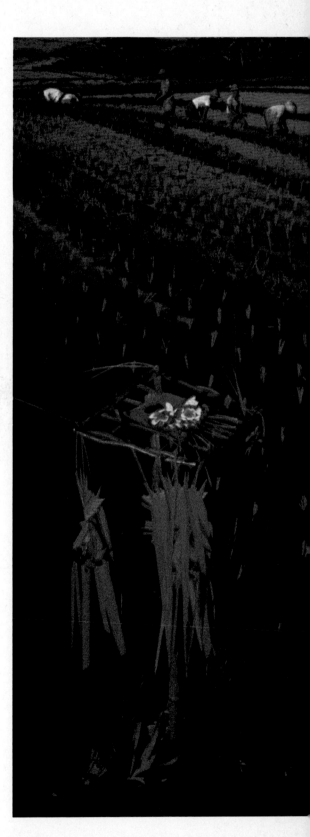

cremation site. As in India, cremation is
not only a sacred duty but also a joyous
occasion, marking the soul's release.

Hinduism made its deepest inroads into
Bali's native faith in the 16th century by
way of Java. Fleeing the armies of Islam,
deposed Hindu princes crossed the reef-
strewn, mile-wide strait to Bali.

The Balinese accepted the royal refugees
—and their gods. Brahmin priests took a
key role in island affairs. Scholarly prayers
lent prestige to temple cleansings, crema-
tions, house purifications, even such indigenous rites as tooth-filing at puberty. To
qualify for cremation a Balinese has his
six upper front teeth filed down, lest the
gods take him for a fanged demon and
deny him entrance to the spirit world.

Each good thing has its evil counter-
part, even direction. Left is bad, right is
good. Villagers orient family compounds

*F*air devotees bear godly fare to a temple fete. Pillars of fruit
and pressed rice may weigh up to 150 pounds; Bali's queenly women,
trained in grace since childhood, balance such burdens with ease.

*H*oly seance begins a trance dance, traditionally staged in Kintamani
to combat pestilence. Young girls don ritual garb; then incense, prayers,
music, and the mesmeric jiggling of sacred puppets on a string invite the gods
to enter their bodies. Wraithlike they rise, entranced; atop men's shoulders
they sway through classical Balinese patterns. While the spirits
move them, they may even walk barefoot on smoldering coals, feeling no pain.

82

toward Agung and away from the demon-filled sea. To confound demons, an inner wall looms just inside the compound gate. Evil spirits, who can't turn corners, barge in, bump the wall, bounce out. Thoughtful folk leave a bit of demon food outside.

Annually, even the most cautious villagers brave the demons' stronghold in the Indian Ocean for the ritual bath of temple deities and fearsome but friendly animal spirits called *barongs*. For days women bustle about the temple preparing elaborate offerings of food and flowers. At last the altars are laden. Gaily clad gamelan musicians stand by their gongs and cymbals. The huge barongs, animated fore and aft by men inside them, prance impatiently. They snap wooden jaws, tossing red tongues and black beards, as if eager to match magic with Rangda, their evil opposite. Reminiscent of India's destructive goddess Kali, Rangda rules the *leyaks,* bewitched spirits who haunt back roads.

At the appointed time women don the towering offerings like hats and a mile-long montage of color surges toward the sea. The trek ends where black-sand beach meets roaring blue-gray ocean. When the cleansing ends, feasting begins. Conveniently, the spirits eat only the invisible essences of the offerings. Jubilant worshipers down what's left.

According to Hindu teaching, this modern era is a time of trouble. Change is imminent, certainly, in the jet age. But the resilient Balinese, buoyed by their faith, have preserved their culture despite conquest and natural disaster. Confidently looking to Agung, young and old play their traditional roles with dignity and a fine sense of drama befitting an island called "the morning of the world."

Dainty vessel of a visiting god, a child dances for hours oblivious of the strain that moistens her headdress. A priest will free her — unharmed — from the spell. During other dances the entranced speak for the spirits, allaying villagers' fears, in Bali's ceaseless quest for communion with deities.

DONNA K. GROSVENOR

BUDDHISM

Bright as Buddhists' hope for nirvana, flowers adorn stylized footprints of Buddha at Buddh Gaya, India, where he attained enlightenment; William MacQuitty

THE EIGHTFOLD PATH TO NIRVANA

Joseph M. Kitagawa

"*L*et my skin wither, my hands grow numb, my bones dissolve; until I have attained understanding I will not rise from here." Dusk had come, and the resolute prince—the day was his 35th birthday—sat down cross-legged beneath a leafy pipal tree. He touched his right hand to the ground so Earth could bear witness and began to meditate. Through the watches of the night, under a full moon, he sat. And when he finally rose, there arose with him a new religion. For he was Siddhartha Gautama and the understanding he attained in a night of transcending revelations made him Buddha, "awakened"—the Enlightened One. Out of the mission he then set for himself—to impart the secret of enlightenment to all who desire salvation—came the faith we call Buddhism.

Today that faith counts some 180,000,000 adherents. Most dwell in countries on the rim of eastern Asia. But even in the United States it calls to 100,000 followers with a spiritual philosophy holding that "as each man creates for himself his own prison, so may he also acquire a power superior to that of the gods."

Of the historical Siddhartha Gautama modern scholarship sifts from the veil of time—and from legend and word of disciples—a few hesitant facts. He was born about 563 B.C. in what is now southern Nepal; a pillar erected in the third century B.C. commemorates the site. His father, highborn in the Kshatriya caste of warriors and rulers, was chief of the Sakya clan; moss greens an outline of stones described as ruins of his palace. In his maturity Gautama Buddha wandered a region along the middle Ganges, preaching. About 483 B.C., having reached the age of 80, his body like "a worn-out cart," he died.

89

Prayer wheels, oil lamps, and meditation grace devotion at the Buddh Gaya shrine where Buddha, seated beneath a pipal tree, made a vow to achieve understanding. A type of fig, the pipal is known also as the bo tree, from bodhi—*enlightenment.*

Such essentials hardly presage a revolutionary impact. But northeastern India at the time was a ferment of religious and political turmoil and experimentation. Theological sects abounded, with charismatic leaders. Many people had grown discontented with the external formalities of Brahmanic sacrifices and the salvation-through-knowledge dispensed only to the chosen few.

Against this background Buddha preached. Brahmanic religion had shaped a resignation toward suffering in this life; it bound man in the collectivity of caste. Buddha built on the old faith but developed its dharma—*dhamma* in the Pali of Buddhism's early scriptures—into a new doctrine, a new code of living. It recognized man the individual and showed him a way to end suffering and the wheel of rebirth, a way to overcome, through right conduct, the profaneness of existence. Its deepest insights—now as in Buddha's day—voice a salvation and compassion capable of inspiring political, social, and religious renewal.

About the personality that proffered this revelation Buddhist tradition weaves a rich tapestry of belief. The child who at birth announced "this is my last existence" grew up amid the pleasures of the palace, carefully shielded from all suffering and misery. At 16 he married, winning his bride by besting other suitors in remarkable trials of physical and intellectual powers. Then followed merry years at court, depicted by sensuous scenes in Buddhist art.

On a chariot ride one day the young prince saw an old man burdened with the weight of years. "Why is that man suffering?" he asked his charioteer.

"That is old age, my lord. It is the sorrow of man, the depriver of his pleasures, the ruination of memory." Troubled, the prince returned home.

On other rides he met a sick man and a funeral and learned about illness and death. Then he encountered an ascetic in rags, serene happiness lighting his face. Moved, Siddhartha pondered the vanity of earthly pleasures. That night, his 29th birthday, he said goodbye to his slumbering wife and new-born son and set out on a pilgrim's search for the essential truth.

First he studied with two yoga masters. But when their teachings did not satisfy his spiritual needs, he turned to extreme asceticism. Sometimes he ate but a grain of rice a day, or stood for days on end. Yet five years of this brought him no nearer his goal, so he gave up austerity. And then, in a forest at Buddh Gaya, he sat down on a grass mat spread beneath the pipal tree.

During meditative trances in the night's three watches he recollected his previous existences, acquired the "divine eye" by which he envisaged the death and rebirth of all creatures of all time, and at last reached a higher state in which the "outflows" of his life—his ignorance and desires—were finally quelled. It was then he grasped the Four Sacred Truths of the way to enlightenment; seven thousand heavens exulted and celestial beings wept for joy, Buddhist legend holds.

*Demon "armies of Mara, terribly arrayed,"
leap to the Evil One's command in hopes
of swerving Buddha from his resolve
for enlightenment (below). This high relief—
and scenes showing Buddha's death
(lower right) and his miraculous birth from
his mother's side—reflect Greco-Roman
influences in Gandhara sculpture
of northwest India. Earliest Buddhist art
had shown the Enlightened One only
by symbols; Gandhara marked a high point
in the transition to later brilliance of
art in Southeast Asia, China, and Japan.*

May's full moon bathes the tiered shrine of Borobudur in Java as monks and nuns observe Wesak — holy days commemorating Buddha's birth, enlightenment, and death. Ninth-century Borobudur encases a hill with terrace upon terrace of stone, elaborate with carvings and spired domes. Its name means "shrine of the many Buddhas."

The Enlightened One had often stressed he was not divine. But the common man came to regard him as much a savior as a sage. In time this bhakti, devotion, became puja, actual worship. And a Mahayana Buddhist pantheon grew — saints, deities, compassionate beings. Among the most revered: Avalokiteshvara, merciful redeemer who in China as Kuan-yin and in Japan as Kannon took female form; Maitreya, a Buddha-to-be who in China became the round-bellied Laughing Buddha; Amitabha, who rules an eden attained by faith and good works.

Later, in a sermon at a deer park near Banaras, he revealed those truths to five former companions who had left him when he gave up his "holy" asceticism.

"This is the Noble Truth concerning sorrow," he told them. "Birth is sorrow, age is sorrow . . . death is sorrow" — all in the world is sorrow and suffering. The second Noble Truth holds that all suffering stems from craving the pleasures of life. Thirdly, the end to suffering can come only by ending craving. And the final Noble Truth reveals that the way to end craving lies in an Eightfold Path whose steps are Right Views, Right Resolve, Right Speech, Right Conduct, Right Livelihood, Right Effort, Right Mindfulness, and Right Concentration.

By such steps Buddha decreed a path of spiritual improvement based on acceptance of the Four Sacred Truths and on such things as avoidance of ill will, malicious talk, lust, and hurt to living things. The path stressed mindful concentration — insight through meditation — in gaining understanding. It is the Middle Way between asceticism and worldly life, Buddha preached. It unseals the eyes of the spirit, leads to peace of mind, to knowledge, to enlightenment, to nirvana. For his followers, nirvana meant the state of bliss or emptiness — the zero and infinity — attained by escaping the wheel of rebirth. It has been likened to extinguishing a flame: A man afire with craving and wrong inclination will flame

again in a new life; cut off the fuel, and the flame goes. The word "nirvana" comes from a root meaning "blown out."

After his Banaras sermon, "Setting in Motion the Wheel of Righteousness," Buddha spent the remaining 45 years of his life as "the Tathagata, the one who has come to teach you the way, the dhamma." For some of those years he wandered, preaching, using keen parable and living example to impart his message of compassion and selflessness to a flawed and troubled world. The rest he spent in monastic centers, busy with the thankless task of forging a life of right action among followers of all conditions and castes, women as well as men, who flocked to the primitive Buddhist community that has emerged as the *sangha*, the brotherhood of monks. Then, feeling his end near, he traveled to a forest retreat not far from modern Gorakhpur. Sickened by tainted food, he died. His last words to those gathered around him were "Decay is inherent in all . . . things. Work out your own salvation with diligence." And the earth shook, the skies darkened; men wept, and the trees shed their leaves.

Disciples passed along Buddha's teachings orally; the first written canons of the faith date from the first century B.C. In them he made no claim to divinity. Nor did he offer reliance on any gods for aid; because of this, Buddhism has

95

DEAN CONGER, NATIONAL GEOGRAPHIC PHOTOGRAPHER. MAP BY BETTY CLONINGER, GEOGRAPHIC ART DIVISION

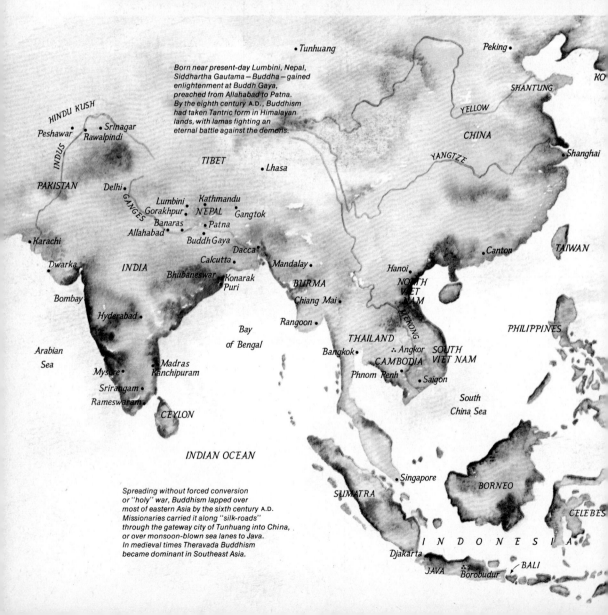

Born near present-day Lumbini, Nepal,
Siddhartha Gautama — Buddha — gained
enlightenment at Buddh Gaya,
preached from Allahabad to Patna.
By the eighth century A.D., Buddhism
had taken Tantric form in Himalayan
lands, with lamas fighting an
eternal battle against the demons.

Spreading without forced conversion
or "holy" war, Buddhism lapped over
most of eastern Asia by the sixth century A.D.
Missionaries carried it along "silk-roads"
through the gateway city of Tunhuang into China,
or over monsoon-blown sea lanes to Java.
In medieval times Theravada Buddhism
became dominant in Southeast Asia.

Domed towers of Wat Arun, Temple of the Dawn, soar above the Chao Phraya River in Bangkok, Thailand. Such spires trace their architectural beginnings to primitive mound worship of monsoon Asia; masonry stupas were built later in mound shape to enshrine Buddhist relics. Gradually profuse adornment and symbolic superstructures enriched the venerated sites. Tradition says that the Indian king Asoka in the third century B.C. divided Buddha's ashes into 84,000 parts for stupas throughout Buddhist lands.

JAPAN
HONSHU
Kyoto •
+ Mt. Koya
• Tokyo
SHIKOKU

Mahayana Buddhism reached China about the first century A.D., Korea in the fourth, and Japan in the sixth. Its appeal won savants first, then the people.

PACIFIC
OCEAN

NEW GUINEA

been called atheistic. Rather than rejecting theism, however, it is indifferent to traditional gods as the means of obtaining salvation. A Buddhist may pray to the deities of his land, but usually for such immediate benefits as rain, or good harvests, or children. He does not pray to the gods for enlightenment. For the core of Buddha's message is that only the individual can walk the path to inner understanding and ultimate truth.

Buddha's dhamma set explicit rules. "Let a man overcome anger by love, let him overcome evil by good; let him overcome the greedy by liberality, the liar by truth," he taught. "Shame on him that strikes; greater shame on him who, stricken, strikes back," he said. "Since, for each one of us, our own self is the most important, respect the self of your fellow man as you respect your own."

Over the centuries in India and Southeast Asia Buddhism became essentially a religion for monks. But in India monasteries grew wealthy, owned land and slaves, paid little heed to laymen. Scholars suggest that when Moslem invaders sacked the monasteries late in the 12th century, the laity had little incentive to restore the faith; Buddhism almost disappeared from the land of its birth.

But Buddhism also was a missionary faith. Buddha himself commanded his disciples to "go forth . . . for the help of the many, for the well-being of the many, out of compassion for the world." In the third century B.C. the great king Asoka, who welded most of India into an empire, became a convert and by his patronage made Buddhism an adjunct to the throne and a sweeping movement. Tradition says he sent missionaries to preach throughout Southeast Asia, had contact even with Egypt and Greece. Tolerant of other gods and ideas, Buddhism flowed and absorbed and diversified. And in the 2½ millenniums since Buddha it has split into three main streams.

One, Theravada Buddhism, calls itself the Way of the Elders. Detractors labeled it Hinayana, the

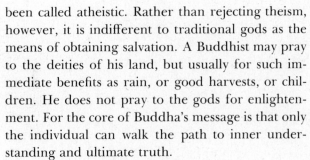

Kipling's "beautiful winking wonder," the Shwe Dagon Pagoda in Rangoon, Burma, tops its spire with a jeweled hti, symbol of Buddha's umbrella. The stupa, said to hold eight hairs Buddha plucked from his head for two Burmese, is one of Buddhism's holiest sites. The faithful coat its 326-foot height with gold leaf. ▶

97

OVERLEAF: W. E. GARRETT, NATIONAL GEOGRAPHIC STAFF

Flames at dawn warm pilgrims atop Adam's Peak in Ceylon. Its crown cradles a depression three feet long, shaped like a footprint. Buddha's followers believe he left it, Hindus see it as a sign of Shiva, Moslems hold Adam landed here when cast from Eden; certain early Christians thought Thomas, the doubting disciple, made it. Such shrines draw the devout from afar; Buddhist texts say that he who braves a difficult pilgrimage will gain nirvana. The climb to the 7,360-foot pinnacle tests severely, though stairs and handrails replace footholds and dangling chains. A bonus: the peak's shadow afloat on mist at sunrise.

At shrines Buddhists place offerings—often a lotus, symbol of purity since, like Buddha who rose above the mire of worldly desires, it blooms unsullied by muck from which it grows.

Lesser Vehicle. It prevails today in Ceylon, Burma, Thailand, Cambodia, and Laos. Theravadins stress the sangha as the means of following the dhamma; a monk who succeeds in reaching nirvana becomes an *arhat*, or saint. At the same time Theravada Buddhism gives the layman a positive role in supporting the sangha, winning merit to better his own karma.

In the first century B.C. arose a division of Buddhism known as Mahayana, the Greater Vehicle, because it offered a broader means of gaining the ultimate goal —a goal open both to the pious monk and to any layman. Further, the goal could be not only nirvana but also a godly existence of self-sacrifice and compassion. The ideal saint became not the arhat, but the *bodhisattva*—he who at the threshold of nirvana postpones his own entry to help others to salvation. Such bodhisattvas acquired an infinite store of merit that could be imparted to the worshiping faithful. A deification resulted—particularly of powerful bodhisattvas deemed Buddhas-to-come. Mahayana Buddhism, once centered in China, now predominates in Korea, Japan, and parts of Viet Nam. In each, indigenous religions added their influences, and numerous sects developed.

The third branch of Buddhism, Tantric, sprouted around the sixth century A.D. and finds its chief expression in Himalayan lands. It interlaced Mahayana Buddhism with Tantric cults of India that invoked deities by magic and rituals. And it expanded the pantheon with an array of new divinities—personifications of Buddha's thoughts and acts, female counterparts of deities, even demons.

Each division of Buddhism musters claim that it represents the original or true form. Actually, each developed by stressing specific elements within the early faith. And as Buddhism spread, it articulated its insights in words and symbols that differed from country to country. In Southeast Asia it learned to speak the language of kingship. In Tibet it learned to speak with shamans. In China it picked up the language of the family. But its essence remains the message of Siddhartha Gautama: "Seek in the impersonal for the eternal man, and having sought him out, look inward—thou art Buddha."

Michael Kuh

Saffron Robes in Gilded Thailand

*T*he gray rain that has overlaid Bangkok since my arrival yields before shafts of sun this Sunday afternoon in mid-October. A stylized bronze lion at the temple steps takes on life as the light brightens. Behind him the gilt encrusting the intricate temple carvings is kindled. I watch in wonder, my Western eye still unaccustomed to religious settings of such great but graceful brilliance. Grace, I note for the hundredth time since arriving in the city, is the enchanting quality that sets the Thai apart from peoples of my previous experience.

I have come to Thailand curious about the religion whose strengths underlie the serene grace and equanimity of the people. I plan to photograph the daily routine of the monks whose omnipresent garb of saffron—a sacred color honored as symbolic of humility—has made this centuries-old kingdom known as the land of the golden robes. That religion is Theravada Buddhism.

The temple steps where I wait climb to the tiered beauty of a *wat* called Phra Keo; wat, in Thai, means a walled compound with its temple and related buildings. Faithful who have come to pay homage to the wat's Emerald Buddha brush past me.

Then the monk I am expecting appears at the temple threshold. A shy half-smile of recognition acknowledges my respectful ritual salute. The entire disciplined spirit quintessential to Theravada Buddhism seems to move in the few flowing, barefoot steps Phra Maha Sathienphongse takes toward me.

POISE OF A BUDDHIST *monk upon the lion-guarded stairs of Bangkok's royal temple affirms the dignity of a disciplined faith. The Way of the Elders, Theravada, binds the Thai— king and commoner—to the life of the* wats, *or monasteries.*

Building or gilding temples earns religious merit. King Rama I built Wat Phra Keo in 1785; the reigning king ceremoniously changes the robes of its green jasper buddha three times a year.

MICHAEL KUH

103

Maha Sathienphongse speaks in English, perfected while studying Sanskrit at Cambridge University in England. To my tentative question about his Theravada faith he replies: "Ours is the old, indeed very old, more orthodox interpretation of Lord Buddha's teachings. It is called the Way of the Elders. We seek to follow Buddha's original rules of conduct, stressing the significance of the sangha, or brotherhood of monks, and the observation of certain basic principles for the pursuit of the monastic life.

"In Europe I have heard these principles called ascetic because we deny ourselves certain so-called pleasures. We in the sangha—I speak as one who has been in the order since the age of 10—hold a different view. We consider Buddha's teachings to be a logical guideline to peace of mind. By the disciplines which Westerners consider austere we believe that we gain rather than sacrifice.

"To be a monk during some period of his life is almost as normal for a Thai as, say, for an American to own a car. In my own part of northeast Thailand a man who has never served as a monk is known as *khon dip*, an 'unripe' person. Girls prefer not to marry him. Even our king was ordained a monk, in 1956. Each dawn he walked barefoot, carrying his alms bowl as we all do. By the way, His Majesty will distribute new robes next week to inaugurate the national round of *kathin*—robe-giving—ceremonies."

BOWING OUT *after three months in the monastery, young monks (below left) observe the rites of return to the laity. Confessing their shortcomings to settled members of the brotherhood, they exchange saffron robes for white and go outside to be anointed. Then they are doused with pots of holy water, shown on the floor. After this they don civilian clothes.*

At a royal kathin *ceremony in Bangkok's Wat Po, King Bhumibol Adulyadej, Rama IX, bestows new garments and other gifts on monks at the end of the rainy season retreat. Hereditary Upholder of the Faith, he himself once served as a monk. Here he speaks to the abbot of Wat Po, whose ornate fan marks his exalted rank in the order.*

I had read about these rites held at the end of the Rains Retreat, which Westerners sometimes refer to as the Buddhist Lent. It coincides with the wet monsoon and lasts from about mid-July through mid-October. During this period monks retire to their monasteries and spend their days in meditation. Rice sprouts grow new in the paddies, agricultural chores weigh light, and laymen are freer to enter the monkhood for varying periods. While their families manage at home, these short-term monks study, recite Buddhist texts, and maintain rigorous discipline. Usually no village social life, marriages, or festivals take place during the Rains Retreat. But at its end occurs one of the year's biggest festivals, centered around the kathin with its offerings of alms and new robes to the monks.

I go to the Ministry of Foreign Affairs for permission to photograph the king's bestowal. A portly official receives me. "Yes, His Majesty's presentation

GOOD KARMA *flows with the morning current as a* bhikku *— monk — from one of 400 wats in the Bangkok area embarks to gather food. He does not beg but silently accepts what waiting patrons offer.*

Though monks may eat meat or fish, they themselves may not take life. Rice is the mainstay in this Southeast Asian kingdom, three-fourths the size of Texas and the Orient's leading exporter of the grain. Food donors win blessings in this life and the next.

Monks offer the laity further merit-making opportunities when they chant appropriate scriptural texts at a wedding, cremation, or housewarming — even the dedication of a new locomotive.

The most joyous of popular rituals occurs when a boy first enters the wat. After ceremonies re-enacting Gautama's palace life, the candidate is borne amid pageantry to the monastery. There he exchanges his princely costume for the saffron robe.

will touch off other kathins all over Thailand," he says. "These are joyous ceremonies by which we lay people demonstrate our pleasure in supporting the sangha. The monkhood is, you might say, a flesh-and-blood manifestation of Buddha's teaching. We all hope to follow his dhamma — doctrine — to the best of our abilities, but we infinitely respect our monks for devoting their lives to this endeavor. By their example we are encouraged to be better. And by receiving our alms the members of the brotherhood confer on us a favor greater than whatever we are privileged to give them."

I make my request to take pictures. In time, approval comes from the royal household, a rare honor for a foreigner. But almost my first step at the ceremony proves a faux pas. I put my foot on the carpet runner that leads from the curb at Wat Po's ornate gate to the doorway of the temple within. The same portly, gentle foreign affairs official — now resplendent in gilt-encrusted white tunic and striped black trousers — registers shock.

"No, no! Not on the carpet! No one but His Majesty may step on the carpet." I look down on this untouchable strip and suddenly what has been for me the bookish theory of Buddhism as a state religion—which once regarded the king as a demigod whose exalted rank was won by merit earned in past lives—becomes a statement of living fact.

In another building within Wat Po's sprawling grounds I have previously admired the famed Reclining Buddha. It lies with monumental grace on its right side, head propped on bent arm, its gently smiling face radiating peace of mind. Now, in the temple where we await the king's arrival, it strikes me that this same peace of mind is reflected in the impassive faces of Wat Po's monks, seated in formal posture on a dais along one wall. Army officers and government officials, burdened with medals, fidget in their chairs near the door.

Then a sudden bustle outside, and into the temple strides King Bhumibol Adulyadej. Behind him a string of attendants bear folded robes. The king sinks

107

into a cushioned throne. The monks begin to chant, a rolling, repetitive refrain like the liturgy of wavelets on a deserted beach. They speak in Pali, an ancient tongue dead now except for its use as the ecclesiastic language of Theravada Buddhism. According to legend, Buddha used this old vernacular of northern India for his sermons, arguing that the courtly Sanskrit was the speech of the intellectuals but that his teachings were meant for all.

Impressively the ritual moves to its climactic distribution of the new robes. Then the king stands before Wat Po's abbot, who is seated first in the line of monks. For a long, electric moment the only sound in the temple is their hushed exchange of whispers. The young man leans solicitously toward the old abbot. I see before my eyes the respect inspired by the saffron robe, even in a god-king.

I learn more about robes and the sangha when I visit the monastery in which the king was ordained. Bangkok, once called the Venice of the East because of its canals, has become a sprawling city of

"MEDITATE, O BHIKKUS, *and be not heedless.... Stop the stream valiantly, drive away the desires," advised Buddha in the Dhammapada, or Path of Virtue.*

Locked in silent meditation at Wat Santi Tham Nakhon in the northern city of Chiang Mai sits 17-year-old Praves Chanla. In training for the past six years, the novice plans, upon reaching the required age of 20, to take the 227 vows of a full-fledged bhikku.

A monk has few possessions beyond his alms bowl, a sling to carry it, and a single set of saffron robes marked with a circle "not smaller than a bedbug, not larger than the pupil of the eye of a peacock."

Shaven heads bared to rain or sun, monks go forth at dawn to gather food, which they eat back at the wat. Solid food is forbidden after noon. The man who becomes fat, warns Buddha, is born again and again.

MICHAEL KUH

RULES OF THE ROBE *guide
a novice's routine. Accepting alms
from a villager, Praves (above)
stands at arm's length; a member
of the order should avoid touching
a woman, even his own mother.*

*Mindful not to injure any living
creature, even the tiniest, monks
often strain water they drink or use
for showers and shaving. Obeying
a centuries-old precept, they shave
heads and eyebrows twice a month,
before the Uposatha ceremony held
on days of new moon and full moon.
Then monks confess to each other
infractions of their religious code.
Their penance varies according
to the gravity of their sin.*

*Even the most pious finds
occasional time for recreation.
Praves (right) shows quiet delight
at his encounter with elephants
working in a nearby forest.*

110

three million, prey to traffic jams and unplanned expansion. Carbon monoxide seals the city's envelope of sweaty air. But inside the whitewashed walls of Wat Bovornives one finds an oasis of shrubs and songbirds and soothing quiet.

My saffron-robed guide is paler than his fellow *bhikkus* (Pali for monk), who walk so gracefully past us that they almost glide. Self-consciousness of one's every movement accounts for this Theravada grace. I feel burdened by shirt, trousers, shoes, possessions. We talk, and I jot in my notebook: "Bhikku Dhammaramo, age 22, born Douglas Johnson in Midland, Michigan. Always interested in religion, read intensively about various beliefs, particularly Buddhism. At age 18, on a visit to Washington, met Theravada monks from Ceylon. Speaking to them confirmed earlier decision to enter the sangha, which he did two years ago at Wat Bovornives."

"What attracted me most toward Buddhism was

111

the freshness of its teaching," he tells me. "It was like a gust of air blowing into a stuffy room. Something I could grasp and test and understand. A plan to live by. Buddha's message places squarely on the individual complete moral accountability for his own actions. You either make good or bad karma in this life according to what you do each day. The sangha does not assure success in achieving nirvana by following Buddha's Eightfold Path, but it offers an ideal environment in which to seek it. Here I find a happiness that increases every day."

Bhikku Dhammaramo introduces me, too, to a monk's simple life and to his few possessions. Among them: a square of cloth to sit on; another to strain drinking water. Washcloth, towels, bed covering. Robe—three large rectangles of cloth, one each for the upper and lower body, a third to drape over the left shoulder. Five-quart bowl made of iron.

"The bowl is used for our daily *pindapata*—that's Pali for our morning alms collecting; you ought to see it done by the monks who go by canoe," he says.

I take his advice. The turbulent surface of the Chao Phraya River is a steady stream of motley boats and barges in the pre-dawn darkness. Great green clumps of vegetation, uprooted by floods upcountry, threaten to foul our outboard propeller as we rip across the current and enter the main *klong*, or canal, of Thon Buri, Bangkok's sister city. Barge families brush their teeth in the wine-dark water. Naked children take a morning dip before their breakfast bowl of rice. The dawn comes up like Kipling thunder, great and golden, behind the stepped and spired temple roofs. Then, on the narrow stretch of a side canal, this whole watercolor comes to a sudden, saffron focus.

An elderly monk paddles his pod-shaped craft across the brightening klong. The saffron ripples of his robe pass like a flower or a poem, so flowing is the stroke of his teakwood paddle. On the opposite bank a young girl waits. The old monk stops and impassively raises his bowl. Into it she ladles cooked rice from an earthenware pot. She presses her palms together at her forehead, gesturing thanks for his acceptance of the alms. And then she reverently lays a lotus blossom on the worn thwart of the small canoe.

*F*rom Bangkok I fly three hours north to Chiang Mai, Thailand's second city, a provincial capital surrounded by cool green mountains. I go directly to Wat Santi Tham Nakhon, a compound near the city's outskirts. Two banyans and a cluster of smaller trees shade its fringes; most Thai wats offer a grove of green for man's repose. I note that the earth within the compound's walls has been swept scrupulously clean—no leaf left under which an insect might accidentally be trod upon. Buddha's precepts forbid a monk to kill any creature.

MISSIONARY MONK *attracts an entourage of Meo children adorned with solid-silver necklaces favored by young and old of both sexes. One of many hill tribes in northern Thailand, Meo trace ethnic roots to China. They raise opium poppies as a cash crop, though the Thai government encourages growing fruits and vegetables instead. Maha Tawin, the only bhikku from Wat Santi Tham who speaks the Meo language, began his mission voluntarily, seeking to root out tribal superstitions and implant Buddhist ideals.*

MICHAEL KUH

MICHAEL KUH

In villages the wat may serve as community center, dispensary, employment and news agency, home for the aged and the mentally ill, place of safe deposit for valuables, school, warehouse, recreation center, and lodging place for guests. In larger cities, the wat's religious role dominates.

I speak to Santi Tham's athletic-looking young abbot. "But of course," he replies, "we have an empty *kuti* — hut — you are welcome to use as long as you care to stay with us. I will introduce you to Praves, one of our novices, who will show you the way. He will profit from your visit; he reads English well but needs practice in conversation."

The monks' kutis are small one-room buildings of teak, neat and uncluttered rather than Spartan. Furniture is minimal: small altar, table and chair,

EARNING MERIT and making merry go hand in hand when visitors and villagers of the Chiang Mai area gather for Tot Kathin. *A ceremony dating back almost to Buddha's time, the term means "to lay down a wooden frame on which to cut cloth." Monks of an earlier day cut, sewed, and dyed their own robes from donated cloth. A few still do.*

Poorer temples depend on proceeds from the annual kathin and other festivals for candles and incense, robes, food, utensils, building materials, and other needs. After the ceremony the monks usually retire, leaving the laity to an afternoon of music and dancing.

low, mattressless rattan bed—"refrain from sleeping on a high or wide bed," Buddha admonished the sangha. The weathered brown of the building's walls blends with the brown of the wat's grounds, and my days blend with the 2,500-year-old rhythm of Theravada's graceful pace.

It is still dark when I awake, wash quickly in cold tap water outside my kuti, and join Praves. He makes his pindapata with two fellow novices along Chiang Mai's flower-fringed paths. Rice, curries, and sometimes fruits and vegetables collect in their bowls. Then they return to the wat to eat. No bhikku may eat before it is light enough to perceive the leaves on the trees, or after noon. Some eat twice during these hours, once after pindapata and again before the midday deadline. Others, like Praves, eat but once. After noon, monks are permitted to take tea, coffee, or soft drinks.

Like other body movements, Praves explains, eating has been disciplined to enhance awareness—the heart of meditation. "My mind tells me 'Now I raise the food to my mouth, now I chew, now I swallow,'" he says. "This thinking while I eat—this thinking of my legs while I walk or of my breath when I meditate—

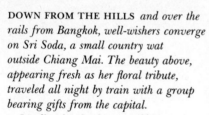

DOWN FROM THE HILLS *and over the rails from Bangkok, well-wishers converge on Sri Soda, a small country wat outside Chiang Mai. The beauty above, appearing fresh as her floral tribute, traveled all night by train with a group bearing gifts from the capital.*

Lending local color, an Akha woman wearing a wealth of silver jewelry offers packets of Chinese green tea; men from the Karen contribute music of gong and a lute-like instrument. Tribal delegations receive goodwill gifts of blankets from the monks.

Gold talons flashing, garlanded girls (far right) weave sinuous patterns to dreamlike music. The Thai fingernail dance once figured in temple rites. Later, danced by princesses, it graced palaces of Chiang Mai kings. When it is performed in darkness, flickering candles held between the fingers replace the curved thimbles.

116

has become as much a part of me as my bowl or my robe." And accounts perhaps, I tell myself, for the grace of movement as natural to a Thai monk as breathing.

After morning food there is chanting in the wat's high-beamed temple. With the help of Praves, I have come to understand a bit of Pali. *"Buddham saranam gacchami,"* the monks intone. *"Dhammam saranam gacchami. Sangham saranam gacchami*—I take refuge in the Buddha. I take refuge in the dhamma. I take refuge in the sangha." Then the same three refrains are repeated—a singsong rather like chants I've heard in the gray stone abbeys of France.

Study, prayer, self-examination, tutoring, lectures, and meditation crowd a bhikku's day. In meditation he sits as if frozen—merely breathing. "It is very hard to empty your head when you are a beginner," Praves says. "Mine was full at first—thoughts of my seven brothers and sisters, the paddies around our house, silly things like the sweetness of fresh sugarcane. But I would try to push these away and remember how my *adjan*, my teacher, had taught me to think of nothing but my breathing—'Now I am breathing in, now I am breathing out.' And finally it was easier to empty my head. Then one day I felt such a happiness my body and my head floated away. Like sleep, but no dream has ever made me so happy. I knew I had at last managed several minutes of meditation. That day was like arriving home after a long journey."

A bhikku's routine includes officiating at various ceremonies—marriages, housewarmings, funerals—serving on *Wan Phra* (the Buddhist Sabbath), protecting against ill omens, propitiating spirits. In the villages, too, the bhikku may participate actively in community projects—helping direct the building of a well, a new road, a dam, or a school. Some monks may serve as missionaries. With

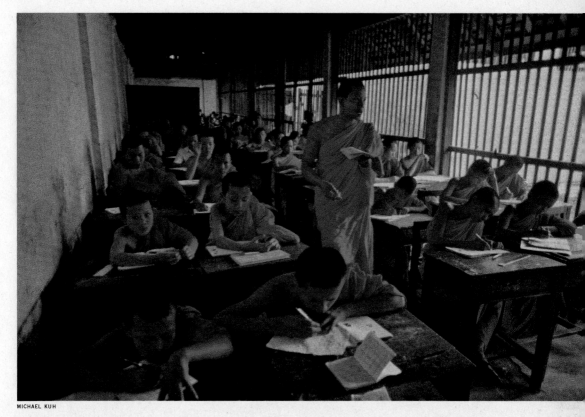

LEARNING THE "THREE BASKETS," *or categories of the Buddhist canon, along with the three R's, novices attend public school classes taught by a monk at Wat Phratad Haripunchai. Monastery schools pioneered in bringing literacy to Thailand's youth; some state schools still operate within wats. The main* vihara, *or temple, here at Lamphun (opposite) displays the carved and inlaid facade adorning many of the nation's 24,000 temples.*

Praves I walked through fields of white opium poppies on the slopes of 5,500-foot Doi Pui to visit one. Two years earlier Maha Tawin had left Wat Santi Tham to live among the Meo hill tribes. "They do not speak Thai," he said. "I am closer to them now, but the old people do not care for what I try to teach. Maybe the children will grow up to understand Buddha's way."

In their daily routine novices follow ten precepts set out by Buddha; ordained monks follow 227. Any man can resign from the sangha anytime he chooses. A novice quits merely by declaring his intentions and removing his saffron robe. The bhikku exits by declaring at a simple ceremony, "I hereby take leave of the sangha, may you all remember me as a layman." But so intense is the experience of life in the order that monks have been known to choke up at the leave-taking ceremony, unable to say the words that will release them.

Praves and I return to Chiang Mai in time for activities connected with the full moon. On this day each month—and again at the new moon—monks and novices all over Thailand have their heads shaved. "Is it a practice rooted in health reasons, say, relief against heat and insects?" I ask the abbot of Santi Tham.

119

"No," he answers. "Buddha taught that vanity is destructive. Hair is a distracting adornment." I watch the shaving until it is Praves's turn on the stool beneath the banyan's shading branches. A cap of lather first, then the razor uncovers a strip of scalp that quickly widens to a naked patch. More deft strokes and both eyebrows disappear. The transformation in the youth's good looks is startling. I think of a butterfly turned back into a caterpillar.

*L*ack of vanity, chasteness, poverty, inner serenity—these are among the pillars that make the bhikku an exemplar of moral conduct. His is an ideal the layman respects, knowing from his own frailties how difficult it is for men to overcome the craving that—as Buddha taught—is the root of all suffering. Avoiding emotional extremes and social disharmony minimizes craving, and hence suffering. Thais call control of the emotions "keeping a cool heart"—not in the sense of being coldhearted, but of keeping one's cool.

I get a lesson in the broadness of the phrase when Praves and I attend a Buddhist funeral. Theravada followers look at death as inevitable, that it is in the nature of all composed things to decompose. They accept the belief that when one's body dies the life-force shaped by one's karma appears again in reincarnated form. Thus sorrow over a death is carefully controlled, and every effort made to banish it with fellowship and ceremony.

"We are late; already the funeral procession is starting," Praves says as we drive into the town of Lamphun, where the body of the abbot of Wat Phratad Haripunchai is to be cremated. We park the car and skirt the crowd following the teakwood-and-gilt spire of the dead abbot's ceremonial bier. We climb the temple steps and overlook a phalanx of saffron robes shaded by black umbrellas. One young novice, perhaps 12 years old, stands spotlighted by the hot Thai sun. His young face is solemn, looking forward. It is only a moment, then the sangha moves ahead. Its pace is Theravada's grace.

Watching, I remember a classroom here in Lamphun where the sun threw stripes from a lattice wall across the saffron robes of novices gathered in an English class. I had been invited to speak to the group in my native language, and I wondered what I could say. I decided to read a translation from their own Pali scriptures and turned by chance to verse 165 of the Dhammapada:

> *By oneself indeed is evil done;*
> *By oneself is one defiled;*
> *By oneself is evil left undone;*
> *By oneself indeed is one purified.* . . .

I looked at the politely smiling boys—future bhikkus—so serene in this credo I was quoting. And I suddenly felt our roles reversed. I had nothing of value to teach them. I was their pupil.

ALONE IN A CAVE *that serves as a shrine, a forest monk meditates as he paces to and fro. Renouncing worldly pursuits, monks in Thailand today follow a regimen Buddha set for his disciples 2,500 years ago: "Be a light unto yourself, a refuge unto yourself."*

Wing-tsit Chan

The Orderly
Realm of
CHINESE SAGES

T he Duke of Lu acceded to an unusual request, according to tradition, and
granted Confucius a carriage with two horses and a page for the 300-mile
journey. Off rode the respected teacher, up the broad valley of the Yellow
River to the capital at Loyang, to a meeting with Lao Tzu, the curator of royal
archives. Confucius was 34 at the time (518 B.C.), Lao Tzu several decades his
senior. History honors the two sages as founders of the great philosophical movements Taoism and Confucianism. These combined with Buddhism to give East
Asia its moral and spiritual base.

Confucius went to Loyang to study ancient rites and ceremonies with Lao Tzu.
It happened that a funeral took place during the visit. A partial eclipse darkened
the sky and Lao Tzu had the bier stopped on the side of the road until the sun
reappeared, saying that no dutiful son would bury his relatives in darkness. Only
a criminal or a disrespectful person would commit such an evil, he said.

In all this Confucius apparently agreed, but we have only a few accounts to
verify that distant meeting. Indeed, we know little about the life of the man

named Lao Tzu. But of the philosophy attributed to him we know much: It extolled the Tao, the natural way. In contrast, Confucius' philosophy was concerned with human society and duty, education and moral perfection. Confucius looked to man to understand nature and heaven; Lao Tzu examined nature to understand man. Yet Confucius and Lao Tzu complemented each other, like two sides of the Chinese mind. The sages respected the traditional ceremonies and fundamentally agreed that theirs was an orderly realm in which man, nature, and heaven were tightly and inextricably bound.

The concept of heaven went far back into China's antiquity, back into the Bronze Age around 1500 B.C. At that time rulers who called themselves sons of heaven traveled with elaborate trappings to Mount T'ai in northern China. There they built an altar, made sacrifices, gave thanks, played sacred music, and took part in ceremonial dances. Until the early 20th century Chinese emperors followed that tradition on the outskirts of Peking; only they could initiate this service addressed to heaven, an act that reaffirmed their right to rule.

Shang Ti (Lord-on-High), an anthropomorphic god, lived in heaven and watched over the actions of the people, rewarding or punishing them for their deeds. The sky swarmed with mythical creatures such as the benign dragon who guarded the hoard of heavenly gems and treasures. To interpret heaven's will, priests resorted to divination. They carved grooves in tortoise shells or animal bones; then, after applying red-hot rods, they read the resulting cracks as messages from above. The will of spiritual beings rigorously controlled the life of man—spirits commonly identified with one's ancestors. Perhaps even Shang Ti was an ancestor, the greatest of them all. Then, about 1000 B.C., a gradual shift from fear of spiritual beings to stress on human behavior began to occur, providing the background for Confucius' humanistic thoughts.

*"In ancient times men found . . .
all excellent qualities in jade.
Soft, smooth, and glossy,
it appeared to them like
benevolence; fine, compact,
and strong, like wisdom . . .
bright as a brilliant rainbow,
like heaven . . . esteemed by all
under the sky, like the path
of truth and duty."*

Confucius in the Li chi

Symbol of heaven, this yellow jade disk from the third or fourth century B.C. served as ornament or religious device; Nelson Gallery-Atkins Museum, Kansas City. Bronze chimera from the Han dynasty (206 B.C.-A.D. 220) evoked nature gods; Freer Gallery of Art, Washington

Eternally intertwined, the two dolphin-shaped parts of yin-yang *represent the prime pre-Confucian forces of a divided but complementary universe. Yin stands for earth, darkness, female, autumn; yang for heaven, brightness, male, spring. Eight trigrams for divination border the symbol in this carving from the Wellcome Museum, London. Opposite: Sons in sackcloth honor their deceased father in Singapore; Winfield Parks, National Geographic photographer*

In the small feudal state of Lu on Shantung Peninsula, the boy was born to the impoverished but noble K'ung family in 551 B.C.—the boy who in his manhood would teach the divine right of all men of ability to be educated. He became a teacher, a meticulous observer of rituals, a critic of tyrannical government, and eventually won recognition as Grand Master K'ung (K'ung-fu-tzu; in Latin, Confucius). But when given a government post as minister of justice, he concluded that even this did not allow him to effect the reforms he had preached. So, in his fifties, he forsook his native state and set out to travel through Lu's neighboring realms with some of his students. Later disciples of those disciples compiled his teachings and his conversations with officials along the way. Together with ancient Chinese scriptures and later Confucian writings those teachings became the basic text of classical Chinese education.

The teachings of Confucius may be summed up in one word: *jen* (humanity, love, humaneness). He sought to train youths to be men of nobility. The superior man is "a man of wisdom without perplexities, a man of humanity without worry, a man of courage without fear." The perfect prince.

At the base of his moral system rested the individual and the family. "When the personal life is cultivated, the family will be regulated; when the family is regulated, the state will be in order; and when the state is in order, there will be peace throughout the world." Filial piety assumed the proportions of a commandment—"an unalterable principle of heaven and earth and the norm of people's conduct." Should a child ever break the pattern? Hardly ever. A son "never disobeys" but sometimes "remonstrates with his parents gently" if they are wrong. And to make the system work, Confucians established the Five Relationships with rules for the behavior of sovereign and subject, parent and child, elder and younger brother, husband and wife, friend and friend. The individual and society balanced each other and received equal weight.

Because of this humanistic emphasis, many have questioned whether Confucius concerned himself with religion and whether, without creed, church, or clergy, Confucianism ranks as a religion. Although neither Confucius nor great Confucians of later centuries posed as prophets or religious leaders in the Western sense, they did advocate reverence and promote traditional religious rites. Confucius never used the ancient word *Ti,* "Lord," but the less personal *T'ien,* meaning "heaven." For him heaven reigned but did not rule. He said, "Respect spiritual beings but keep them at a distance." He intended that man take care of his own affairs, not rely on his ancestors for decisions and help.

Moral behavior was crucial to him: "A man of humanity, wishing to establish his own character, also establishes the character of others." But he also stressed

"Those who are born wise are the highest type of people; those who become wise through learning come next; those who learn by overcoming dullness come after that. Those who are dull but still won't learn are the lowest type of people....

I won't teach a man who is not anxious to learn, and will not explain to one who is not trying to make things clear to himself. If I hold up one corner of a square and a man cannot come back to me with the other three, I won't bother to go over the point again."

Confucius in the Analects

religious acts. "When parents are alive, serve them according to the rules of propriety. When they die . . . sacrifice to them according to the rules of propriety."

After his death in 479 B.C., educated Chinese honored him with increasing reverence and made his temple in Shantung a goal of pilgrimage. Government officials, building a state doctrine based on his teachings, ordered that temples be erected in his honor in every administrative district.

The sayings and writings of Lao Tzu came to be collected at the behest of a frontier guard, legend tells us. Lao Tzu, having retired as royal archivist, was withdrawing to the west through mountain passes. Yielding to the guard's request, he wrote some 5,000 words for the benefit of posterity. They set forth the Tao, the Way, "which existed before heaven and earth." Tao does not control actions; rather it allows them to develop naturally, spontaneously.

The story of the sage's withdrawal and his passive philosophy suggests that Taoism teaches a rule primarily for hermits and retired scholars. Yet Lao Tzu also spoke out as a severe critic of conventional Chinese morality and political control: "The more laws and order are made prominent, the more thieves and robbers there will be." Unlike Confucius, he upheld nature as the guide; and, speaking as a moralist for all time, he urged, "Repay hatred with virtue." Around this simple philosophy grew a popular religion presided over by a multitude of gods, a religion broad enough to encompass even ancient practices of divination and the search for a longer life through alchemy.

In their active careers China's scholar-officials tended to follow Confucius' precepts; in retirement they sought seclusion to contemplate the mystical writings of Lao Tzu. And after the first century A.D. some Confucian and Taoist scholars found it fashionable to seek sublime truths in Mahayana Buddhism, a religion that travelers and traders brought from India over the great silk routes and mountain passes of Central Asia. The new religion's many saints and its doctrine of personal salvation also appealed strongly to the less educated.

All three systems advanced the age-old Chinese belief in the orderly universe. The pious learned to obey Confucianism, Taoism, and Buddhism all at the same time and could find temples dedicated to the three sages in most parts of their land. Typically, the devout wore a "Confucian crown, a Taoist robe, and Buddhist sandals." When the scholar Chang Jung died in A.D. 497, he was holding in his right hand a copy of Buddhism's Lotus Scripture; in his left, two books, the Confucian *Classic of Filial Piety* and Lao Tzu's *Classic of the Way and Virtue*.

Buddhism affected popular Taoism dramatically, providing the model for worship in temples. For the peasants, Taoism and Buddhism merged in a phantasmagoria of myth and magic. But a certain quality remained, a simple piety.

Well do I remember an unlettered country woman who, because of her good and devotional character, was asked by her fellow villagers to go to the shrines and worship for them. She usually went to the shrine of the Buddhist goddess Kuan-yin. Her young son carried the basket of incense, candles, paper money, pastries, fruits or meat, and tea, wine, and firecrackers. Entering the low-roofed shrine, the boy burned the incense, lit the candles, and spread the offerings. The woman knelt before the clay image. Speaking in a soft voice, bowing repeatedly, she threw two wooden blocks for divination. On more than one occasion the boy's mother emerged in tears: Her mission had been fulfilled; she had communicated with the spirits. She asked no pay for her services, though the villagers usually gave the boy fruit, a piece of meat, or a coin for good luck.

That I remember particularly well, for I was the boy.

"The highest good is like water. Water benefits all things generously and is without strife. It dwells in the lowly places that men disdain. Thus it comes near to the Tao. The highest good loves the [lowly] earth for its dwelling. It loves the profound in its heart, it loves humanity in friendship, sincerity in speech, order in government, effectiveness in deeds, timeliness in action. Since it is without strife, it is without reproach."

—Lao Tzu in the Tao Te Ching

Wending through the wild, cloud-shrouded mountains of a Taoist landscape in a painting by an unknown artist from the T'ang dynasty (A.D. 618-907), an emperor's entourage recedes amid the vastness of nature. Lao Tzu himself rides a water buffalo in the portrait at left from the Sung dynasty (A.D. 960-1279). The painting is by Ch'ao Pu-chiu, whose literary name is Wu-chiu, and epitomizes the scholar-recluse. Both in the National Palace Museum, Taipei

Pilgrims' Path

Buddhist Japan

Oliver Statler

We climb for 20 minutes up the steep pilgrim path from the road to the temple set amid pines and sheer rock walls. An old woman, bent almost double by rheumatism, toils up painfully: "My legs and feet are bad, but Kobo Daishi is pulling me." A 73-year-old man, making the pilgrimage to give thanks for his recovery from a stroke the year before, brings up the rear, almost carried by two guides but still on his feet, his face radiant.

The faith that drives them has brought thousands of Japanese each year for centuries to Shikoku, smallest of Japan's four main islands, to trace the footsteps of one of that nation's greatest religious leaders, Kobo Daishi. A convert to Buddhism who spent years wandering and meditating on the island, he spearheaded the growth of that religion in ninth-century Japan and helped give it a distinct Japanese character. Today some 11,000,000 of his countrymen belong to his Shingon sect, one of the six major Buddhist divisions in Japan.

Intrigued by the pilgrimage and the remarkable man who inspired it, I have come to Japan to live and to study the pilgrimage at first hand. I began at the sage's grave in the great monastery he founded at Mount Koya on the island of Honshu. Here his blessing, protection, and company are sought by the pilgrim — for on this journey one always travels with Kobo Daishi. The pilgrim's staff symbolizes his presence, and on the pilgrim's sedge hat are written the words

"We Two." After staying the night on Mount Koya, the pilgrim comes down, crosses the choppy channel to Shikoku by steamer, and near Tokushima begins a circuit of 88 temples—one to remedy each of the major illusions of the soul.

I have walked most of the route, trying to feel what it was like in the old days when all pilgrims went afoot. Often on the island as I traverse a silent cypress forest or a shore with the whisper of the sea in my ears, I feel a special closeness with this man who drew so much inspiration from nature and hymned its beauty in poems:

> *From the mountain temple the morning fog*
> *is like the ocean,*
> *The breeze among the pines makes waves.*

Kobo Daishi was born on this lovely island in 774. The family was prosperous; the men served as Confucian scholars and imperial officials. But the

FLICKERING FLAMES *consume sin on Mount Koya, traditional starting point for pilgrims tracing the footsteps of Kobo Daishi. In the* goma *ceremony—derived from ancient Vedic fire worship— the priest burns oil, grains, and 108 pine sticks representing arrogance, anger, greed, and 105 other defilements. Kobo Daishi founded this monastery on Honshu in 816 for his Shingon sect; he rests entombed on grounds that hold some 120 temples and welcome a million visitors a year.*

Women ladle water from basins onto statues of Jizo (right), guardian deity of children and travelers; washing him, they purify themselves. Wood strips in the statues' laps bear the names of the dead for whom pilgrims pray.

133

times were convulsive. Struggles for succession wracked the court. Buddhism, which had reached Japan only two centuries earlier, had become the court religion and challenged the ancient cults of the people. A brilliant student at the university on Honshu, Kobo Daishi could not escape the ferment. He withdrew from the university, converted to Buddhism, and returned to Shikoku to enter the mountains. He wandered, scantily clad, eating meagerly, pushing body and spirit to the limit. At last revelation came; in a ballad's words, "A bright star fell from heaven and entered his mouth."

He was ordained a priest and went to China to study. Returning, he brought back a doctrine tinctured with Indian mysticism. It became known as *Shingon*, the True Word. Through mystical priestly rites and by meditation the devotee could attain Buddhahood in this life. While the mystical elements may appeal to some intellectuals today, millions of other followers are guided toward Buddhahood by leading a moral life and through a belief in the power of prayer and of faith.

Kobo Daishi won favor at the Japanese court, served succeeding emperors,

pioneered in educational and social work, and gained fame as a writer, painter, sculptor, and (by no means least to the Japanese) a calligrapher of genius. Legends clustered around his name: He plunged his staff into the dry earth and springs gushed forth; he took the bitterness from bracken and made trees bear sweeter fruit; he built roads and bridges, introduced tea to Japan, and invented the Japanese syllabary. Known as Kukai in his lifetime, he was by imperial decree awarded the posthumous name Kobo, which means "Propagator of the Buddhist Law," and the title Daishi, "Great Teacher" or "Saint."

Little wonder that places associated with his early asceticism and the temples he founded became objects of pilgrimage. Probably disciples began the treks. But it was not until the 17th century, when the Tokugawa shoguns came to power and brought peace and stability to the war-ravaged country, that common folk could do much traveling. The earliest guidebooks for pilgrims date from then. Their pages reveal that it was a rugged trek. Accommodations were in vermin-infested farmhouses and temple sheds. Many made their way by begging, either to

WOODCUT FROM AN 18TH-CENTURY PILGRIMS' GUIDEBOOK, COURTESY JUN'ICHIRO KITAGAWA, MATSUYAMA, JAPAN. LEFT: GORDON W. GAHAN

CLUTCHING STAFFS *that symbolize Kobo Daishi's presence, pilgrims climb to one of his 88 temples on the island of Shikoku. Ribbons identify their group; envelopes hanging from necks hold* ofuda, *name slips, to leave at temples. Buses take the devout to the gates of most temples. Earlier pilgrims (above) walked the 850-mile route, packing food on chest, bedding on back. Seat flap provided scant comfort at rocky way-stops.*

135

AROMA OF SANCTITY *rises above temple eaves as pilgrims thrust incense into a* koban,
a stone basin, abrim with ashes from offerings to Yakushi-nyorai, buddha of healing and
"Lord of the World of Pure Emerald in the East." Sign on post advises "Beware of pickpockets."
Priest (above) inscribes the record book of a woman clad in traditional white garb,
with prayer beads, ofuda box, and a small brass bell to ring while she walks and prays.

demonstrate humility or because few had—or dared carry—the necessary cash.

To walk the route takes about two months. While some temple-goers still hike it today, most of them travel comfortably on tour buses. I have found it easy to feel superior to those bus pilgrims, telling myself they are cheating themselves of the physical exertion and closeness with nature that brings a glimmer of the saint's asceticism. Now and then I have hitched a ride, and I've been grateful. But the question nags me: Have buses and packaged tours made it so easy that the spirituality of the pilgrimage has been diminished?

*T*hus, out of curiosity, I have signed up with a bus tour. Completing the circuit by bus requires two weeks, but one agency has divided the pilgrimage into five sections, each taking but a long weekend. I find that next on their schedule is the fourth section, covering temples 44 through 70.

When I meet my fellow pilgrims at a Shikoku port early on a gray October morning, I see with disappointment that few wear the pilgrim's traditional white robes, almost none the sedge hat. At least everyone has the essential staff; the tour agency provides these. As we pile into the buses we seem a very "middle" group: middle-class, middle-aged, middle-income. Most are city folk with city folk's reserve. But camaraderie will grow. Morning and evening as we ride we chant together the "Hannya-Shingyo," a prayer verse known as the "Heart Sutra" that packs the essence of Mahayana Buddhism. In time we will even join in a little contest to see who can be first to ring each temple's bell.

I ask my companions what has brought them. One man says: "To train my mind and spirit. I believe if we older people set a good example, the young will learn from us." An attractive young woman tells me she is a follower of one of Japan's new sects—some aggressive and evangelical, like Soka Gakkai—which have flourished amid the country's vast social changes since World War II. "I come to compare the new with the old, my faith with the Buddhism of my family." She does not say so, but I suspect she has come also to heal a family rift.

Others seek a simple enrichment of life. A schoolteacher tells of his shock at a brother's sudden death a few years ago. "It seemed so sad that all his life he had only worked, worked, and worked, never taking time to enjoy himself. His widow shared my feeling and, having made a pilgrimage herself, urged me to do so while I could. So here I am."

Our first stop is Taisanji (the suffix *ji* means "temple"), built in the sixth century and visited by Kobo Daishi. As at every Japanese Buddhist temple, its main hall enshrines an image of the buddha or bodhisattva to whom it is dedicated—in this case Kannon, a bodhisattva who embodies the love and compassion central to the faith. But we worship also at a small hall dedicated to Kobo Daishi. Before it some pilgrims bow briefly, some light candles, some burn incense, others pray

PILGRIM'S WAY *through fog-mantled cedars to a remote temple recalls Buddha's words: "The man who walks in the noble path lives in the world, and yet his heart is not defiled by worldly desires." Folklore says the towering* sugi, *whose needles supply incense and flavor saké, sprang from the bristly beard of Prince Susa-no-o, a mythical founder of Japan.*

GORDON W. GAHAN

or softly repeat the invocation *Namu Daishi henjo kongo*. Like any Buddhist formula it has layers of meaning. To one man it may imply simply veneration of Kobo Daishi; to another it may mean veneration of the saint and, beyond him, the Absolute; to yet another it may also call on his own Buddha-nature to manifest itself.

At both halls we each leave a coin and a slip of paper on which we have written name, address, age, and date. Thus we indicate repentance of sins and also satisfy that deep-seated compulsion to scrawl "Kilroy was here." In the old days pilgrims used wooden blocks which they nailed to temple walls. Our paper slips are certainly less trouble and we are assured that at season's end they will be respectfully disposed of—burned or cast into the sea.

We have pilgrim books in which the priests certify our visit to each temple. Many a pilgrim has been buried with this precious document. If we traveled individually, we would present our book to the priest, who would raise it to his forehead in respect and, with bold calligraphy and vermilion stamp, certify our visit. But there are so many of us that our books are carried by the tour escorts, who present them to the priests. This is sensible, yet I miss the little ceremony and the sense of completion it brings.

We lodge the night in the handsome reception hall of a mountainside temple, surrounded by giant cedars and cypresses. Following a custom harking back to when travelers wore straw sandals and washed their feet before entering a house, we first wash the ends of our staffs—symbolically washing Kobo Daishi's feet. Slipping off our shoes, we enter the building and gather around big kettles of hot green tea. Then comes an announcement: There is only one bath, to be used by both men and women. No question who takes possession first; this is Japan. The men stampede for the steaming water while the women pour themselves another cup of tea. I dally in the bath and am still dressing when the women mount an invasion of their own. If men are allowed precedence, they are not allowed advantage. The men give way with some mildly ribald joshing. Both sides preserve modesty with small towels.

Dinner appears to be Buddhist, or vegetarian; boiled rice and pickled vegetables, side dishes of *tofu* (bean-curd cake) with a large mushroom and taro (a starchy tuber), boiled spinach with sesame seeds, fern shoots, noodle soup with green onions, and a cucumber salad. In the salad I discover a bit of boiled fish—our meal is not strictly vegetarian after all. I learn also that while most on the pilgrimage are Buddhists, only a minority belong to Kobo Daishi's sect. No matter, I'm told; everybody reveres Kobo Daishi.

Afterward a priest exhorts us to put our whole spirit into the pilgrimage, to forget rank and position, and to abandon daily concerns. "Do not just go

UNDER BOBBING UMBRELLAS, *pilgrims reach a* Daishido, *a temple sanctuary dedicated to the sage they honor. Rooftop ornament symbolizes the five elements in the Buddhist cosmos: sky, wind, fire, water, and earth. At another temple, a girl pulls the log clapper away from a bell (far left), then releases it to toll her arrival; on New Year's eve the bell booms 108 times to banish the past year's sins. Suppliants (lower) light candles in quest of wisdom.*
GORDON W. GAHAN

141

with Kobo Daishi; *be* Kobo Daishi." Bedding is laid on the *tatami* (straw matting) and we sleep 20 to 30 to a room. (The Japanese do not expect privacy.)

*D*imly the sunlight plays on translucent paper temple doors. The morning service reflects Shingon's emphasis on art: Candles glow on a gilded altar; behind it hang paintings of profound symbolism. Drums and bells accent the priest's chanting of the "Heart Sutra." Such services give the pilgrimage a special character, for in Japanese Buddhism it is not customary to worship in a group. The priest usually performs his temple rites alone while individuals come and go through the day. Perhaps this will change. Priests can see the response of groups such as ours, and the success of the new sects has demonstrated that many people feel a need to worship together.

CONVIVIAL CUP *of green tea revives road-weary pilgrims at their temple lodgings. After dinner, bedding will convert the tearoom into a dormitory. Guests leave their shoes outside, a time-honored custom that may cause momentary confusion in the morning (above).*

After the service, buses bear us toward a temple trail still deeper in the mountains. It is on this climb that I notice the bent woman and old man persevering to the top. Surely they find the temple's natural setting reward enough. It perches on a high mountain ledge, walls of wind-scoured rock rising 600 feet above it. Yet there is more: a tunnel carved by the saint which widens into a chapel, and an almost inaccessible eyrie where he meditated. But if the site brings us closer to Kobo Daishi, it also tells us a great deal about Japanese religion.

One senses that this place was sacred long before Buddhism reached Japan. The deep feeling for nature in the indigenous Japanese religion—primitive Shinto—would have made this awesome spot the dwelling of a hallowed spirit. Indeed, when the saint arrived he found a woman mystic living on one of the peaks. He converted her and founded the temple; she lived out her life as a

143

SIGHTS AND SOUNDS *of a pilgrimage: Kneeling woman prepares to post her prayer with others on a temple wall. Priest at altar displays the word* waku, *illusion of the soul, and explains that pilgrims shed one illusion at each temple in the circuit. Bishop on motorcycle roars to a memorial service. Group leader at temple gate summons his flock with a flag.*

devotee and is buried here. A place already sacred was thus consecrated to Buddhism. It was Kobo Daishi's innovation to identify Shinto spirits as manifestations of the buddhas and bodhisattvas. The result was a fusion.

Today Shinto and Buddhism continue as separate faiths—the former with its shrines, the latter with its temples—but in the minds of the Japanese they have become irretrievably intermingled. A majority utilize both faiths, celebrating marriage and birth with Shinto rites, funerals and memorial services with Buddhist rites. When one sees a Buddhist priest cycling along a country road or riding on a city bus, one knows instinctively that he is bound for someone's home to conduct a memorial service at the family altar. How incongruous that Buddhism, with its concern for this life, should have the tint of death in Japan.

The blending of faiths worries the Japanese not a whit. As one pilgrim told me, "What religion you have is not important. All paths lead to the same goal."

As we move on to other temples I notice a pair of elderly ladies who paste copies of the "Heart Sutra" on each temple door. They belong to a group that makes copies of the sutra as a religious exercise and presents them as offerings on pilgrimages. "My calligraphy is so clumsy I use copies made by another," one woman explains. "But my friend brushed her own—she writes beautifully." The artist smiles shyly and turns back to the door hung with a clutter of objects— calling cards, portraits of Kobo Daishi, photographs of loved ones, straw sandals offered with a prayer that a leg ailment be cured, and crutches and braces no

PAGODA-LIKE *pile of ofuda stacks a spindle in a temple hall. Symbol of a spiritual quest which brings 50,000 pilgrims yearly to Shikoku, each name slip signifies the bearer's repentance of sins.*

Their sojourn at an end, pilgrims clad in the yukata, *an informal kimono, relax with a banquet and floor show (opposite) at a resort inn. Yet even here they carry Kobo Daishi's words in their hearts: "Not just in a dream, but in our deep thought, let us meet often hereafter." Tradition says he lies uncorrupted in his tomb awaiting the coming of Maitreya, buddha of the future.*

longer needed because the pilgrimage—with its exercise, sunshine, mountain air, and faith—brought a cure. And why should not that cure be called a miracle?

That night the priest centers his talk around the "Heart Sutra" and its universal application. He emphasizes the last line: *Let us go, let us go, all of us, helping each other, to the other shore*—to spiritual awakening, to the ideal world where there is no envy and no dispute, to nirvana, which was Buddha's goal. He mentions the next day's climb to Yokomineji, the toughest on our itinerary. "When you become weak and weary, repeat those words. Share your strength with each other. Take your time. With steady steps it will be easy."

The next morning we start up the trail together, but as each settles on his own pace, we stretch out, a line of umbrellas weaving through firs and cedars dripping with rain. A swollen stream tumbles down its rocky course beside us. Everything is wet, everything glistens—except, dry in a grotto, a stone Jizo, the bodhisattva who protects children and travelers. He is often found along roadsides, always provided with clothing by the local people. This one wears a jaunty cap and cloak of red. I'm always glad to see him; he is said to have a special compassion for the wicked, and there are so many of us.

Swirling mist envelops us. Emerging, we come to a *torii,* a Shinto gate, framing a view of the island's highest and most sacred mountain, Ishizuchi. We recall that Kobo Daishi meditated here, and then we struggle onward. An hour and a half after our start, the first of us reach the temple and set its bell booming encouragement to those still climbing. At last we all make it, the hard climb! In my mind echo the words of the sutra: *Let us go, let us go, all of us, helping each other, to the other shore.* Suddenly the sun breaks through for the first time.

Doubts about the spirituality of motorized pilgrims vanish with the gray skies. The exultant faces of my companions tell me that if their faith is often simple and without doctrinaire complications, it springs from the heart. Tomorrow, when we disband, I will miss them. In them, Buddhism—and Kobo Daishi—live.

ZEN'S
Disciplined Way to
Sudden Light

Oliver Statler

*T*hey were dressed simply—slacks, sweatshirts or sweaters, the girls with no makeup. But they sat formally, their legs folded, at the long rows of low wooden tables. At the priest's signal they unwrapped bowls and chopsticks. A signal, and servers moved down the rows. Another signal, and the 100 youths picked up their handbooks and recited thanks for the food before them.

They were all 20 years old, all employees of the Matsushita Electric Company, all volunteers for this long weekend of Zen training at Kyoto's temple of Nanzenji. Curiosity had brought them here; also a desire to test themselves. Many had felt traditional values missing from their lives; they hoped to find their "true selves" through this regimen of instruction, cleaning the temple grounds (Zen

*T*his garden's everlasting

stones of gray;

*B*ecalmed in sunshine

through the long spring day.

*P*oetic understatement of a haiku echoes the
austere beauty of the Ryoanji garden,
tranquil haven to a Kyoto monk awaiting satori,
a flash of insight into the unity of all nature.

*Tea ceremony, reflecting Zen
ideals of harmony, reverence, purity,
and tranquillity, provides respite from
the turmoil of the temporal world.
Amid the chaste and serene setting*

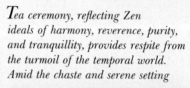

*prescribed by Zen tradition, a monk at
Kyoto's Keishuin temple dips hot water
from a cast-iron kettle, pours it over
finely ground leaves, and whisks it
into a thick, green, bitter-tasting
"froth of the liquid jade."
A single spray of color, the chuckle of
boiling water, and the pungent smell
of a charcoal stove punctuate the simple
yet courtly ritual every move of which
is decreed by centuries of custom.*

teaches "No work, no food"), and purging the mind in *zazen,* sitting in meditation.

I knew that Zen had come to Japan from China, shunning dogma, developing self-reliance, fusing thought and action in a direct and unhesitating style of life. Two main schools arose, *Soto* holding that this enlightenment can be gradually attained, *Rinzai* that it comes in a flash of insight. The latter sect—then as now more austere and with fewer followers—admirably suited Japan's samurai. Rinzai masters dealt stern discipline, spoke in paradoxes, jolted students with sudden blows to help them free mind from self and become one with the universe. To temples of this school such companies as Matsushita today send employees.

But weekend Zen? And for young adults of Japan's postwar generation, who found sitting in formal manner on the tatami as uncomfortable as I did?

I watched them eat their simple food in the absolute silence Zen discipline imposes. Tea was served last. They cleaned the bowls with it, wiped and wrapped

them, recited phrases of gratitude, and quietly filed outdoors to a large chapel. There they placed cushions on the stone floor and sat in rows facing the master. The heavy doors were closed against the night and the lights dimmed.

"Zazen is of no use unless you do it the right way," the priest said softly. "Don't think why you do it. Don't think about your family, your career, your interests. Be *nothing*. Think *nothing*." Once more he told them how to breathe and how to sit, erect but without tension. Silence engulfed the room. The robed priest with chiseled face and spare body became a Buddhist statue.

Two monks with staffs began noiseless progress. A sitter would bend forward to receive two sharp blows across the shoulders. "A strange experience but good," one participant described it. "You reach your limit, yet can't make a sound. You yearn for the beating which pulls you up straight again."

At the end of the hour a bell brought relief. "Relax," the priest said.

They would leave richer, these 100 initiates, as thousands have in recent years. Some would continue to practice zazen, finding it helps awaken mental powers, gives new confidence. More would return to prior ways, for many Japanese — as does the average Westerner — find Zen an insight difficult to achieve.

Japanese business leaders favor its training. Enthusiasm, discipline, and loyalty are virtues Japan's new samurai need as they go forth to conquer the market. And as one successful manager said to me: "This is the spirit of Zen—to be set for what is coming, to fill your responsibility to the limit."

*S*ting of a baton may shock
to sudden enlightenment this young
office worker. She and other employees
(opposite) of the giant Matsushita
Electric Company undertake Zen
training to hone mental discipline and
heighten self-understanding. Zen's
Rinzai sect relies on blows, shouts,
seemingly unanswerable questions
(What sound is made by the clapping
of a single hand?), and grueling
hours of zazen — seated meditation —
to trigger flashes of intuition.

Tradition holds that Zen's
first great patriarch, the Indian
sage Bodhidharma, sat staring at
a cave wall in China for nine years.
He cut away eyelids grown heavy
with weariness, eventually
lost the use of his legs.
Tiny round-bottomed, tip-proof
daruma dolls (his name in Japanese)
recall his single-minded quest
for transcendental truth.

Important in Japan since the
12th century, Zen now numbers
ten million adherents. Its stark
simplicity and orderliness mark
Japanese culture — in archery
as in architecture, in calligraphy,
ceramics, drama, flower arranging
as well as swordsmanship and judo.
For Zen stresses not retreat from
life but full immersion in it.
It rejects the shadow world of
concepts and categories (How can
words about food satisfy hunger?)
to perceive the world directly.

153

He was born of a lotus budded by a red ray of light emanating from Buddha. A king discovered him — sceptered and shining like a small god amid the petals — and adopted him as a son. But like Gautama 12 centuries earlier, the lotus-born youth traded royal robes for a pilgrim's rags.

So begins the legend of Padma Sambhava, the eighth-century Indian guru who spread the enlightenment of Buddha in Himalayan lands rife with worship of spirits, demigods, and demons. He founded the Tibetan form of Buddhism with its priesthood of lamas, or superior ones.

Before Buddhism came, Tibetans had no writing. The world was what they saw and what their minds made real. Hill folk found it easy to believe that potent spirits haunted the hazardous steeps and deep lost valleys, bedeviling man with earthquake and avalanche, blight and disease.

Native shamans fought the evil spirits with witchcraft and blood sacrifice — to small avail. When King Trisong Detsan, inclined to Buddhism by his Chinese mother, tried to build a monastery, he could not keep stone on stone. Night-roaming demons knocked down each day's work.

Padma Sambhava was already famed as a demon tamer when he answered the king's call in 747. He had walked unscathed, it was said, through an adversary's thunderbolts. Again, tied to a pyre, he turned the flames to water. In each case the tormenting demons had yielded to Buddha.

In Tibet he lived up to his fame, subduing defiant demons, accepting those who agreed to defend his faith. Blending native beliefs with the Hindu and Buddhist cults of Tantrism, he employed spells, mystic diagrams, intricate hand movements, and ritual. In Tantrist teaching the contemplative male gods gain power through union with their female counterparts. Devotees seek to attune themselves with this primal power through elaborate rites, some involving sexual union as well as use of wine, meat, fish, and parched grain.

Demons and Lamas in the High Himalayas

JOHN SCOFIELD, NATIONAL GEOGRAPHIC STAFF

Dancing lama flaunts the face and phurbu, or magic dagger, that doomed a thousand Himalayan demons. The rite at Rumtek monastery in Gangtok, cloud-mantled capital of Sikkim (above), honors Padma Sambhava, who 12 centuries ago rooted the gentling beliefs of Buddhism in neighboring Tibet. His mystic powers comforted simple folk beset by devils in a lonely mountain realm.

155

As Padma Sambhava's mission grew, touching Nepal and eventually Bhutan and Sikkim, the once-warlike Himalayan people embraced a peaceful, religious life with sincerity and zest. By the 11th century Tibetan history had changed from a chronicle of conquest and defeat to a narrative of missionaries, monks, and monasteries and the culture they dominated.

By 1950, when Chinese Communists began uprooting Tibetan society, religious orders included about a fifth of the population. A single monastery, Drepung near Lhasa, harbored 10,000 monks. Even brigands who preyed on rich caravans prayed before they set out to rob; they gave part of their booty to support monks and lamas.

Pyre of a princess awaits the flames in Sikkim's royal cremation ground. Red-robed lamas will fuel the fire with grain, consecrated oil, offerings of molded butter. White scarfs guide the soul through bardo, *the dreamlike realm between death and reincarnation. By right thinking the roaming spirit can free itself from base desire and seek a better rebirth or even an end to the cycle — nirvana. As friends pray to ease the way, 10-foot trumpets moan and conch-shell horns simulate the windsong of the forest. Young trumpet bearer has already begun monastic schooling in a sect to which each family customarily dedicates a son for the priesthood.*

JOHN SCOFIELD, NATIONAL GEOGRAPHIC STAFF

Masked deities, led by lamas swinging censers, depict a demon-filled day in the life of the founder of Lamaism. A dark Buddha flanked by disciples looks on from a balcony banner in this Gangtok monastery.

The theory of reincarnated lamas gained acceptance in the 15th century after the rise of the Yellow Hat reformist sect. (Reforms included a ban on some public practices of Tantrism.) Adherents believe that when a lama dies his soul passes to a newborn boy who becomes his successor. The Dalai Lama, god-king to Tibetan Buddhists, ranks highest on the roster of incarnations. His title Dalai means "ocean," suggesting the vastness of his wisdom.

In the search that led to recognition of the present Dalai Lama — the fourteenth — oracles were consulted. A certain holy lake high in the mountains yielded an image of a turquoise-edged roof that led to the farmhouse where the boy, then two years old, was found and tested.

Among signs of spiritual merit in a child are prominent ears, shoulder marks that might indicate remnants of a deity's extra pair of arms, and the ability to recognize objects from a former life.

Amid Earth's highest peaks — supernally beautiful, eternally harsh — man is a fragile being and knows it. The cold wind can kill. A quicker end waits but a step off the thread-thin trails. And so, within and without the cloisters that hug the heights, prayer murmurs a constant counterpoint to the traffic of daily life. Lips of votaries move as rosary beads slip through fingers. Tattered flags whisper pious messages to the tireless winds. And prayer wheels, whirled by hand, transmit their inscribed litany, *"Om mani padme hum* — Oh, the jewel in the lotus," hundreds of times each turn.

Lamaists, like other Buddhists, believe that all beings strive through many lives to achieve the peace of perfection. Some, like Padma Sambhava, who have won release through good works choose to return — for the good of man — for yet another turn on the wheel of life.

159

Sacred Writings of the East

"Ｆrom the unreal lead me to the real; From darkness lead me to the light. . . ." Thus the Hindu prays, questing for ultimate truth. For him the answers lie in wondrously diverse scriptures whose composition may have begun before 2000 B.C. and has continued through the centuries. He divides these into *shruti,* what is heard or revealed — the most sacred — and *smriti,* what is remembered. Shruti includes the ancient Vedas, or sacrificial hymns; the Brahmanas that explain them; and the Aranyakas (Forest Books) and Upanishads that transform the earlier rituals into symbols of deeper theological truth. All four are also collectively called Vedas. Smriti embraces the great epics and the Puranas — tales of gods and ancient kings — as well as philosophical and sectarian texts. Each sacred book, Hindus believe, holds truth by which men can mold their lives.

Theravada Buddhists revere the Tripitaka (Three Baskets), named for the containers in which Ceylonese monks placed their palm-leaf scrolls when Buddha's teachings were written down in the first century B.C. The Mahayana canon shares much of the Tripitaka but adds the Vaipulya and Prajnaparamita Sutras, which set forth doctrines on the bodhisattvas. Other sects offer their own versions of scripture; the immense total defies mastery by a single scholar.

Confucian wisdom lies in the Five Classics, ascribed to the Master's time and earlier, and the Four Books, assembled by disciples. One of the latter, the *Analects,* distills the essence of his teachings. Taoists turn first to the *Tao Te Ching* or *Classic of the Way and Virtue,* probably written down in the third century B.C. Mystical, poetic, full of jolting paradox, it contrasts with and complements the down-to-earth teachings of Confucianism; together the two philosophies inspired Chinese thought and life for more than two thousand years.

The Vedas

Creation Hymn

Seeking the origin of creation, Vedic thinkers found a rich variety of answers. From the gods' sacrifice of a Primal Man, Purusha, says this hymn from the Rig Veda, sprang the sun and moon, all animal life, ritual, and the division of society into four major orders, later called castes:

housand-headed Purusha, thousand-eyed, thousand-footed—he having pervaded the earth on all sides, still extends ten fingers beyond it. Purusha alone is all this—whatever has been and whatever is going to be. Further, he is the lord of immortality and also of what grows for food.... All creatures constitute but one quarter of him, his three quarters are the immortal in heaven.... When the gods performed the sacrifice with Purusha as the oblation.... from that wholly offered sacrificial oblation were born the verses and the sacred chants; from it were born the meters; the sacrificial formula was born from it. From it horses were born and also those animals who have double rows of teeth; cows were born from it, from it were born goats and sheep. When they divided Purusha, in how many different portions did they arrange him?...

His mouth became the Brahmin; his two arms were made into the rajanya [Kshatriya]; his two thighs the Vaishyas; from his two feet the Sudra was born. The moon was born from the mind, from the eye the sun was born; from the mouth Indra and Agni, from the breath the wind was born. From the navel was the atmosphere created, from the head the heaven issued forth; from the two feet was born the earth and the quarters (the cardinal directions) from the ear. Thus did they fashion the worlds.

The Duty of Charity

The ancient bards stressed the need for gift offerings to the gods, but the Rig Veda here also makes clear the rich man's duty to share his bounty with the lowly as well:

Bounteous is he who gives unto the beggar
  who feebly comes to him in want of food.
Success attends him in the shout of battle.
He makes a friend of him in future
  troubles.
No friend is he who to his friend and

comrade, who comes imploring food,
  will offer nothing.
Let him depart—no home is that to rest
  in—and rather seek a stranger to
  support him.
Let the rich satisfy the poor implorer,
  and bend his eye upon a
  longer pathway.
Riches come now to one, now to another,
  and like the wheels of chariots
  are ever moving.

Hymn to the Cow

Plow-puller, load-bearer, source of food and fertilizer, the cow was early revered as the possessor of great powers. In this Atharva Veda hymn, she is compared to the universe:

Worship to thee, springing to life, and
  worship to thee when born!
Worship, O Cow, to thy tail-hair, and to
  thy hooves, and to thy form!
Hitherward we invite with prayer the Cow
  who pours a thousand streams,
By whom the heaven, by whom the earth,

by whom these waters are preserved....
Forth from thy mouth the songs came,
  from thy neck's nape sprang
  strength, O Cow.
Sacrifice from thy flanks was born, and
  rays of sunlight from thy teats.
From thy forequarters and thy thighs
  motion was generated, Cow!
Food from thine entrails was produced,
  and from thy belly came the plants....
She hath become this universe: all that the
  Sun surveys is she.

The Upanishads

Karma

The Upanishads probe underlying truths of human existence. The selections below deal with the related concepts of karma and transmigration. Every action holds its inevitable result; traveling through many bodies, a soul reaps in one life what it has sown in the past:

According as one acts, according as one conducts himself, so does he become. The doer of good becomes good. The doer of evil becomes evil. One becomes virtuous by virtuous action, bad by bad action.

But people say: "A person is made not of acts, but of desires only." In reply to this I say: As is his desire, such is his resolve; as is his resolve, such the action he performs; what action he performs, that he procures for himself. On this point there is this verse:

Where one's mind is attached — the inner self
Goes thereto with action, being attached
*   to it alone.*
Obtaining the end of his action,
Whatever he does in this world,
He comes again from that world [the realm
*   of the dead]*
To this world of action.

— So the man who desires.

Now the man who does not desire — He who is without desire, who is freed from desire, whose desire is satisfied, whose desire is the Soul — his breaths do not depart. Being very Brahman, he goes to Brahman.

Transmigration

Accordingly, those who are of pleasant conduct here — the prospect is, indeed, that they will enter a pleasant womb, either the womb of a Brahmin, or the womb of a Kshatriya, or the womb of a Vaishya. But those who are of stinking conduct here — the prospect is, indeed, that they will enter a stinking womb, either the womb of a dog, or the womb of a swine, or the womb of an outcaste.

Four Stages of Life

Sometime between 300 B.C. *and* A.D. *300 the sage Manu set down an ethical code — the* Manu Smriti — *which specifies the duties of each caste and (in this excerpt) delineates stages of life:*

One should devote to a life of Vedic study with a teacher a period of 36 years, or half of it, or one-fourth of it, or until the Vedas are finished. After studying all the Vedas, or two of them ... one, with celibacy unbroken, should take to the life of the householder.

After obtaining the permission of the teacher, the twice-born should bathe, dress himself according to his family traditions, and marry a girl, beautiful and belonging to his own caste. ...

When the householder observes wrinkles on his skin and white hair on his head, and sees also a son to his son, then he should take refuge in a forest. Leaving the vulgar food and all his external appendage [like clothing, attendants, and so on], he should go ... either with his wife or after entrusting her to his son. ...

There he should continue performing the five great sacrifices as prescribed, and live on the different kinds of pure food of the hermits or with leafy vegetables or fruit. ... He should sit amidst the five fires [four fires around him and the sun above] in summer, under the sky in the rainy season, and with wet clothes in winter. Thus he should increase his penance. ...

Having spent the third part of his life in this way, one should give up all associations [duties and responsibilities] and renounce the world [become a wanderer] for the fourth part. ...

He is without fire, without an abode. He approaches a village only for food. He is detached. ... He is silent and enters the Brahman in meditation.

The Bhagavad-Gita

Duty of a Warrior

Millions of Hindus draw their teachings from the Bhagavad-Gita, *part of the smriti. With armies arrayed for battle, the hero Arjuna in this excerpt lays down his arms, refusing to slay his kin. The god Krishna, serving as his charioteer, dispels the illusion behind his concern and urges him to do his duty as prescribed for his caste:*

Your words are wise, Arjuna, but your sorrow is for nothing. The truly wise mourn neither for the living nor for the dead. There was never a time when I did not exist, nor you, nor any of these kings. Nor is there any future in which we shall cease to be.

Just as the dweller in this body passes through childhood, youth and old age, so at death he merely passes into another kind of body. The wise are not deceived by that.

Feelings of heat and cold, pleasure and pain, are caused by the contact of the senses with their objects. They come and they go, never lasting long. . . . Bodies are said to die, but That which possesses the body is eternal. It cannot be limited, or destroyed. Therefore you must fight. . . .

You ought not to hesitate; for, to a warrior, there is nothing nobler than a righteous war. . . . Die, and you win heaven. Conquer, and you enjoy the earth. . . . Realize that pleasure and pain, and gain and loss, victory and defeat, are all one and the same: then go into battle. Do this and you cannot commit any sin.

A Gandhian View

Though the Bhagavad-Gita *inspired Gandhi, he rejected killing. For him the battlefield was* politics, his weapon ahimsa, *nonviolence. In his* Autobiography *he explains his involvement:*

My uniform experience has convinced me that there is no other God than Truth. . . . To see the universal and all-pervading Spirit of Truth face to face one must be able to love the meanest of creation as oneself. And a man who aspires after that cannot afford to keep out of any field of life. That is why my devotion to Truth has drawn me into the field of politics; and I can say . . . in all humility, that those who say that religion has nothing to do with politics do not know what religion means.

Theravada

Buddha's Last Instructions

In this discourse from the Tripitaka, the dying Buddha—as the "Tathagata, the one who has come to teach you the way"—instructs a monk. He urges self-reliant striving against craving, a major doctrine of Theravada Buddhism:

I am old now, Ananda, and full of years: my journey nears its end, and I have reached my sum of days, for I am nearly eighty years old. Just as a worn out cart can only be kept going if it is tied up with thongs, so the body of the Tathagata can only be kept going by bandaging it.

Only when the Tathagata no longer attends to any outward object, when all separate sensation stops and he is deep in inner concentration, is his body at ease.

So, Ananda, you must be your own lamps, be your own refuges. Take refuge in nothing outside yourselves. Hold firm to the truth as a lamp and a refuge, and do not look for refuge to anything besides yourselves. A monk becomes his own lamp and refuge by continually looking on his body, feelings, perceptions, moods, and ideas in such a manner that he conquers the cravings and depressions of ordinary men and is always strenuous, self-possessed, and collected in mind. Whoever among my monks does this, either now or when I am dead, if he is anxious to learn, will reach the summit.

The Sermon at Banaras

The Tripitaka also preserves Buddha's first ser- *ascetics. In it he reveals the Middle Way, the*
mon, which tradition says he preached to five *Eightfold Path, and the Four Sacred Truths:*

here are two ends not to be served by a wanderer.... The pursuit of desires and of the pleasure which springs from desire, which is base, common, leading to rebirth, ignoble, and unprofitable; and the pursuit of pain and hardship, which is grievous, ignoble, and unprofitable. The Middle Way of the Tathagata avoids . . . these ends. It is enlightened, it brings clear vision, it makes for wisdom, and leads to peace . . . enlightenment, and Nirvana. What is the Middle Way? . . . It is the Noble Eightfold Path — Right Views, Right Resolve, Right Speech, Right Conduct, Right Livelihood, Right Effort, Right Mindfulness, and Right Concentration....

And this is the Noble Truth of Sorrow. Birth is sorrow, age is sorrow, disease is sorrow, death is sorrow; contact with the unpleasant is sorrow, separation from the pleasant is sorrow, every wish unfulfilled is sorrow — in short all the five components of individuality are sorrow. And this is the Noble Truth of the Arising of Sorrow. It arises from craving, which leads to rebirth, which brings delight and passion, and seeks pleasure now here, now there — the craving for sensual pleasure, the craving for continued life . . . for power.

And this is the Noble Truth of the Stopping of Sorrow. It is the complete stopping of that craving, so that no passion remains.... And this is the Noble Truth of the Way which Leads to the Stopping of Sorrow. It is the Noble Eightfold Path....

Teachings on Compassion

The compassionate nature of Buddha's teach-
ings is reflected in these short passages from
the Tripitaka; one advises "turning the other
cheek," the other softens the concept of caste:

Never in this world is hate
    Appeased by hatred;
It is only appeased by love —
    This is an eternal law.

No brahmin is such by birth.
No outcaste is such by birth.
An outcaste is such by his deeds.
A brahmin is such by his deeds.

Victory breeds hatred
    For the defeated lie down in sorrow.
Above victory or defeat
    The calm man dwells in peace.

Consequences of Karma

The Questions of King Menander *records*
conversations between a Greek ruler of north-
western India in the second century B.C. *and*

a Buddhist sage who, tradition says, converted
him. Here the sage explains to the puzzled
European some of the consequences of karma:

"Venerable Nagasena," asked the King, "why are men not all alike, but some short-lived and some long, some sickly and some healthy, some ugly and some handsome, some weak and some strong, some poor and some rich, some base and some noble. . . ?"

"Why, your Majesty," replied the Elder, "are not all plants alike, but some astringent, some salty, some pungent, some sour, some sweet?"

"I suppose, your Reverence, because they come from different seeds."

"And so it is with men! They are not alike because of different karmas. As the Lord said . . . 'Beings each have their own karma. They are . . . born through karma, they become members of tribes and families through karma, each is ruled by karma, it is karma that divides them into high and low.'"

"Very good, your Reverence!"

Mahayana

The Bodhisattva

Mahayana Buddhists revere the bodhisattva — a perfected being who helps others to salvation. The Prajnaparamita Sutras, early Mahayana texts, exalt the bodhisattva's love for mankind:

He looks on all beings as though victims going to the slaughter.... He is filled with great distress at what he sees, for many bear the burden of past deeds which will be punished in purgatory, others will have unfortunate rebirths which will divide them from the Buddha....

So he pours out his love and compassion upon all those beings ... thinking, "I shall become the savior of all beings, and set them free from their sufferings."

The Lotus Sutra

The Lotus Sutra, bearing the name of Buddhism's sacred flower, was compiled before A.D. 250. A basic Buddhist scripture in East Asia, it includes the key Mahayana doctrine that salvation is open to all who express their faith, even to children who sketch Buddha with sticks:

Those among the living beings,
Who have come into contact with former
  Buddhas,
And have learned the Law and practiced
  charity,
Or have held on to discipline and endured
  forbearance and humiliation,
Or have made serious efforts
  at concentration and understanding,
Or have cultivated various kinds of blessing
  and wisdom —
All such beings as these
Have already achieved Buddhahood....

Men who possess a tender heart....
Those who have offered relics,
Or have built hundreds of millions
  of pagodas....
Those who have had pictures of the
  Buddha embroidered,
Expressing the great splendor
Which he achieved from a hundred
  merits and blessings,
Whether embroidered by himself
  or by others,
Have all achieved Buddhahood.
Even boys at play
Who have painted Buddha figures
With straws, wooden sticks, brushes,
  or finger nails —
All people such as these,
By gradual accumulation of merits
And with an adequate sense of compassion,
Have already achieved Buddhahood.

Most Happy Land

The Pure Land sect, nurtured in China and still important in Japan, offers the hope of rebirth in a pure land under a Buddha called both Amitabha and Amitayus — Infinite Light and Infinite Life. The Amitabha Scripture, composed around the fourth century, describes that land:

Beyond a trillion Buddha lands west of here there is a world called Most Happy Land.... Sentient beings in that land have no pain of any kind but enjoy all kinds of pleasure only.... There are seven rows of balustrades ... and seven rows of trees. They are all of four kinds of gems and surround the land.... There are lakes of seven gems filled with water.... The bottoms of the ponds are completely covered with gold dust, and the paths and steps on the four sides are made of gold, silver, beryl, and crystal....

Heavenly music always goes on.... It showers mystical flowers from heaven.... There are always all kinds of wonderful birds of mixed colors....

If there is a good man or a good woman, who, upon hearing of Buddha Amitayus, recites the Buddha's name for one, two, three, four, five, six, or seven days with a single and undisturbed mind, when he or she approaches death, Buddha Amitayus and the many other holy beings will appear before him, and when death comes, he, with his mind not at all upset, will be immediately born into Buddha Amitayus's Most Happy Land.

Confucius

Born into chaotic times, Confucius sought order and peace through reverence of custom, concern with human society rather than the supernatural, and the practice of jen—*perfect virtue. His humanity and reasonableness shine in nuggets from the* Analects, *a record of his conversations and activities compiled by his followers:*

zu Yu asked about filial piety. Confucius said: "Nowadays a filial son is just a man who keeps his parents in food. But even dogs or horses are given food. If there is no feeling of reverence, wherein lies the difference?"

Tzu Kung proposed to do away with the sacrificial lamb offering at the announcement of each new moon. Confucius said: "Tzu! You love the lamb, but I love the rite."

Tzu Lu asked about the worship of ghosts and spirits. Confucius said: "We don't know yet how to serve men, how can we know about serving the spirits?"

"What about death?" was the next question. Confucius said: "We don't know yet about life, how can we know about death?"

Fan Ch'ih asked about wisdom. Confucius said: "Devote yourself to the proper demands of the people, respect the ghosts and spirits but keep them at a distance—this may be called wisdom."

Tzu Kung asked: "Is there any one word that can serve as a principle for the conduct of life?" Confucius said: "Perhaps... 'reciprocity': Do not do to others what you would not want others to do to you."

Someone inquired: "What do you think of 'requiting injury with kindness'?" Confucius said: "How will you then requite kindness? Requite injury with justice, and kindness with kindness."

Tzu Kung asked about the gentleman. Confucius said: "The gentleman first practices what he preaches and then preaches what he practices."

Confucius said: "The young are to be respected. How do we know that the next generation will not measure up to the present one? But if a man has reached forty or fifty and nothing has been heard of him, then I grant that he is not worthy of respect."

When Confucius was traveling to Wei, Jan Yu drove him. Confucius observed: "What a dense population!" Jan Yu said: "The people having grown so numerous, what next should be done for them?" "Enrich them," was the reply. "And when one has enriched them, what next should be done?" Confucius said: "Educate them."

Tzu Kung asked about government. Confucius said: "The essentials are sufficient food, sufficient troops, and the confidence of the people." Tzu Kung said: "Suppose you were forced to give up one of these three, which would you let go first?" Confucius said: "The troops." Tzu Kung asked again: "If you are forced to give up one of the two remaining, which would you let go?" Confucius said: "Food. For from of old, death has been the lot of all men, but a people without faith cannot survive."

The Book of Mencius

Second sage of Confucianism, Mencius (372-289 B.C.) saw China's chaos as a perversion of an earlier Golden Age, and evil as a perversion of human nature, which is innately good. In his collected writings he details man's virtue:

We see that no man is without a sense of compassion, or a sense of shame, or a sense of courtesy, or a sense of right and wrong. The sense of compassion is the beginning of humanity; the sense of shame is the beginning of righteousness; the sense of courtesy is the beginning of decorum; the sense of right and wrong is the beginning of wisdom. Every man has within himself these four beginnings, just as he has four limbs. Since everyone has these four beginnings within him, the man who considers himself incapable of exercising them is destroying himself.

The Mean

Tradition ascribes the Chung Yung (The Mean) *to the disciple Tzu Ssu. One of Confucianism's Four Books, it proposes moderation, balance, and suitability as a moral concept — and informs man how to achieve this harmony:*

efore the feelings of pleasure, anger, sorrow, and joy are aroused it is called equilibrium. When these feelings are aroused and each and all attain due measure and degree, it is called harmony. Equilibrium is the great foundation of the world, and harmony its universal path. When equilibrium and harmony are realized to the highest degree, heaven and earth will attain their proper order and all things will flourish....

The superior man does what is proper to his position and does not want to go beyond this. If he is in a noble station, he does what is proper to a position of wealth and honorable station. If he is in a humble station, he does what is proper to a position of poverty.... If he is in the midst of barbarian tribes, he does what is proper in the midst of barbarian tribes. In a position of difficulty ... he does what is proper to a position of difficulty.... He can find himself in no situation in which he is not at ease.... He rectifies himself and seeks nothing from others, hence he has no complaint to make. He does not complain against heaven above or blame men below. Thus it is that the superior man lives peacefully ... and waits for his destiny, while the inferior man takes to dangerous courses and hopes for good luck.

Lao Tzu

The Eternal Way

Tradition links the Tao Te Ching *to Lao Tzu, sage of the sixth century* B.C. *It posits a mystical Tao — or Way — as the source and governor of all being. Man is enjoined to embrace* wu-wei, *nonaction — letting things happen naturally and responding selflessly to them:*

The Tao [Way] that can be told of is
   not the eternal Tao;
The name that can be named is not the
   eternal name.
The Nameless is the origin of Heaven
   and Earth;
The Name is the mother of all things.
Therefore let there always be nonbeing
   so we may see their subtlety,
And let there always be being so we may
   see their outcome.
The two are the same,
But after they are produced, they have
   different names.
They both may be called deep and
   profound.
Deeper and more profound,
The door of all subtleties!

When the people of the world all know
   beauty as beauty,
There arises the recognition of ugliness.
When they all know the good as good,
There arises the recognition of evil.
Therefore:
Being and nonbeing produce each other;
Difficult and easy complete each other;
Long and short contrast each other;
High and low distinguish each other;
Sound and voice harmonize with each other;
Front and back follow each other.
Therefore the sage manages affairs without
   action
And spreads doctrines without words....

The Great Tao flows everywhere....
Always without desires, it may be called
   The Small.
All things come to it and it does not
   master them; it may be called
   The Great.
Therefore [the sage] never strives himself
   for the great, and thereby the great
   is achieved.

Demon of impermanence grasps the Wheel of Life, fraught with pitfalls through which Buddh
   wisdom leads to enlightenment; 19th-century Tibetan painting in the British Museum, Lond

JUDAISM

Tradition fortifies an ancient faith with rituals symbolized by the Passover plate, the Esther scroll for Purim, the cup for wine blessing, the spice box for Sabbath's end, the citron case for Sukkot. European artifacts of silver and gold in the Israel Museum, Jerusalem; Ted Spiegel, Rapho Guillumette

"HEAR, O ISRAEL"

Elie Wiesel
Historical sections by Rabbi Herbert Weiner

Auschwitz 1944.

"Do you know who's more to pity than we are?" he whispered.

"Who?"

"Those who converted. Hitler did not recognize their conversion. And so, here they are. With us. Suffering without knowing why. Without even being Jewish."

The man who said these words had once been *Rosh-Yeshiva,* dean of a religious school, in Polish Galicia. I liked to listen to him. He had become my new, though nameless, teacher.

"And the Jews," I asked, "do you know why they are made to suffer so?"

He waited a moment before answering: "Suffering always means question, for us and for them alike. Only their question is not ours."

Once upon a time there was a small Jewish boy who, living far away in his town somewhere beyond the mountains of central Europe, thought himself capable of discerning good within evil, of distinguishing dawn from dusk and, in general, of deciphering the symbols, both visible and hidden, that destiny was heaping upon him. Everything seemed simple. He felt secure in his own surroundings. Yet, everything alien frightened him. And alien meant the priest all dressed in black, the watchman with his rifle, the woodcutter and his ax, the schoolteacher and his stick. They all exuded a hostility he considered natural and therefore without remedy.

Man hates only that which disturbs or eludes him. And though we were dependent on our neighbors' tolerance, our lives unfolded independently of theirs, a fact, it seemed, they resented. Our concerted determination to safeguard a separate existence confused and irritated them as much as that existence itself: a living Jew, a believing Jew. According to their calculations, this chosen and accursed people should long ago have ceased to haunt a mankind whose salvation was linked to the cross.

173

I felt no animosity and surely no hate toward them. In truth, I was profoundly
ignorant not only of things Christian but of the non-Jewish world in general.
I did not know that Christians and Moslems both saw their roots in the history
of my people, that the land of Israel was the spiritual cradle of nearly half the
world, that the role Jews played in history and civilization was so out of pro-
portion to their actual numbers—today some 14 million—as to evoke strange
ambiguities of feeling even among their friends.

My knowledge of the Jew, on the other hand, drew from seemingly inexhaus-
tible sources. It came from stories and legends, eyes and silences. It poured into
me daily, continuously, even as the sap of a tree feeds a leaf. And that was just
how I felt—like a leaf on a tree of history whose roots reached back through

many centuries, whose limbs had spread into many lands, and whose power to produce new blossoms in every age had never ceased.

*A*braham, Isaac, and Jacob were the patriarchal roots of the Jewish tree of life. The originating seed was a call bidding Abraham to leave his Mesopotamian homeland and seek a promised land then known as Canaan. There he would found a people. This people was to be locked forever in a special relationship with the creator of heaven and earth whose oneness they would be the first to recognize, whose desire for justice and mercy they would try to fulfill. And their existence would be a blessing to "all the families of the earth."

This is the essence of the covenant which, some 3,700 years ago, set apart and unified the seminomadic tribes who would call themselves the children of Israel. Several centuries later—scholars suggest that the exodus from Egypt might have taken place around the time of Pharaoh Ramesses II—this covenant was renewed and expanded at a desert mountain called Sinai. Jewish tradition agrees that what took place there gave Jews both their reason and power for survival as a people; that is, Israel received its Torah.

Torah has several meanings. It can mean the parchment scroll kept in the synagogue Ark; or the five books of Moses (the Pentateuch) inscribed on this scroll, the "written" Torah which Orthodox Jews believe is the literal word of God. It can include the Talmud, the "oral" tradition which Orthodoxy also traces back to Sinai—legends, laws, and customs that explain the written Torah. In its broadest sense, Torah is every word or act which reveals the power and presence of God—from the preaching of the prophets to the simple statement of an anonymous cowherd: "Lord of the universe! It is known to you that if you had cattle and gave them to me to tend, though I take wages from all others, from you I would take nothing because I love you."

SYRIAN FERTILITY FIGURINES, 2ND MILLENNIUM B.C., IN THE LOUVRE; ERICH LESSING, MAGNUM

The Pentateuch, the other books of the Bible, the Talmud, the prayer book —these are the basic texts of Judaism. But there is more—commentaries on the law, mystical and philosophical writings, the sayings of inspired teachers.

From all these a Jew learns that holiness belongs not only in the synagogue but also in the home and marketplace. When, long ago, a pagan demanded to be taught the essence of Torah while he stood on one foot, the wisdom of Rabbi Hillel's reply was not only in the advice, "What is hateful unto yourself, do not do unto others," but even more in the afterword: "This is the whole Torah, the rest is commentary. Go and study." The concrete and detailed application of principles like love and justice—this is the real wisdom of Judaism.

As I grew older I learned the more abstract concepts of my faith. Thus I was told that to be a Jew means placing the accent on the verb *to be* and the noun *Jew* equally and simultaneously, to guard that one does not exclude the other or become fulfilled at the expense of the other. That to be a Jew means to serve God by taking sides with man and acting as his witness while affirming God's right to judge him. And, finally, that to be a Jew is to opt for God and creation alike—it is a refusal to oppose one to the other.

177

An idealized concept of man and his relationship with God and his fellowman? Perhaps. Still, it was a concept tested every day, almost every hour, in every possible manner and circumstance. At school I read in the Talmud: Why did God create only one man? So that no person could later claim superiority over others. All men have the same ancestor. Also: Suppose the arsonist guilty of setting the Temple in Jerusalem on fire is caught. He is punishable with only 39 lashes of the whip. Let a fanatic kill him and *his* punishment will be death. That is because all the temples in the world are not worth the life of one single man—though he is a criminal.

Painful irony: We were chased from country to country, our sanctuaries were burned, the young and the old among us killed—and yet we went on tirelessly, fiercely, praising the inviolate sanctity of life and proclaiming faith in man, any man, whoever he may be or whatever he may do, to us or to himself.

I shall never forget Shabbat—the Sabbath—in my town, my *shtetl*. With the advent of Shabbat the town became a kingdom whose madmen and beggars were princes. All ordeals and anxieties, past and future, receded into the background. Appeased, man invoked the divine presence to express his gratitude.

A dream of freedom dies in the flames of Jerusalem's holiest shrine as Titus' legionaries crush a revolt by nationalist Zealots. Solomon had built the first Temple; Nebuchadnezzar destroyed it. Zerubbabel raised the second, rebuilt by Herod the Great only 90 years before this siege. Now the center of worship falls under Roman pounding, to rise no more. The year: A.D. *70 (70* C.E., *or Common Era, in Jewish usage; 3830* anno mundi, *in the year of the world, by traditional Jewish reckoning from the creation). Yet a fragment remained—the Western or Wailing Wall, where Jewish pilgrims through the centuries decried their loss.*

The Temple was served by priests, kohanim, *and their assistants,* Levites, *whose duties the Bible had assigned to descendants of Aaron and their kinfolk in the tribe of Levi. With the Temple gone, leadership swung to the studious rabbi (my master) as the teacher of Judaism. Priestly tradition lives on— in family names like Cohen and Levy and in rituals like the blessing offered at the Western Wall (right): "The Lord bless thee and keep thee....The Lord lift up His countenance upon thee, and give thee peace" (Numbers 6:24-26).*

178

"DESTRUCTION OF THE JERUSALEM TEMPLE BY TITUS," 17TH-CENTURY ENGRAVING BY AN UNKNOWN DUTCH ARTIST; ISRAEL MUSEUM, JERUSALEM. BELOW: TED SPIEGEL, RAPHO GUILLUMETTE

Roman victors parade their spoils. Treasures from the Temple include the sanctuary's seven-armed menorah

The mood in the most humble dwelling was festive and serene. The services in the synagogue, the songs of the devout Hasidim and the radiance of their rabbis were dazzling. The jealousies, the hatreds and rancors of the neighbor could wait, so could the debts and worries. Shabbat enveloped all of creation, conferring upon it a dimension of peace and a sense of the absolute.

Let those who are hungry come and eat; let those who are or feel abandoned accept the hand stretched out to them; and let those who hide their pain and fight back tears defy solitude by sharing in the collective joy of Shabbat.

All this I learned, not as one learns some external knowledge, but in living with our traditions, reliving the great scenes of our past, and listening for the sounds handed down by generations of ancestors. My head was filled with memories, stories of prophets and kings and tragic tales about the "remaining

180

lamp that came to symbolize the Jewish people — a scattered folk sustained by the guiding light of their God.

few," over and over the remaining few. I was forever breaking away from Egypt, liberating myself from bondage. I heard Jeremiah lamenting the fall of the first Temple to the Babylonians. And the voices of little children crying the keynote of Judaism through the ages — "Hear, O Israel: the Lord our God, the Lord is one" — as Crusaders set fire to medieval synagogues. And I heard the prophets holding out the bright promise of the Messiah, the Lord's anointed, who would bring an age of universal peace and plenty, when there would be "no sound of weeping, no voice of crying."

For all this I was the messenger, symbol of memory and promise, vessel of continuity, and the creature lending meaning to God's creation. All this I knew and I burrowed in this knowledge as though to measure its awesome depth where all is beckoning and all is presence.

181

*Ship-shaped rock of Masada
simmers in the Dead Sea doldrums,
a derelict of history salvaged
by Israeli diggers. In this desert
citadel, fortified by Herod, diehard
Zealots held out for three years
after the Temple fell. Gripped by
a vise-like siege, Masada's leader
Eleazar Ben Yair concluded "that
a death of glory was preferable to a
life of infamy." Warriors slew their
kin, then themselves—960 in all.
Arrayed for battle, the Romans met
a deathly silence—and a handful
of survivors who had hidden away.*

*The turncoat Jew Josephus
recorded their tale; 19 centuries
later a two-year siege of science
recaptured the drama. The noted
soldier-archeologist Yigael Yadin
unearthed the casemated fortress
wall, storerooms and baths at the
northern tip, the Herodian palace at
the western bulge, the Roman camps
below. Diggers found human bones,
armor, scrolls of scripture, and—
most spectacular of all—part of the
apocryphal Book of Ecclesiasticus
in the lost original Hebrew text.*

*At Jerusalem's Shrine of the Book
visitors scan the ancient Masada texts
as well as the Dead Sea Scrolls
(below), hidden by an ascetic Jewish
sect—the Essenes—in caves at
Qumran, 32 miles north of Masada.*

TED SPIEGEL, RAPHO GUILLUMETTE

A saving remnant shall always remain, the prophet Isaiah assures Israel as it confronts catastrophe. "Even before God strikes the blow," said a rabbi in later times, "he provides a healing." The rabbis themselves were such a healing. Neither wealth nor social position entitled a person to be called rabbi—only recognition that he was an authentic receiver and transmitter of Torah.

Even while the priests were still offering Biblically ordained sacrifices in Herod's golden Temple, the rabbis had begun to transmute Judaism into a faith which was not dependent upon any one place or even one land. The ingredients for this metamorphosis were always present; the Biblical God, though making special demands upon his chosen people, was a universal God. In the time of the second Temple, Jews who lived in Babylon and had no easy access to Jerusalem had substituted small sanctuaries. The rabbis, however, went further. "Wherever ten men gather in My name," they taught, "there will I cause My Presence to descend." It was as if they knew that Jews, soon to be scattered, would need Torah-teachings in their wanderings.

Not that they made light of the Psalmist's oath, "If I forget thee, O Jerusalem, let my right hand forget her cunning." When a Jew prays, they declared, he must face toward the holy city. Nevertheless, the rabbis said, when the Holy of Holies went up in flames, a spark of this flame descended into the synagogue, a place which men can sanctify by their prayers. The basic forms of liturgy were also fixed by the rabbis. The prayer book which emerged was never sealed; it could grow with the inspiration of spiritual genius. But a fixed liturgy meant that a Jew in 6th-century Babylon, in 14th-century Cordova, and in 20th-century Poland were united by words, thoughts, and moods which could annul the disintegrating effects of time and space. Most important, the rabbis spelled out every detail of the law and showed by example how study of the law could be not only a guide to life but in itself life's peak experience.

The result of their labors girded Jews for the long trial of exile that followed the Roman conquest of Judaea 19 centuries ago. Though it lacked a common soil, a common language, a common sovereignty, Judaism had been supplied with a portable homeland whose pillars were "Torah, prayer, and good works." Love of God and man, respect for the life of the mind and for spiritual strivings structured by the wisdom of earlier generations—this was the atmosphere of life within that homeland. Those who lived outside and observed the Jewish ghetto from afar were rarely aware of these things. But those who lived within had no trouble repeating daily, "Blessed are we and blessed is our lot."

To be sure, even a portable homeland required some space and security. And history seemed to decree that every Jewish community in the Diaspora—the dispersion—was to come to an end, usually a catastrophic end. Still, there was the strange fact: before every blow, a healing. Thus, even as the once fruitful community in Babylonia began to fade in the ninth century, vigorous new centers of Torah arose in North Africa and western Europe. Before Spain's thousand-year-old community was ended by Ferdinand and Isabella's decree of exile in

Through the harsh centuries dispersed Jews clung to their identity. Beard, side-curls, and garb betoken the Hasid—"one who is pious." Hasidic style of joy in worship swept eastern Europe in the 1700's; close-knit communities, ultra-orthodoxy mark the movement today.

A HASID PRAYS NEAR THE WESTERN WALL IN JERUSALEM; TED SPIEGEL, RAPHO GUILLUMETTE

1492, eastern Europe was already witness to an efflorescence of Jewish life which, despite poverty and pogrom, was as bright as any in Judaism's long saga.

Beginning with the French Revolution, European Jewry entered into what seemed like a new and shining period. Ghetto walls fell and Jews rushed out to identify with lands that seemed prepared to accept them as full citizens. Many of the freshly emancipated Jews refused to use words like "exile," disclaiming the slightest desire to return to Zion. From now on we shall call our synagogues "temples," said the new Reform religious groups in Germany, for many laws in the Bible and Talmud are outdated and we no longer look forward to rebuilding the Jerusalem Temple. From now on we are Germans or Frenchmen of the Mosaic persuasion—if we still care for that persuasion.

In the West, the period of emancipation was often accompanied by an exodus from Judaism. But in eastern Europe, where the tsars permitted no such release, Jewish masses maintained strong ties to the historic tree of Jewish life. There the call for emancipation produced a new reaction, a movement late in the 19th century urging Jews to return to the ancient land of their fathers, to rebuild it and their own souls. In 1896 Theodor Herzl, a Viennese writer, came to the same conclusion in his pamphlet *The Jewish State*, and modern Zionism was born.

About the turn of the century, small pioneer groups arrived in what was then the neglected lower part of greater Syria. They laid the foundation for the rebirth of Jewish sovereignty in its ancient homeland. In the same period, immigration of Jews from Europe to the West reached a crescendo: The largest and freest Jewish community in history was growing in the United States. Was all this historic coincidence? Was it again the "healing" that was to precede a "blow"? If so, it would have to be the greatest healing that man could conceive, for the blow which awaited was almost beyond human conception.

*E*verything had seemed simple to me, real and vibrant with truth. Every being had its place, every object its usefulness. Then came Nazism and the holocaust and turned everything upside down. By its sheer magnitude and goals the event was eschatological. "Concentrationary" man had just discovered the anti-Messiah. And yet, the effect of Auschwitz and the other death camps was, at first, one of oversimplification. The executioners on one side, the victims on the other. I knew that to be Jewish was to belong to the latter, to accept their fate, their agony, to assume their condition to the end.

And to resist—no matter how. To resist simply by refusing death. By continuing to be. Literally. For the enemy was bent on destroying the Jew by annihilating his being, by refusing him the very right to possess a name, a language, a face. In the kingdom of barbed wire, all subjects were alike and all words were equal. The hours succeeded one another and so did the days, empty and meaningless, until the inmates lost all notion of time.

The adolescent I was ceased to understand. He began to doubt himself and others and especially the peculiar relationship God maintained with his creatures. Was this a punishment God was inflicting upon them or upon himself?

In either case, for what sins and for what crimes? Is there today a crime heinous enough to deserve such reprisal? Is it possible to speak of justice, of truth, of God, and of the death of one million children in a single breath?

I wondered if this was to be the end of the Jewish people — or the end of the human adventure, period. But even in the shadow of the pyre there were Jews who persevered in their defiance; they recited their morning and evening prayers, they sought to observe the dietary laws, they studied Talmud from memory. And one of my workmates — we were carrying stones weighing more than we did — would say: "Let us assume that our people did not give the Law to others, let us forget Abraham, Moses, and the prophets. Our contribution to philosophy, science, and the arts — let us pretend it was not made. Let us say that, from David to Einstein, we have done nothing to make the human race progress even one step. Only one thing will not be contested: Of all the great killers, of all the bloody assassins of history, from the pharaohs to Nero, to Tamerlane, to Hitler, not one ever came from our ranks." I shall remember his words as I shall remember his face, a face wearing the mask of an old, old man, though he was only my age.

15TH-CENTURY ILLUMINATION FROM MAIMONIDES' "MISHNEH TORAH"; BRITISH MUSEUM

The most bewildering aspect of what we call the mystery of the holocaust is that our enemies were average, mediocre men, not intellectual giants. We were victims of stupidity — theirs. The farcical tenets of their "racial science" were applied to determine the degree of Jewishness in an individual; the element of choice did not enter the equation. Today, after the upheaval, that element again prevails. In most parts of the world the Jew is free to cut his ties or claim them as his own and strengthen them. Yet, as before, the catastrophe brought about not a decline but quite the opposite: a renaissance of Jewish consciousness, collective as well as individual. Not only did he not give in to pressures, the Jew showed himself more determined than ever. Auschwitz, instead of destroying him, somehow made him stronger, perhaps by increasing his awareness of his vulnerability.

A new situation not without its complexities: It suddenly became too easy for a Jew to define himself as such. No longer was he required to accept total commitment or to conform to a set tradition. To be Jewish, he needed only to say he was. Nothing complicated about that, other than that it set off a number of heated debates in Israeli rabbinical circles.

Names crowded on a wall barely hint at the millions murdered when Adolf Hitler's genocidal fury fanned guttering sparks of anti-Semitism into a holocaust. Of European Jewry only a scarred remnant survived, to mourn, and to cry with the Psalmist, "We are accounted as sheep for the slaughter. Awake, why sleepest Thou, O Lord?" (44:23-24).

I confess that these debates, which regularly though infrequently raise storms in Jewish religious circles, neither trouble nor interest me particularly. I prefer to marvel at the phenomenon itself: That in a world in turmoil young people, speaking all languages and from all social and economic groups, join in the adventure that Judaism still represents to them.

To prepare these introspective and purely subjective notes on Judaism, I had to undertake a kind of pilgrimage into time, halting in places where my mind had been formed, stimulated, or tested: my native town—Sighet in Transylvania—Paris, Moscow, and Jerusalem.

In my town, which is no longer my town, I met a Jew, one of the rare survivors in the region. With him at my side, I walked through the cemetery, thinking that the real cemetery of Sighet was elsewhere, up there in the sky, or in the memory

of the children crowding the altar, or in the flames reflected in the shining eyes of old men. Once we had been 10,000 Jews here, out of a total population of 25,000. The population is still 25,000 or more, but there are fewer than 50 Jewish families left. "To be a Jew," I asked, "what does that mean to you? Does it mean turning your heart into a cemetery?"

"No," my companion said. "The heart of man is a sanctuary and the dead, by definition, have no right to be there. To be a Jew is to fill the sanctuary with light, without betraying the cemetery."

In the Soviet Union I felt the tide of a Jewish awakening which defies rational explanation. In the larger cities young Jews gather by the thousands to celebrate the festivals with more fervor than anywhere else. Yet they have access to neither religious books nor teachers. Our poets and philosophers? Never heard of them.

MEMORIAL TO CZECH JEWS IN PINKAS SYNAGOGUE, PRAGUE; JAMES P. BLAIR, NATIONAL GEOGRAPHIC PHOTOGRAPHER

Joyous prayer resounds against hallowed stones where generations mourned as Israelis commemorate t

Our guides and masters? Unknown. I talked to young Marxists who felt themselves vitally linked to Israel's community and fate, without knowing why or even wishing to know. To feel the link was enough.

And in Paris, with rediscovered classmates, I recalled our tumultuous discussions of the early postwar years: Should one go to Palestine? Or choose the "universal" message of Marxism? Or perfect one's religious knowledge? Or become a mystic? Having survived by sheer chance, how was one to justify each day, each moment of this reprieve we had been granted? As a famous Hasidic rabbi used to say: "The questions remained questions but we were obliged to continue." And Israel? What about Israel? I asked myself. Why am I living here, in America, and not there, in the land I knew long before I ever visited it? How can I identify with its destiny from afar? And, in truth, Israel to me *is* question rather than answer. And so it is to most Israelis: cabinet ministers, officers, soldiers, judges, farmers, intellectuals, and dreamers. Sooner or later, they all agree: Yes, Israel is a constant interrogation precisely because it cannot be made

nning of the Western Wall in the 1967 war. Beyond gleams the Dome of the Rock, sacred shrine of Islam.

to fit any category. To the religious Jew, Israel shows its secular side; to the rationalist, its mystical dimension; to the pacifist, Israel exhibits its military might; while to the nationalist, it stresses the humility of its warriors. Israel can be approached from more than one side but somehow you always end up in Jerusalem. In Jerusalem the Jew in me feels at home, not geographically but, more important, historically. At home in his history.

In Jerusalem the Jew understands that there is a time for introspection and a time for action; but whether he is doing one or the other, he must see himself as spokesman for all Jews—for all those whose secret must be guarded in order for them to go on living and imposing a meaning on their lives.

In Jerusalem he understands that Jerusalem is everywhere, wherever men aspire to dreams binding them to other men and other dreams, wherever men open themselves to prayer. For every man is a high priest and every hand, stretched out to friend or stranger alike, is an altar; and this one learns in Jerusalem, ancient symbol of peace and fervor.

Herbert Weiner

A Kibbutz Where Work Means Worship

At first glance it looked like any other small community enjoying the golden light of late afternoon—young mothers in slacks wheeling baby carriages, loungers in deck chairs in front of white cottages, elderly strollers. Externally, I could see only one sign of difference: All the males wore some kind of head covering—usually a knitted circular *kipah* bobby-pinned to the back of the head.

But the young girl from New Haven with whom I stood outside the visitors' rooms had found much more at Yavneh, a religious kibbutz on Israel's coastal plain some 14 miles south of Tel Aviv. "It must have been something like this in Biblical days," she said. "Life close to the soil, a sense of real community, religion natural—not strained."

She had come here before starting college to seek a way of living that combined *avodah*, physical labor, with Torah in its broad sense—the religion of Judaism defined by the holy writings and rabbinic sages. Yavneh seemed to suit her purpose—and mine.

Israel's religious scene, so packed with contrast and contradiction, had long fascinated me. It includes Jews who will not touch the official currency because the state whose sovereignty it symbolizes should, they believe, have awaited the arrival of the Messiah. Others, while learning about the Bible in their schools, insist that God had nothing to do with the events described in that book. I explained to Shimon, the official in charge of visitor housing, that I wanted to dig deeper into what the 12th-century

SHOULDER TO SHOULDER *Israelis blend skill and muscle to raise a new chicken house for bustling Kibbutz Yavneh, a religious commune where automatic tools and ancient custom go hand in hand. Though shirts disappear in the heat of the day, skullcaps stay on; Orthodox Jews keep heads covered as a sign of reverence for the Lord.*

Struggling pioneers began the first kibbutz 60 years ago on the socialist ideal: "From each according to his ability, to each according to his need." Now more than 200 dot Israel, differing widely in ideology; yet all believe that Jews can best redeem their nation—and their souls—by labor on the land.

TED SPIEGEL, RAPHO GUILLUMETTE

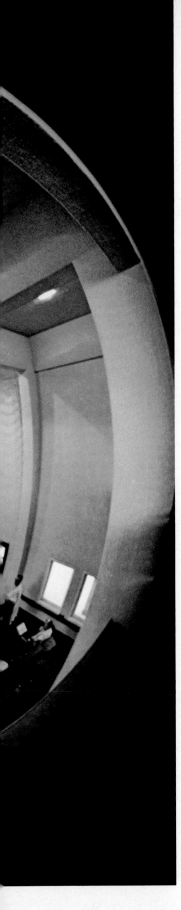

philosopher Yehuda Ha-Levi called the connection between Jews, the land of Israel, and "the Divine Matter." And what better place to contemplate this relationship than a kibbutz called Yavneh? Shimon needed no further explanation. He is a *sabra*, as native-born Israelis are called, after the prickly pear whose tough skin and soft inner fruit are supposed to resemble the Israeli character.

Every Israeli schoolboy knows the Talmudic story of ancient Yavneh. When Roman besiegers were about to destroy the Temple 1,900 years ago, Rabbi Yochanan Ben Zakkai was slipped outside Jerusalem's walls in a casket. Appearing before the Roman commander, he won approval of a seemingly unimportant request: to establish a scholarly academy in the village of Yavneh, or Jamnia as it was called in Greek. What happened at that academy set its seal upon ensuing centuries of Jewish history.

"Yavneh and its sages" perfected that style of life and values known as Rabbinic Judaism. From that time on, prayer took the place of temple sacrifices, the study of Torah became the highest concern of every Jewish community, the ideal Jew became the *talmid chacham*, student of the wise. For the rabbis of Yavneh, life's grand imperative—to serve the Lord—was spelled out in 613 commandments plus

SYNAGOGUE SERVICE *begins Yavneh's workday; prayer book guides worshipers with devotional writings from scripture and sages. Leather-thonged* tefillin *and fringed shawl remind the wearer of his duty to love the Lord and fulfill his commands.*

TED SPIEGEL, RAPHO GUILLUMETTE

numerous customs and traditions. Such was the "Yoke of Heaven" which every Jew bore with joy and pride and, if necessary, with courage unto death.

All this Shimon understood, and also the question it implied: Were the ideals of ancient Yavneh still viable in a modern state or even in modern Yavneh?

*D*uring the first few days of my visit it seemed that traditional Judaism and modern life had achieved a comfortable synthesis. The work schedule was hard—beginning before sunrise for most and continuing into late afternoon. Yet every morning at 5:30 and again around sunset a sizable number gathered in the spacious but simply designed synagogue. In Jewish orthodoxy women are exempt from the daily obligation of communal prayer; yet most services find a few worshipers in the women's section fenced by low latticework.

At evening prayers a worshiper might ascend the pulpit to offer "a word of Torah"; on some nights there were lessons in the Bible or the Talmud, the great compilation of ancient rabbinic teaching and commentary. After a day in the fields, pious study does not come easy. Heads nod, eyes droop; often a man will

pray at home. Yet on the whole Yavneh's farmers do not let weariness detract from "labor of the heart."

But service to the Lord, in classical Judaism, is not confined to synagogue or study; it is required everywhere—even in the fields and barns of Yavneh. Only here the synthesis of religion and life becomes more difficult. The Bible forbids the mingling of different species of seed in the same field and, by implication, prohibits the grafting of one kind of fruit tree or vine to another. It commands that the land lie fallow every seven years. Most difficult are the problems growing out of one of the Ten Commandments: "Remember the sabbath day, to keep it holy. Six days shalt thou labor ... but the seventh day is a sabbath unto the Lord ... in it thou shalt not do any manner of work" (Exodus 20:8-10).

"WALK IN MY STATUTES ... *then I will give your rains in their season, and the land shall yield her produce*" (*Leviticus 26:3, 4*).

Bright as the Biblical promise, Yavneh's green fields and olive groves quilt the ancestral soil of Israel. Some 330 members share ownership, chores, and profits; their children, workers preparing to launch new settlements, and visiting students total another 500. Formed in 1941 by pious German Jews, Yavneh— unlike most other kibbutzim—seeks to walk with religious statutes. Some laws touch even the sower of beans (opposite). Scripture permits only one kind of seed in a field; mixing kinds is "an abomination to the Lord."

The problems range from the Biblical ban on lighting fires to intricate rabbinic instructions covering almost every activity during the holy day of rest.

So long as Jews lived in minority groupings outside Israel, many of the forbidden tasks could be performed by non-Jews. But in modern Israel Jews are a majority, and religious communities like Yavneh must seek other ways to reconcile the laws of their faith with those of economics.

Cows don't stop producing milk on Saturday and the milk must be taken to avoid injury to the animals, but Sabbath restrictions forbid switching on the milking machines. Alex Bekker, a young American who had studied animal husbandry in Illinois, told me how Yavneh met the problem: On the Sabbath a spring clock activated the mechanical milkers.

Yavneh owns the largest hatchery in Israel, producing 6,000,000 chicks a year. In one of the coops Tzuriel Admonit showed me the long automatic feeding belt that takes care of the chickens' needs for the 24-hour Sabbath period when nobody works here. I also saw the conveyor belt which carries off and deposits the eggs. True, not all the chickens lay their eggs on the belt; thousands of

eggs are crushed because religious law does not permit handling the eggs on the Sabbath. "But," said Tzuriel, "at least we're working on it."

I heard Tzuriel called "a kind of wild heifer in the religious movement," and at dinner one night in the bright, modern dining hall, I began to see why. Like all else, the dining room lies within the reach of religious commandment. The rabbis taught that the dining table should be treated as a sacrificial altar over which a Jew must consider himself a presiding priest. No one, therefore, comes to table without pouring water over his fingers and reciting the appropriate blessing. The plates are either blue for a dairy meal or white for meat: Orthodox Jews do not mix the two. At each table plastic cards are inscribed with the after-meal blessing, for the Bible

"AN EXCELLENT THING," *wrote a sage centuries ago, "is the study of the Torah combined with some worldly occupation." Folk of Yavneh strive for such excellence: The mechanic who changes tractor tires also imparts Talmudic lore to youngsters; the botanist who guides apple harvesters freshens the shawls which mantle her menfolk at worship; the panelist who ponders the Talmud's words in the evening spends his days teaching grammar. He uses passages from the Torah, where it is written: "Thou shalt love the Lord. . . . And these words . . . shall be upon thy heart, and thou shalt teach them diligently unto thy children" (Deuteronomy 6:5-7).*

199

says, "Thou shalt eat, be satisfied, and bless the Lord" (Deuteronomy 8:10). Yet for all its efforts Yavneh occasionally finds itself at odds with Israel's religious establishment and men like Tzuriel Admonit find themselves embroiled in controversy. "Most religious youth," he told me, "serve in the Nachal, which combines army with agricultural work. But if a boy or girl serves in another division — my son, for example, is in the artillery — he can be very much alone. The army permits a soldier to say his prayers instead of doing morning calisthenics. But the boys don't like to shirk obligations, so they take on double burdens." Tzuriel felt the rabbinate could provide stronger religious support for these youths.

At a second meeting I told Tzuriel how a rabbi from a nearby institution had been scandalized by the sight of men and women swimming together in Yavneh's pool. "They even dance together," the rabbi had said, "and you will see unmarried boys and girls from the kibbutz movement walking hand in hand."

Tzuriel recognized that Yavneh had its critics among Orthodox rabbis. But, he insisted, "how can we tell boys and girls who work together, serve in the army together, that they may not, if they like each other, walk hand in hand?"

Why, he went on, did the critics not notice the creative accomplishments of the religious kibbutz, the decorum and aesthetic beauty of its worship services — all carried out within the traditional law and not as "Reform" Jews.

Generally the attitude of Israelis toward religion parallels that of people in any modern land. A minority, which includes the people of Yavneh, believe as earlier generations have believed. Others disbelieve. Many doubt. Yet Judaism is very much a part of the Israeli Jew's life. A schoolboy need only look out the window to see places where Biblical events occurred. The language he speaks, revived as a living tongue within the past century, is the language of the prophets.

GEARED TO THE FUTURE,
*a junior kibbutznik enjoys a lesson
in jockeying heavy farm machinery.
But the end of a synagogue service
shows Yavneh's young ones (opposite)
as eager as any to romp and play.
They live in dormitories—joining
parents in leisure hours—and run
their own farm, where self-reliance
grows along with the quack grass
they pull up for transplanting (below).
To reclaim barren land, Israelis
sow grass and legumes to stabilize
the soil; plowed under, the plants add
organic content. After a few years'
enrichment the soil yields crops,
and the words of Isaiah come easily
to mind: "The desert shall rejoice,
and blossom as the rose" (35:1).*

*Choicest blooms of the kibbutz
are the children themselves.
Eligible to become members at 18,
many defer the decision until after
military service, required of both sexes.
From sturdy kibbutz stock, a small
fraction of the population, have
come many of Israel's scientists,
leaders, soldiers (including
Moshe Dayan), and the idealism
vital to the nation's rebirth.*

The holy days sanctified by Biblical and rabbinic tradition are national holidays. "For us," Israelis like to say, "all the land is a temple."

How does education differ in a religious kibbutz? "We begin in the *gan*, the kindergarten," said Moshe Cohen, a lean, courtly gentleman who administers the lower grades. "The day begins with a gathering for prayer. Each boy wears a fringed undergarment, as the Torah commands. The main difference between Judaism as it is taught here and in nonreligious schools is that we have no gap between learning and doing. The children know that even as they are cleaning their quarters to welcome the Sabbath their parents are doing the same at home."

As we talked on the sun-drenched porch of the science building an elderly man in a black suit approached and asked if he could do his "research."

JUBILATION *in the house of prayer marks completion of the reading of the Pentateuch. As the final weekly segment ends, the first verses of Genesis follow; Yavneh's worshipers whirl with joy, raise high the precious Torah scrolls in this fall festival of Simhat Torah.*

The lunar calendar sets festival dates. In ancient Jerusalem officials announced each new month at the rise of the crescent moon. But when the Jews were dispersed, uncertainty led to adding an extra day to some holiday observances outside Israel, a custom still current. To keep festivals in season and bridg the 11-day gap between lunar and solar years, the Jewish calendar adds a month 7 times in a 19-year cycle.

Moshe led him into the laboratory and helped him arrange tubes and a micro-scope. "He's a retired doctor," the educator explained, "the parent of a member." Ten minutes later the man came out, lifted his hat in thanks, and went on his way. Obviously the "research" had more to do with an old man's dignity than with science. Torah, after all, also commands, "Thou shalt respect the aged."

Over the traditional afternoon cup of tea one day Principal Mordecai Chayot told me that male graduates of his high school face three years in the army, followed by a fourth year of "voluntary" service in some young kibbutz. "That's why our young people, when they finally get to the university, have no time for demonstrations or protests." This led us to a discussion of the anti-army, pacifist feelings of so many youngsters in America. "Pacifism," said Chayot, "is good for parlor talk. Here it would mean simple and speedy destruction."

Whatever transformation Judaism has undergone in modern Israel, one tradi-tional value has been absorbed into the texture of life—the Sabbath. To be sure, the expression of this value, its taste and flavor, varies widely. On Tel Aviv's Dizengoff Street it means bright lights, horrendous traffic, crowded sidewalks. In a border bunker it may mean only the symbolic touch of flickering Friday

203

evening candles. But Yavneh preserves the Sabbath in all its traditional glory.

Ten minutes before sunset on Friday a siren wailed a warning that labor must cease. My neighbors in the guest house checked the clock which would automatically turn off the lights at 11 p.m. Then the husband ran to pick some flowers for his room. The last tractor clanked its way to the garage and an almost tangible stillness descended. From all directions people converged on the synagogue, the elderly in jackets and hats, the girls in sweaters and skirts, the boys in spotless white shirts. Soon the murmur of prayers swelled, full-bodied yet restrained— for the "joy of the Sabbath" has more to do with holiness than with hilarity.

"Come in peace, Sabbath queen, come in peace," sang the prayer leader as the congregation rose and turned in symbolic welcome toward the back doors.

Afterward in the dining room Sabbath loaves and wine were set on white tablecloths. This night families made a point of sitting together, and though the blessing over wine was publicly chanted by one member, most husbands repeated it. After dinner the young people gathered in their quarters, adorned by candles lit in honor of the Sabbath, and over soda pop and cake they began the singing and clapping that enlivens youth gatherings in Israel.

*T*he next evening, Sabbath over, I met Yoram Zamash, "the captain," a steady-eyed tractor driver who led the paratroop company which reached the Western Wall of the ancient Temple in Jerusalem during the six-day war in 1967. Within an hour after gaining the cherished wall, he had sent for two elderly rabbis, his former teachers and disciples of Israel's first chief rabbi, Abraham Isaac Kook. Sniper fire was still crackling. Why had the captain summoned the sages at such a perilous moment? "I knew it was right for them to be there," Zamash said.

For me the incident had the touch that distinguishes the people of a religious community like Yavneh. On the surface their lives seem so ordinary; yet there is always that bit of difference—whether in the dining room or in the milking barn or on the battlefield. And this bit of difference, affecting every aspect of existence, can change the quality of that existence.

Rabbi Kook once wrote something along those lines: "The light of Israel is not a Utopian dream.... It does not wash its hands of the material world or leave the flesh and society to wallow in impurity. It is rather a raising of all life."

For Jews, the rabbi taught, this raising of life could best take place in the land of Israel, which was as a body to Israel's soul. "And though this work be carried on by few and though its accomplishments be involved with much dross, it would succeed, for 'the Presence of God dwelt within it.'"

I think of these words when I recall Yavneh's green fields, its glorious Sabbath, even the conveyor belt in its chicken hatchery.

"THE SUN ARISETH. . . . *Man goeth forth unto his work," sang a psalmist (104:22, 23). A man of Yavneh, a worker in the land where the psalmists sang, pauses in the early light, dons symbols of his faith, and renews the mystical bond affirmed more than 30 centuries ago on the heights of Sinai. With the words of King David he voices the prayer: "Let us fall not into the hand of the Lord . . . and let me not fall into the hand of man" (II Samuel 24:14).*

TED SPIEGEL, RAPHO GUILLUMETTE

Ted Spiegel

Days of Joy and Lamentation

For a child of the Jewish tradition the festivals are both holy days and holidays. There's always the gladness of coming together, the excitement of preparation, the respite from school, the haunting synagogue melodies, the delicacies of feast days, and—after a youngster turns 13—the dull ache of fast days.

In my youth my grandfather Moses Spiegel impressed me with the idea that for Judaism time is infinite. He described the events embodied in our festivals with such immediacy that I began to think of myself as a part of them. As each new *yom tov* appeared on the calendar, I said to myself, "This is what happens to us now"—never, "That is what happened to them then."

At Hanukkah I rose with the Maccabees against the Seleucid oppressors of Israel, and witnessed the rekindling of the Temple's eternal light with one day's supply of holy oil—that burned miraculously for eight. During the Purim reading of the Book of Esther, I hissed at Haman, the wicked Persian vizier, and cheered the beautiful queen as she thwarted his genocidal plot against our people. As we fasted on Tish B'Av, the ninth day of the month of Av, I could hear the clattering Roman legions destroying our Temple, one of the calamities bemoaned in the dirges of Tish B'Av. On Simhat Torah, Grandfather clasped the Torah to his broad chest and we danced about the synagogue, rejoicing in the completion of the annual reading of God's word.

As with these minor festivals, so the past came alive in major festivals evolved from those ordained in Leviticus 23: Passover; Shavuot, the Feast of First Fruits that also commemorates the giving of the Law on Mount Sinai; Sukkot, the Feast of Booths; and the High Holy Days—beginning with the New Year, Rosh Hashanah, and ending with the solemn Day of Atonement, Yom Kippur.

I have shared the joy and duty of our observances in home, synagogue, and seminary across America, in the traditional rites of the Orthodox as well as in the modern adaptations of the Conservative and Reform movements created by the currents of our times. Whatever the way of worship, all were striving to be a part of that rainbow which stretches from Sinai to a distant Judgment Day.

"WHY IS THIS NIGHT
DIFFERENT FROM
ALL OTHER NIGHTS?"
FROM THE SEDER OBSERVANCE

"Seven days shall there be no leaven found in your houses." In accord with the divine edict of Exodus 12:19, Al and Esther Lott scrupulously prepare their Seattle, Washington, home for the spring festival of Passover, making the customary candlelight search for the last morsel of leavened, or yeasted, bread. Mrs. Lott exchanges her everyday dishes for sets preserved leaven-free, and stocks up with unleavened *matzah* in memory of the time when Hebrews could not tarry to let their dough rise as they fled from Pharaoh. Then, on the eve of Passover, surrounded by savory aromas, this Conservative family conducts the Seder, or Order of Service, with its bountiful meal.

Al Lott holds aloft the Seder plate of symbolic foods, including the roasted egg that recalls ancient Temple offerings and the lamb shank, reminder of the sacrificial lambs whose blood marked the houses of the children of Israel as Moses prepared to lead them to freedom. These houses the Lord "passed over . . . when He smote the Egyptians. . . ." The meaning of the other symbols emerges when ten-year-old Jeff Lott, exercising the youngest's privilege, proudly asks: "*Ma-nish-ta-naw* . . . Why is this night different. . . ?" His father replies, in essence: "The matzah is our forefathers' bread of affliction. The bitter herbs remind us of their lives as slaves. The *haroset* your mother made from apples, nuts, and wine represents the mortar used to erect Pharaoh's cities. We dip the herbs in haroset to evoke the oppressed life, the greens in salted water to bring back that tearful spring. And the pillow I lean on signifies freedom. Slaves ate standing; only free men reclined." Thus Passover provides an enduring reminder of man's struggle for liberty.

"AT 13 THE AGE IS REACHED FOR THE FULFILLMENT OF THE COMMANDMENTS"

RABBI JUDAH BEN TEMA, SECOND CENTURY

"It will be the pinnacle of his boyhood—but just the beginning of his manhood," explains Bobby Abolofia's father. The boy will achieve that pinnacle on the Saturday after his 13th birthday; then the services of Sabbath, the weekly festival, assume new meaning as he comes before Seattle's Bikur Holim congregation to be recognized as Bar Mitzvah—Man of Duty, or popularly, Son of the Commandment.

Endless hours of study precede that day. Sunday religious school from age five has taught him his heritage and the Hebrew language of the Orthodox prayer book. With special tutoring by Cantor Isaac Azose (opposite, lower) he has learned to sing from the unvoweled lettering of the Torah scroll. He has come to understand the meaning of the *tefillin* laced on forehead and arm (opposite) used in weekday morning worship—that they constitute a physical reminder of the spiritual responsibilities of manhood. The black boxes of the tefillin contain verses from Exodus and Deuteronomy ordaining use of the tefillin and including a passage from Judaism's credo, the Shema: "Hear, O Israel. . . ."

On the Thursday morning before the big day, Bobby, with his new prayer shawl and joined by his father Sam (below), is counted as one of the ten worshipers—the *minyan* or quorum—needed for communal prayers. In grandfather Shaya Abolofia's youth in Turkey, to which his Sephardic ancestors had fled from Spain, the Bar Mitzvah ceremony took place during one of the weekday Torah readings. But Seattle's Sephardic community has accepted, as have the more numerous Ashkenazim from central and eastern Europe, the Sabbath ceremonial observed in America. Celebrations accompanying the event date from the Middle Ages; modern affluence has transformed it into a family festival.

TED SPIEGEL, RAPHO GUILLUMETTE

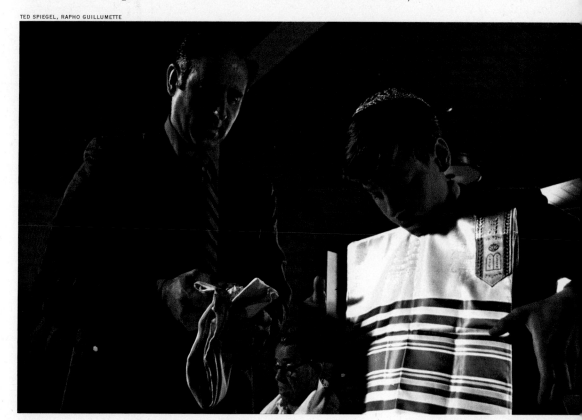

BAR MITZVAH SERVICE RE-ENACTED, AS ORTHODOX LAW FORBIDS PHOTOGRAPHIC WORK ON THE SABBATH; TED SPIEGEL, RAPHO GUILLUMETTE

Family, guests, and congregants now pack Bikur Holim's prayer room. Worshipers lift the Torah from the Ark, bring it to the reading desk with its silver ornaments, remove its blue velvet mantle, and unroll it to Numbers 18. Here begins the segment designated for reading this Sabbath. The words of the *aliyah*, the calling up, ring out and Bobby, rising from the midst of his gathered male relatives, responds. Flanked by his grandfathers, he assumes the entire congregation's duty to read the Torah. As his hand guides the silver pointer across the parchment scroll, his proud alto voice soars in the ancient cantillation: "And the Lord said unto Aaron. . . ." Amid murmurs of approval in the women's balcony Bobby's mother Rae beams with pride.

Among Orthodox Ashkenazim the boy would read the Haftorah, the weekly passage taken from the books of the prophets, and sometimes from the Torah, which includes only the five books of Moses. In most Reform services he would wear neither skullcap nor prayer shawl. Reform Judaism, viewing the Torah as God-inspired rather than God-given, does not recognize the traditional 613 *mitzvot*, or commandments, as divine law; it regards the festivals and ethical teachings as important elements in the fabric of the faith. Men and women sit together and frequently recite English prayers in Reform temples and in those of Conservative Jewry. The latter honors the concept of mitzvot but looks to its rabbis to interpret the tradition in light of modern conditions. Today many congregations observe a ceremony for girls reaching religious maturity—a Bas Mitzvah.

The Torah reading over, the rabbi cedes his pulpit to Bobby for the Bar Mitzvah address. Though the words flow from one young in years, their intent is ageless: "I come before you this morning with a deep sense of humility and reverence, ready to fulfill my duties, obligations, and privileges as an adult Jew. . . ."

Among the duties he will seek to fulfill are attendance at the daily worship (opposite) and the reverent handling and understanding of the law that guides his spiritual life.

"YE SHALL DWELL
IN BOOTHS SEVEN DAYS"

LEVITICUS 23:42

"Hallelujah! Praise, O ye servants of the Lord, Praise the name of the Lord" (Psalms 113:1). The joyous Hallel of festival ritual rises above the gentle rustle of mystical wands (far right) as students of the Jewish Theological Seminary of America, in New York, obey the commands of Leviticus: "And ye shall take . . . the fruit of goodly trees, branches of palm-trees, and boughs of thick trees, and willows of the brook, and ye shall rejoice before the Lord. . . ." Bearing the *lulav*, a sheaf of palm, myrtle, and willow, and the *esrog*, a goodly citron, the students encircle the Torah at the reader's desk. They emulate the procession of people about the second Temple's altar when pilgrims flocked to Jerusalem for the week-long Feast of Booths, Sukkot.

"Saluting with a palm branch is a Middle Eastern form of praise that goes back to antiquity," explains Dr. Saul Lieberman, rector of the Conservative seminary, as we explore the rich garden of law and legend that has grown about the festivals. "Ancient people celebrated in gaily decorated booths at harvest time. Dining in a booth, or *sukkah*, has a combined significance: successful completion of the fall harvest and remembrance of our manner of living during the Exodus."

American observance of Sukkot ranges widely. Many share the synagogue's lulav, esrog, and sukkah; the more devout erect a sukkah at home and take great care to select wands and fruits (opposite) according to Talmudic criteria.

Joining the students in their sukkah (below), I find myself in a cradle of time. Such fragile shelters have harbored our people's thanks for about 3,500 years.

TED SPIEGEL, RAPHO GUILLUMETTE

214

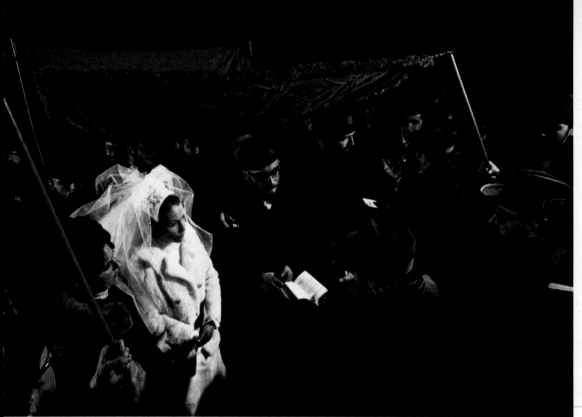

"BLESSED ART THOU, O LORD . . . WHO HAST CREATED JOY AND GLADNESS, BRIDEGROOM AND BRIDE"

FROM THE SEVEN BENEDICTIONS OF WEDLOCK

"I wear skullcap, side-curls, and beard. Bear your Jewishness with pride in America and people look at you and say, 'He's O.K., he's doing his thing.'" Baruch Torenheim's outward appearance bespeaks his inner commitment to observe all the mitzvot of his faith. With a twinkling eye Baruch the bridegroom adds: "And remember, the Torah's first mitzvah is 'Be fruitful, and multiply.'" The twinkle typifies the Hasidim, a sect famed for its charismatic leaders and its singing and dancing in the service of God.

The day before Baruch's wedding to Miriam Scheinfeld had been one of fasting and repentance. They had purified themselves in the *mikveh,* the ritual bath, and prayed at the Lubavitch Hasidic synagogue. Then Baruch examined the *ketubah,* the marriage contract that provides for the wife in the event of divorce or the husband's death.

Now 400 guests, many of them Baruch's fellow students at the Lubavitch Yeshiva, shiver in the 14-degree night outside the Brooklyn wedding hall (above); the setting symbolizes the hope that the couple's descendants be as numerous as the stars in the sky. Beneath the *huppah,* the wedding canopy that represents the future home which Baruch and Miriam will share, Rabbi Tzvi Torenheim blesses wine and gives thanks to God for the institution of marriage; then, at his signal, his son Baruch places the ring on the bride's finger and sanctifies the union with the ancient formula, "Behold, thou art consecrated unto me by this ring, according to the Law of Moses and Israel." The rabbi reads the terms of the wedding contract and afterward recites the lyrical Seven Benedictions of Wedlock, ending in "Blessed art thou, O Lord, who makest the bridegroom to rejoice with the bride." As the final chant fades away, a hush descends and the groom shatters a glass underfoot—solemn reminder of the destruction of the Temple, sorrow amid joy.

"*Mazal tov!*—Good luck!" Now inside at the reception joy reigns, the women on their side of the screen (opposite); Orthodoxy's rules of decorum govern even here. Dancing, whirling, tumbling—the Hasidic zest that uplifted the forlorn ghettoes of eastern Europe two centuries ago comes alive. What a night! And this is only the first of seven.

"...FOR IT IS A DAY...TO MAKE ATONEMENT"

LEVITICUS 23:28

The plaintive tones of the Kol Nidre chant fill high-ceilinged Temple de Hirsch Sinai in Seattle. It is the eve of Yom Kippur, most awesome of holy days. A Jew who does not appear in synagogue all year will yield to the intense appeal of the Day of Atonement, and his heart will fill with nostalgia at the sound of Kol Nidre. This moving plea for the release of rash vows taken under duress gained a special poignancy in bitter days like those of medieval Europe when Jews were forced to forswear their God.

Yom Kippur marks the culminating observance of the High Holy Days, the ten days of penitence of early autumn which begin with the ram's horn sound of the *shofar* on Rosh Hashanah, the Jewish New Year. From dusk to dusk Yom Kippur is a day of absolute abstinence from food and drink. It is a day of sackcloth and ashes for the mind, when each worshiper seeks atonement for humanity's sins as well as his own: "For the sin which we have sinned against thee in secret...in stubbornness...by abuse of power...by disrespect....O God of forgiveness, bear with us, pardon us, forgive us."

At the end of the prayer-filled day the shofar resounds once more through this Reform temple (above), a final blast that marks the closing of the heavenly book of judgment for the coming year. It is a sound from Biblical days, a sound that summoned the hosts to battle, that proclaimed peace, that echoed on Sinai when the Lord spoke to his servant Moses. It will herald that golden time when, the prophets declare, men "shall beat their swords into plowshares, and their spears into pruning hooks; nation shall not lift up sword against nation, neither shall they learn war any more" (Isaiah 2:4).

ISLAM

Blue-tiled dome sumptuous as a Persian carpet
crowns Sheikh Lutfullah Mosque in Isfahan, Iran;
Thomas J. Abercrombie, National Geographic staff

MOHAMMED IS HIS PROPHET

Edward J. Jurji

The hour was sundown. I stood on a hotel balcony in Rabat, Morocco. But it could have been Cairo or Karachi, Djakarta or Istanbul, any of a hundred cities about the globe where the spires of Islam rise. The muezzin's call to prayer floated through the evening hush. Its summons—rolling, alliterative syllables chanted in Arabic, the tongue of the Prophet Mohammed and of Islam's holy book the Koran—is one and the same everywhere, just as Allah, God, is one. When that summons swells from minaret to minaret, the faithful stop whatever they are doing, face Mecca, and spread their prayer mats—worshipers united in reverent act and language.

The communicative magic of the tongue was underscored for me that evening. Prayer time was over, the pious had risen from the last prostration. As the city resumed its business, the devotional mood vanished—or so it seemed. The hotel doorman and the driver of a taxi he had hailed for me got into a violent argument. With a string of oaths, the driver started the cab. Apprehensive of his driving in such a rage, I tried to calm him, first with English, then French. Neither language had any effect, though I'm sure he understood me. Finally I drew a phrase or two from the Arabic of my Syrian-Lebanese childhood.

With a bounce that shook the vehicle, the driver whooped "*Allahu Akbar!*— God is most great!" His anger dissolved in enthusiasm at meeting in the unlikely guise of an American traveler a potential Companion of the Garden—comrade in paradise. A keynote of Islamic parlance, "Allahu Akbar" has many shades of meaning: in war a rallying cry, in peace a prayer, at any time a sign of fraternal goodwill. As a lifelong student of Islam, I felt—here in al-Maghreb al-Aqsa, the "far west" of Arab chroniclers—the magnetic pull of that storied faith and ethos.

I would note it even more tangibly in mosque-studded Fez, Morocco's time-washed cultural capital. There the faith shows on the faces of men in white

223

WINFIELD PARKS, NATIONAL GEOGRAPHIC PHOTOGRAPHER

jellabas who stream into mosques for Friday noon prayers: Almost every brow bears a pale round spot, an indelible souvenir of the countless times that forehead has pressed the ground as a sign of humble obedience to God.

"Islam" means surrender or submission to the will of Allah, in whose eyes all men are equal, in whose service all men are brothers. Newest of the world's major religions and with claim as the fastest-growing, it centers on the simplest, most straightforward of creeds. Murmured in the ear of the newborn child and ideally the last whisper of the dying, that creed rings in a single sentence: There is no god but God, and Mohammed is his prophet.

This latter clause emphasizes Islam's division from other monotheistic faiths. Followers of Islam, or Moslems (the word in Arabic means "one who submits"), revere Mohammed as the greatest prophet who ever lived, the last of the messengers sent by God. But Moslems honor him and the prophets who preceded him —notably Noah, Abraham, Moses, and Jesus—as human, not divine. Allah rules alone. Mohammed's role was to bring to a perverse and materialistic society, through the express mandate of God, an absolute and final revelation: the Koran. The faith thus expounded molded a manifold human community. It galvanized man to action in the worship of God—and in turn shaped the far-flung empire conquered by the word as much as by the sword.

At the time of Mohammed's birth the Arabian desert was a realm of wandering tribes and caravan centers dominated by patrician traders. Men valued manliness

225

and eloquence, demanded fierce loyalty to the clan. They worshiped nature spirits, made pilgrimages to a cube-shaped shrine in Mecca housing scores of gods. In that prosperous crossroads city Mohammed was born about A.D. 570.

Left an orphan, he was reared first by a grandfather, then an uncle. At 12, Moslem writers say, he went with his uncle on a caravan journey to Syria. Not a few Christian hermits then lived on the borders of the Syrian desert; one whom the boy met predicted he would become a prophet. Young Mohammed, quiet and withdrawn, may have shown signs of the deep thought and insights that characterized his adult years. We don't know. Legends of the Prophet eventually filled hundreds of volumes but give few facts on his childhood.

We do know that the massive-shouldered, dark-eyed youth worked hard as a shepherd and camel driver, winning the nickname *al-Amin*, "the trustworthy." A marked change in his fortune came when, at 25, he received this message: "O son of my uncle, I like you because we are relations, and also for your good reputation among the people, your . . . good character and truthfulness." The note, concluding with a proposal of marriage, came from Khadijah, a rich widow for whom he had managed trading caravans. He accepted her offer, though she was 15 years older than he. The marriage brought him domestic contentment, four daughters, and the leisure to meditate on the destiny of man.

A favorite spot for his reflections was a cave on Mount Hira, three miles from Mecca. Here in the month of Ramadan in the year 610 occurred the fateful "Night of Power"—when he saw the vision and heard the voice that were to

"Our abode is transitory, our life . . . a loan." Rootless on a landscape inconstant as the winds, Arabs mae

alter his life and through him divert the course of history. Tradition identifies God's agent as the angel Gabriel. "Mohammed, recite," the voice commanded:

> *Recite: In the name of thy Lord who createth,*
> *Createth man from a clot.*
> *Recite: And thy Lord is the Most Bounteous,*
> *Who teacheth by the pen,*
> *Teacheth man that which he knew not.*

Thus was revealed the first fragment of the Koran, held to be God's eternal and infallible word. Convinced of his mission to proclaim the message anew — man had corrupted the pure monotheism revealed by Abraham and other prophets — Mohammed memorized the words; later they were set down by a scribe. Similarly over a 22-year period came each of the Koran's 78,000 words.

Long before the night of the first revelation, monotheistic trends were astir in and about Arabia. Though many desert people venerated the moon and stars — and at the Kaaba, Mecca's ancient shrine, bowed to many idols — they also recognized a chief god called Allah, or "the God." In Mohammed's time, Biblical ideas were spreading from Jewish and Christian outposts. Too, Arabs and Jews had in Abraham a common ancestor — the Arabs being descended through Ishmael, son of Hagar. In the Koran, Abraham exposes the error of moon worship, but both the crescent moon and the star emblem of the ancient Semites survive as a symbol of Islam; it appears on flags of half a dozen nations.

llah anchor and guide. At sunup, evoking words of Mohammed's successor Abu Bakr, Bedouin strike tents.

"*Mohammed! Thou art the Messenger of God.*" *From two bowshots away on Mount Hira near Mecca the angel Gabriel calls (below). A mission as the prophet of Islam begins for the 40-year-old former camel driver. This new monotheistic faith, spread by sermon and sword, replaced the idolatry of Arabian tribes.*

In an aureole of flame (left)—Moslem artists veil Mohammed's face lest they commit sacrilege—the Prophet prays beside the Kaaba in Mecca. He routed pagan idols from the sanctuary tradition says was built by Abraham and Ishmael.

16TH-CENTURY TURKISH MINIATURES FROM "PROGRESS OF THE PROPHET"; TOPKAPI MUSEUM, ISTANBUL

Against a background of these religious traditions, fired by his own vision and Khadijah's steadfast support, Mohammed eagerly awaited further visitations. He went often to Hira. He meditated. He waited. He hoped. And when more than two years had passed without new revelations, he despaired. A ninth-century biographer records that "he seriously considered . . . hurling himself down to the abyss from either Mount Hira or Mount Thabir. Just as he was about . . . to jump off . . . he heard a heavenly voice . . . and beheld Gabriel, seated upon a throne set between heaven and earth, who said: 'Mohammed! Thou art the Messenger of God and I am Gabriel.' From that moment onward, the Prophet . . . never again faltered. . . . Revelations thereafter steadily increased."

Mohammed was unschooled, but he could preach with eloquence and passion. His first sermons reviled idolatry and all its supporters—including his own tribe, the Quraysh. Its aristocracy turned a handsome profit providing for the needs of pilgrims who came from all over Arabia to worship at the Kaaba. God's wrath would surely overtake men who refused to yield to his undivided sovereignty, Mohammed preached. He proclaimed not a new god but the all-powerful God of creation and judgment, revealing himself to man once more: "Therefore invoke not with Allah another god, lest thou be one of the doomed. And warn thy tribe of near kindred, and lower thy wing unto those believers who follow thee."

The Prophet at first had little impact outside his intimate circle. Converts were few, the earliest being Khadijah, two young wards, and Abu Bakr, a Quraysh merchant. But with growing confidence and a message that gave new values to life, Mohammed drew larger audiences. Arab paganism counted death the end of existence and made wealth a goal; the Koran taught that rich must share with poor, promised glorious afterlife for the righteous and hellfire for others.

In the pilgrimage season Mohammed went among the crowds at the Kaaba, declaring the idols unworthy of worship. Quraysh elders who held concessions to sell ritual robes, "sacred" food, and water saw their profits shrink. The democratic spirit of Mohammed's preaching threatened the power of the upper classes. Thus town leaders turned in fury against the "driveller, star-gazer, and maniac-poet." They stoned and beat converts. Khadijah died, piling sorrow on adversity. In September 622, Mohammed, warned of a plot against his life, obeyed a vision telling him to leave Mecca for Yathrib, an oasis city 250 miles north. This momentous *Hegira,* or migration, marks the start of the Moslem era, for with it Islam grew to political power. And Yathrib became Madinat al-Nabi, "the city of the Prophet," or more simply, Medina.

*H*istory records Mohammed's Medina venture as one of the world's greatest success stories. He began it a fugitive; he ended it ten years later the spiritual and political leader of a new state, a state that in another decade had burst out of Arabia to shake the leading powers of the Western world, a state that in its four centuries of ascendancy wrought an amalgam of cultures vibrant with contributions to the advance of civilization. The Koran, growing piecemeal as Mohammed received each new revelation, constitutes an enduring part of that success. Moslems worship God, but in a true sense they are also Koranists. Through the book

"*Ye have indeed in the Apostle of God
a beautiful pattern. . . .*" Palms uplifted,
knees to the ground—postures set by the
Prophet—Moslems in Teheran, Iran, adhere
to "*the Book in which there is no doubt.*"

Code and core of Islam, the Koran copies
a stone tablet in paradise, revealed to
Mohammed over 22 years. Verses jotted on
parchment, palm leaves, or bleached bones
were compiled after his death into
114 chapters; they set out laws, stories
(some retold from the Bible), prayers,
etiquette, calls to battle. The pages below
are from the chapter "Spoils of War."
Islam's holy book invokes Allah by 99 "most
beautiful names." The camel, legend says,
has aloof dignity because it knows a 100th.

In resonant Arabic the Koran echoes
the rich imagery and rolling cadences of
Bedouin bards. Harsh days on sun-stoked
sands made the wanderers sing the
more sensuously of myrrh-scented nights,
of fine rippled horseflesh and clashing
sabers. At poetry contests, a highlight
of fairs, rival tribes feuded with phrases.
Odes most moving were lettered in gold
on silk and hung in the Kaaba, it was said.
But pagan poetry—considered the work of
wine and jinn—was decried by the Koran
as leading men away from paradise.

THOMAS J. ABERCROMBIE, NATIONAL GEOGRAPHIC STAFF

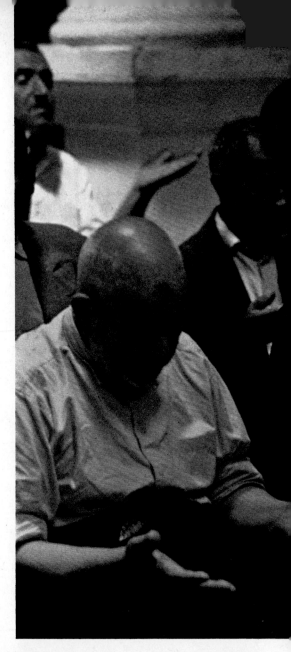

God speaks. Verses, the basic unit, combine in *suras*, or chapters, arranged after the Prophet's death in generally descending order of length.

The early Meccan suras, brief but volatile, brim with urgency: "Nay, I swear by the Day of Resurrection . . . on that day man will cry: Whither to flee? Alas! No refuge! Unto thy Lord is the recourse that day." Vivid images color the passages. A trumpet blast signals the resurrection. The dead rise. Informed of their good and evil deeds as recorded in the book of life, they pass onto a bridge. The righteous cross safely into eternal bliss in lush "gardens underneath which rivers flow." Evildoers are hurled into the abyss where "garments of fire will be cut out for them; boiling fluid . . . poured down on their heads."

From the fervor of religious exhortation, the suras revealed in Medina turn to the building of a community according to divinely ordained rules—some in lessons from lives of the prophets, some explicit on justice, property, personal behavior, the family. Suras grow longer, more didactic. 231

Through revelation and living example, Mohammed tempered social evils and
brought his followers a broader concept of humanity. His rules bettered lives of
slaves, improved the condition of women. Polygamy was taken for granted in a
land where men died young and women needed shelter; the Koran declared
"men are in charge of women" but limited the number of wives to four and
decreed they should be treated equally and kindly. Divorce was permitted by repeating "thou art dismissed," though a wife's property rights were recognized.
To God-fearing women went a promise of paradise on equal footing with men.

Mohammed, after Khadijah died, took ten wives—wed before the Koran's
limiting edict. Some were widows of key followers who fell in battle; others,

daughters of Arab leaders, he married for political reasons. His favorite was Aisha, black-eyed offspring of his close companion Abu Bakr. A tradition attributed to Aisha says that Mohammed's greatest pleasures — after prayers — were sweet odors and the company of women. Desert Arabs prized manly vigor, and legend came to endow Mohammed with this and all other virtues — the ideal man. Traditions recounting his deeds and sayings eventually grew into a supplement to the Koran called the *Hadith*. It helped shape Islamic society, welding faith and law into an all-encompassing system of beliefs and social practices.

Over the centuries power and theological struggles spawned divisions of Islam. Among them: Sunni (from *sunnah*, meaning "custom and law"), orthodox in

doctrine; Shiah (from *shi'ah*, "partisans" of Mohammed's son-in-law Ali), whose leaders are venerated as divinely guided; Sufi (from the *suf*, "wool," of its followers' monkish robes), ascetic and contemplative in practice. But reformers have sought to mold the varying beliefs. In the 12th century Abu Hamid al-Ghazzali, greatest of Islamic theologians, synthesized Sunni dogma and Sufi mysticism to profoundly shape religious thought. In the 18th century Mohammed Ibn Abd al-Wahhab preached strict adherence to the Koran in forming the puritanical Wahhabi creed. Still, schisms remain, though Islam finds powerful unity in its holy book and in its Five Pillars — belief, prayer, almsgiving, fasting, pilgrimage.

In Medina, Mohammed had preached to followers gathered in the courtyard of his home; reputedly today's mosque owes its plan to his modest dwelling. To call his followers to prayer, Mohammed chose not Christianity's bell nor Judaism's ram's horn but a muezzin's cry from a housetop. The first muezzin was a melodious-voiced former slave; today's call may be electronic. Friday became the Moslem Sabbath, with congregational worship at noon. Mohammed's sermons touched any topic: new revelations that had come to him, plans for impending battles, civic projects. Today a *khatib*, or preacher, delivers short stylized sermons consisting of praise to God, a blessing on the Prophet, an admonition to piety, a blessing on believers, and a comment on or quotation from the Koran.

The sermon serves as a prelude to prayers, led by the imam. Though Islam has no formal priesthood—no clergy stands between a believer and God, and theoretically any layman may lead the worship—the imam serves as senior officer of the mosque and spokesman of the faith. He also officiates at weddings and funerals, receives converts, and performs rituals during the fasting of Ramadan. In this ninth lunar month all Moslems except the ill, aged, and those on journeys are exhorted to abstain from food and drink between dawn and sunset.

At one time Mohammed had fasted on the Jewish Day of Atonement and followed the Jewish practice of facing Jerusalem while praying. Some scholars suggest that by such gestures he hoped to attract as allies certain Jewish clans. But they remained aloof. Early in his Medina venture Mohammed broke with these practices, changing fast days and turning his direction of worship toward Mecca. And Jerusalem, with Medina, came to rank after Mecca among Islam's holy cities.

Soon after the Hegira, emboldened Moslems began raiding Meccan trade caravans to retaliate for the city's opposition to the Prophet's mission. In March 624, Mohammed himself led some 300 of the faithful against a larger force sent by Mecca to punish the raiders. He won, and believers took this triumph as divine espousal of their cause. By 628 Mohammed could lead 1,400 to Mecca and secure a treaty that called for a ten-year truce, with permission for Moslems to make a pilgrimage to the Kaaba. But new converts soon tilted the balance of power further in his favor. In January 630, he seized upon an incident as a breach of the treaty and marched on Mecca with a force of 10,000. Warned of the odds, the Meccans offered only token resistance. Mohammed rode triumphantly into his native city.

On camelback he made seven ritual circuits of the Kaaba, ordered all its idols destroyed, and rededicated the shrine to "Allah, the Beneficent, the Merciful." Now the call to prayer sounded throughout holiest Mecca.

The take-over of Mecca set a model of leniency followed by Islamic conquerors; vanquished pagans could embrace Islam, Christians and Jews could keep their own faiths—if they paid a tax. A magnanimous victor, Mohammed succeeded, as had no man before him, in uniting feuding Arab tribes in a virile brotherhood, the *ummah*. His positive system, emphasizing rigid performance of duties set out in the Koran, proved an antidote to social and spiritual anarchy in Arabia.

Now his ministry neared its sunset. From a hill he faced a pilgrim multitude on the plain of Arafat near Mecca. He preached a final revelation, saying "this day [God has] perfected your religion for you . . . and [has] chosen for you . . . Islam." Returning to Medina, he fell ill.

One sunrise in 632 Mohammed struggled from Aisha's chambers to the assembly where his followers had gathered for prayers. He smiled on them and reminded them that the faithful would follow him to paradise. Then he returned and laid his head to rest in his wife's arms. Suddenly he was gone.

Mohammed's companions chose Abu Bakr to succeed him. Thus arose the system of caliphs—successors—who in time guided a theocratic state with wider sway than even Rome's. They ruled with an administrative code based on the Koran and Mohammed's example, adapted to meet changing places and times.

When Abu Bakr first learned of Mohammed's death, he called the people together. "O men," he said, "if anyone worships Mohammed, let him know now that Mohammed is dead. But if anyone worships God, let him know that God is alive and immortal forever." Then Abu Bakr recited a verse from the Koran: "Mohammed is but a messenger, messengers . . . have passed away before him. Will it be that, when he dieth or is slain, ye will turn back on your heels?"

History records the answer: a faith, potent today, that once fused Arab nationalism and devotion to a single God into the most powerful empire on earth.

ISLAM'S FIVE PILLARS OF FAITH

Obligations invoked by the Koran, the "Five Pillars" of Islam give enduring form to a direct and uncomplicated faith.

BELIEF — *Moslems declare acceptance of God and Mohammed as his prophet; they count the Koran God's word and angels instruments of his will.*

PRAYER — *At dawn, noon, late afternoon, sunset, and after nightfall Moslems face Mecca in* salah, *ritual prayer. Ablutions—with sand if no water is available—precede these devotions.* Du'a, *private prayer, may be said anytime.*

ALMSGIVING — *Charity, voluntary or as a tithe, purifies man's remaining wealth, Moslems hold.*

FASTING — *Going without food bends minds to spiritual nourishment, brings man nearer God.*

PILGRIMAGE — *All should make one* hajj *to Mecca. The trip assembles Moslems from afar, boosts brotherhood and the exchange of ideas.*

Thomas J. Abercrombie

The Sweep of Islam

*T*hey were hardly more than a band of Bedouin from the sand and lava wastes of Arabia. Their capital was Medina, a sultry oasis of mud-brick houses surrounded by date palms along the caravan route to Mecca. Here their leader Mohammed had given them a new religion, Islam, then died. Abu Bakr, lifelong companion of the Prophet, was named caliph—successor—and assumed command of the infant Moslem nation, still as threadbare as the austere caliph's single cloak. Few then could have dreamed that these lean tribesmen and their newfound faith would change the course of civilization. The year: 632.

To Europe, Arabia had spelled gold, spices, and the frankincense so prized in Roman temples and Christian churches. Geographers had plotted the coastline of the mysterious peninsula with accuracy before the time of Christ but left the interior blank. Few Westerners had penetrated its forbidding terrain. *Jazirat al-Arab*, the Bedouin called it, the Island of the Arabs—surrounded on three sides by water and on the other by shifting seas of sand. Through its million square miles not one river flowed.

The first Moslem expeditions northward were little more than *razzias*, tribal raids for booty the Arabs had long carried out against each other. Mohammed had converted about a third of the peninsula nominally to Islam, and the Koran forbade the raiding of fellow Moslems. At the same time the holy book enjoined believers to propagate the faith. It recommended mercy for the vanquished. But in battle against unbelievers who resisted Allah's faithful it urged: "Smite at their necks . . . slay them wherever you catch them."

Emboldened and united in holy war, the tribes rode against the infidels to the north—two of the mightiest empires of the time, Byzantium and Persia, now exhausted by long wars against each other. A swift camel, a sword, and a crust of bread was all the Arab warrior had. But against better armed, better trained foes he pitted a devastating mobility and unbridled zeal inspired by the Koran's promise: instant paradise if he fell in battle. For the holy book assured him that "those who are slain in the way of Allah" will be honored in the gardens of delight, "reclining upon couches lined with silk brocade, the fruit of the gardens near to hand, [and maidens] of modest gaze, who neither man nor jinni will have touched before them."

Armies fell like ripe wheat under the flashing Arab blades. First Syria surrendered to the frenzied faithful, then Iraq, Egypt, Iran, distant Morocco. A century after the Prophet's death the Arab world spanned three continents. Five times a day the names of Allah and Mohammed rang from minarets all the way from Spain to the borderlands of China. Arab fleets made the Mediterranean a Moslem sea. By the ninth century the caliph in Baghdad was the most powerful man on earth. The splendid court of Harun al-Rashid, immortalized in the *Arabian Nights*, and the famed libraries of tenth-century Cordova drew poets

*I*n the wake of Sindbad, men of Kuwait ply the Persian Gulf under lateen sail. During Baghdad's golden age, Arab dhows rode the monsoon seas in quest of Zanzibar ivory, Malayan tin, spices of the Indies, and China's silks. Merchant missionaries sowed the first seeds of Islam in Indonesia, today the world's largest Moslem nation.

and savants. Lust for empire gave way to the quest for knowledge. "The ink of scholars is more precious than the blood of martyrs," the Prophet had said.

During Europe's Dark Ages the light of Islam shone, unifying, stimulating the cultures of many lands with the currents of trade and the bond of a common language, Arabic. Ibn Sina of Bukhara, known to the West as Avicenna, wrote his *Canon*, which remained Europe's medical textbook for more than 500 years. Mathematician al-Khwarizmi of Baghdad introduced "Arabic" numerals and the decimal system from India and wrote the standard treatise on *al-jabr*—algebra. Commentaries on Aristotle by the Moorish philosopher Ibn Rushd—Averroës—profoundly influenced Thomas Aquinas and Roger Bacon.

Arab navigators and astronomers brought the compass from China and perfected the astrolabe. Moslem science bequeathed to our language such words as "cipher," "alcohol," "almanac," "logarithm," "soda," "antimony," "azimuth," and

Swift conquest carried impoverished Arabs to a rich empire from the Atlantic to the Indus. Traders spre

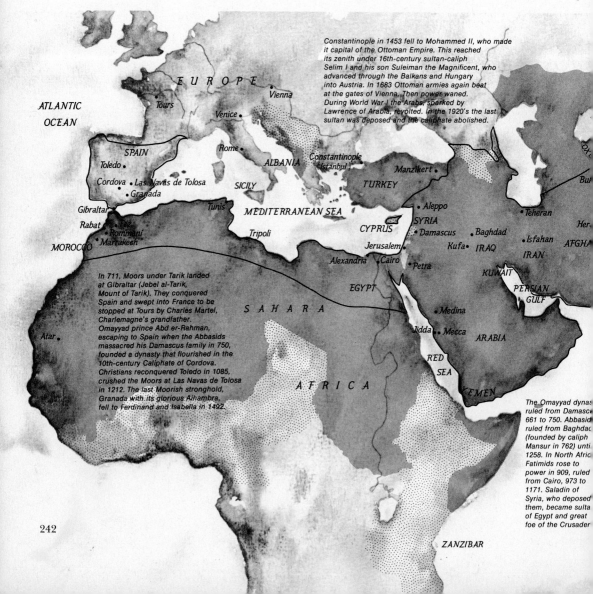

Constantinople in 1453 fell to Mohammed II, who made it capital of the Ottoman Empire. This reached its zenith under 16th-century sultan-caliph Selim I and his son Suleiman the Magnificent, who advanced through the Balkans and Hungary into Austria. In 1683 Ottoman armies again beat at the gates of Vienna. Then power waned. During World War I the Arabs, sparked by Lawrence of Arabia, revolted. In the 1920's the last sultan was deposed and the caliphate abolished.

In 711, Moors under Tarik landed at Gibraltar (Jebel al-Tarik, Mount of Tarik). They conquered Spain and swept into France to be stopped at Tours by Charles Martel, Charlemagne's grandfather. Omayyad prince Abd er-Rahman, escaping to Spain when the Abbasids massacred his Damascus family in 750, founded a dynasty that flourished in the 10th-century Caliphate of Cordova. Christians reconquered Toledo in 1085, crushed the Moors at Las Navas de Tolosa in 1212. The last Moorish stronghold, Granada with its glorious Alhambra, fell to Ferdinand and Isabella in 1492.

The Omayyad dynasty ruled from Damascus 661 to 750. Abbasids ruled from Baghdad (founded by caliph Mansur in 762) until 1258. In North Africa Fatimids rose to power in 909, ruled from Cairo, 973 to 1171. Saladin of Syria, who deposed them, became sultan of Egypt and great foe of the Crusaders

242

"zenith." Brocades from the looms of Moslem Sicily clothed Europe's wealthy. The manufacture of paper, brought from China, entered Europe through Spain, as did the liberating spirit and rich imagery of Persian fables and love poems. Crusaders returned with more ideas from the Moslem world: improved armor and fortifications, military use of carrier pigeons and heraldry, knightly tournaments and concepts of chivalry. The pointed arch, developed in Persia, provided an architectural key to building lofty cathedrals. New foods appeared on Europe's tables: apricots, rice, and *sukkar* — sugar.

Islam's impact quickened the Renaissance that set Europe on its dynamic course into the modern age. Though the power of the caliphs waned, and Arab masters became subjects of Ottoman and Christian, the spiritual unity of Islam remained. Today in independent nations from Morocco to the Philippines Mohammed's message guides 500 million of the faithful, one-seventh of mankind.

faith eastward and south. Christians reconquered Sicily and Spain but elsewhere Islam persevered.

MAP BY BETTY CLONINGER, GEOGRAPHIC ART DIVISION

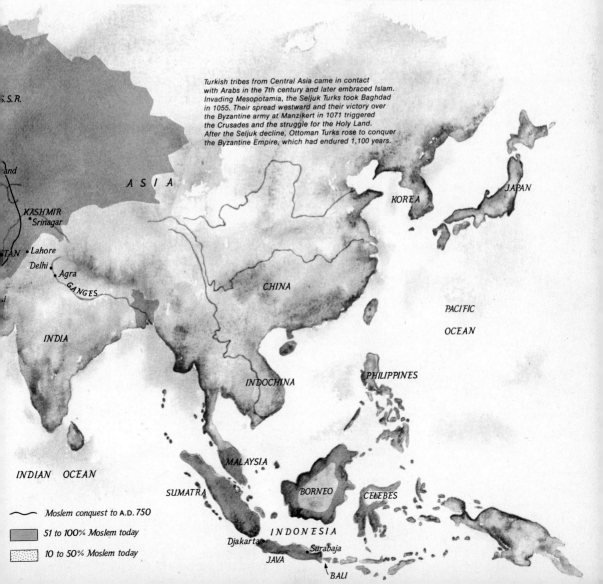

Turkish tribes from Central Asia came in contact with Arabs in the 7th century and later embraced Islam. Invading Mesopotamia, the Seljuk Turks took Baghdad in 1055. Their spread westward and their victory over the Byzantine army at Manzikert in 1071 triggered the Crusades and the struggle for the Holy Land. After the Seljuk decline, Ottoman Turks rose to conquer the Byzantine Empire, which had endured 1,100 years.

S.S.R.

ASIA

JAPAN

KOREA

KASHMIR
Srinagar

Lahore
Delhi
Agra
GANGES

CHINA

PACIFIC

OCEAN

INDIA

INDOCHINA

PHILIPPINES

INDIAN OCEAN

MALAYSIA

SUMATRA

BORNEO

CELEBES

Moslem conquest to A.D. 750

51 to 100% Moslem today

10 to 50% Moslem today

INDONESIA
Djakarta
Surabaja
JAVA
BALI

MOSLEM BOY CELEBRATES
A RITUAL STEP TOWARD MANHOOD

Where an Arab conqueror, sweeping 1,200 miles across northwest Africa, rode his horse into the Atlantic and called God to witness that he had kept his oath to carry Islam to the limits of the world—there stands the Moslem kingdom of Morocco, western bulwark of Islam. Today, 13 centuries after Uqba Ibn Nafi's daring raid, 12 centuries after a descendant of Mohammed founded the city, Fez (opposite) still lives by the Koran. More than 300 mosques grace labyrinthine lanes in Morocco's cultural capital. Principal of these, Qarawiyyin Mosque, shelters the medieval university which drew such famous scholars as historian Ibn Khaldun and geographer Leo Africanus. *Suqs* clustering about it follow Islam's hierarchy of trades: Bookbinders, incense sellers, cloth merchants, and other "noble" trades stand nearest. Farther back congregate coppersmiths, potters, tanners whose skill made "morocco" synonymous with fine leather.

Festivals often break the routine. Dressed in finery, a lad (below) parades with his father on horseback past a *marabout,* a tomb of a local saint, to celebrate his circumcision, performed by the family barber. Family and neighbors surround the proud pair, marching to the beat of drums. The boy's sister (opposite, lower) balances a tray bearing incense and flasks of rose attar to perfume the procession. Incumbent on all Moslem males, circumcision pre-dates Islam. Archeology reveals the rite in Egypt as early as 2400 B.C.

THOMAS J. ABERCROMBIE, NATIONAL GEOGRAPHIC STAFF

CLASSROOMS FOLLOWED CONQUERORS
ACROSS THE VAST SAHARA

"God . . . the Exalted in Might, the Wise . . . has sent amongst the Unlettered an apostle from among themselves . . . to instruct them in Scripture and Wisdom." Words revealed to Mohammed by Allah teach these children in Atar, oasis home of 4,000 in Moslem Mauritania. They learn to read Arabic studying Koranic verses inked on prayerboards. In this crust of land where sheep and goats outnumber people seven to one, literacy barely reaches ten percent. For children of desert nomads the campfire is still the classroom, memory the storehouse of poetry and folklore, the Koran a total way of life. From this western reach of the Sahara, homeland of the Moors, an army of Moslem puritans, the Almoravids, swept north in the 11th century. They founded a splendid capital at Marrakech in Morocco before crossing the Strait of Gibraltar to stem the Christian reconquest and take over Islamic Spain.

A mud-brick minaret (opposite), braced with tamarisk logs, soars above the oasis of Agadès, a sweltering caravan crossroad 1,400 miles eastward in the Republic of Niger. Camel trains wend into the marketplace, where caravaneers barter blocks of salt for swords and saddles, camels or cloth. Blue-veiled Tuareg tribesmen haggle with turbaned Arabs, black-skinned Hausa farmers, Fulani herdsmen in calfskin loincloths, and jeeploads of hardy French tourists following the main north-south track across the world's largest desert. Once unchallenged masters of most of the Sahara, the Tuaregs held off foreign armies for five decades. From his crumbling castle near the mosque, a Tuareg *amenokal*, or sultan, still reigns as spiritual head of a parched district the size of Texas.

ARABESQUES IN TILE AND TAPESTRY
REFLECT PERSIA'S GOLDEN AGE

When Mongol hordes sacked Baghdad in 1258, ending the glories of the Abbasid caliphate, Islam still endured eastward in Persia. There, at the start of the 17th century, Emperor Shah Abbas made Isfahan his capital, lavishing on it Persian art at its peak. Lines of his court poet Saeb might well describe Isfahan's splendors preserved to this day: "Each of its bricks is valuable as treasure. Its jasmine gardens dawning in the heart of night. . . ." Arabesques of inlaid tile emblazon the graceful dome and minarets of Isfahan's Madrasah Mosque (below). Worthy of such mosques are luxurious Persian carpets (opposite) on which the faithful bow in prayer. Nimble fingers of a girl in Kerman can tie knots faster than the eye can follow—325 to the square inch.

Along Isfahan's arcade-lined square where Shah Abbas and his court galloped at polo, women stroll wrapped in cotton *chadors* (far left). In Iran as in most Moslem countries the veil, though mentioned in the Koran, is retreating before liberalizing trends.

THOMAS J. ABERCROMBIE, NATIONAL GEOGRAPHIC STAFF

EMBERS OF ISLAM
SMOLDER UNDER SOVIET RULE

Over the Oxus into the steppes of Central Asia, they had swept with cries of "*Allahu Akbar!*" (God is most great!), those Arab conquerors in the early eighth century. It was here they captured Chinese papermakers, whose art throve in Baghdad seven centuries before it reached England. Samarkand, astride the silk route to China, flourished in trade and culture. In Bukhara's famous library young Avicenna filled his eager mind.

Then the tide turned. Genghis Khan, leader of pagan Mongolian hordes, came ravaging out of the east. In 1369 Timur the Lame—Tamerlane—seized power in Samarkand. A nominal Moslem claiming descent from Genghis Khan, he plundered lands from Syria to India, slaughtered thousands, built pyramids of their skulls. Gathering artists and artisans from afar, he embellished his capital, Samarkand, with palaces and mosques.

Tamerlane's great mosque (opposite, lower) thrusts the wreckage of its vanished glory above the Soviet horizon. At Friday prayers (upper) a newly tailored litany reminds Uzbek merchants in cloaks and traditional turbans, like those worn in the marketplace (below), that "the Soviet Government was sent by Allah" and must be obeyed.

PAKISTANIS FEAST DURING ID AL-FITR
IN "LAND OF THE PURE"

Breaking a four-week fast, Pakistanis dine on curries and kebabs in a Karachi club. Whether they dress in urban finery or desert burnous, most of the world's Moslems do not eat or drink from dawn to sunset during Ramadan, holy month of fasting.

Long before Islam, Arab traders rode the monsoons across the Arabian Sea to India. By the eighth century swords of Islam reached the Punjab; Moslem kingdoms later ruled most of India. But it was not until the 16th century that Baber, a descendant of Tamerlane, established the Mogul Empire, which consolidated Moslem rule over the subcontinent. Nomadic Turks in race, Persians by cultural adoption, the Moguls raised "tents of stone," topped them with Persian domes, graced them with Persian gardens. Exquisite miniatures, in Persian-Hindu art, reveal the splendors of their court. Its language, Persian, mixed with Hindi, forms Urdu, official tongue in West Pakistan today.

Islamic monotheism of the ruling minority influenced Hindu thought; the Sikhs' religion (page 47) sought to unite the two. From the turn of this century Hindu and Moslem worked together toward independence from Great Britain. Sir Mohammed Iqbal, urging that Islam was not only a religion but a distinct social order as well, first voiced the call for a Moslem India in 1930. Honored as the leading Moslem philosopher of modern times, Sir Mohammed lies buried in Lahore's Badshahi Mosque (opposite). Partition under the leadership of Mohammed Ali Jinnah, British withdrawal in 1947, and mass migrations created Pakistan – Urdu for "Land of the Pure."

WITH FASTS AND FLOGGING, A MARTYR IS MOURNED

The one major crack in Islam's orthodoxy appeared less than half a century after Mohammed's death. Muawiya, Arab governor of Syria, refused to recognize Ali, son-in-law of the Prophet, as fourth caliph, or successor to the original Prince of the Faithful. Muawiya took the title himself, moved the seat of Islam from holy Medina to worldly Damascus, and founded the Omayyad dynasty that was to last a hundred years. Ali established a rival capital at Kufa, in Iraq, but was murdered.

After Muawiya's death in 680, Ali's son Husain set out across the desert from Mecca to claim the caliphate. Near Kufa, Husain and his small party were massacred by cavalry of Muawiya's son Yazid; Husain's head was delivered to Damascus. The shock of this murder—of the beloved grandson of the Prophet—caused partisans of Ali, the Shiahs, to break away from the mainstream of Islam (Sunni). Never again would they recognize

a caliph's authority. Today about ten percent of all Moslems call themselves Shiahs — some 50 million, mostly in Iraq, Iran, Yemen, Algeria, northern India, and Pakistan. As Shiah Moslems have each year for 13 centuries, young men in Kashmir parade through the streets of Srinagar (above), wailing and scourging themselves with knives and chains, to lament the anniversary of Husain's martyrdom.

Exalting different descendants of Ali as their imam, or leader, the Shiahs later split further. In the 11th and 12th centuries one branch, the Ismailis, reigned with terror from a string of mountaintop strongholds in northern Persia and Syria. Members of the order, drugged by hashish, sampled the "joys of paradise" before setting out to murder generals, viziers, even caliphs. They were called *hashshashin*, or hashish eaters — hence our word "assassin." Today's Ismailis, several million strong, comprise a merchant class in India and East Africa. In 1946 they collected 243½ pounds of diamonds, a pious offering to match the weight of their imam, the Aga Khan.

Masterpiece in marble, the Taj Mahal in Agra immortalizes a Moslem emperor's love. Shah Jahan lavish

years on this tomb for his wife Mumtaz-i Mahal. Majestic, tranquil, it epitomizes Mogul splendor in India.

HINDUISM AND BUDDHISM COLOR ISLAM IN INDONESIA

Islam from India spread slowly across the 3,000 islands of Indonesia. Marco Polo, return-ing from Cathay in 1292, visited a region of northern Sumatra governed by one of the earliest Islamic rulers. Moslem traders married island wives, converting them and their kin. Gradually Buddhist and Hindu influence, which for centuries had dotted the islands with splendid temples, yielded to growing Moslem power.

Not surprisingly, Indonesians wove local culture into the fabric of their new faith. One early Moslem guru, now venerated as a saint, used gong and xylophone music together with leather puppets—the traditional Hindu shadow plays—to enliven his

lectures on the Koran. Many Indonesian mosques lack minarets; because jungles muffle a muezzin's cry, booming buffalo-skin drums call the pious to prayer. Decorated mounds of rice carried to the mosques on the Prophet's birthday reiterate offerings brought to Buddhist temples. Court costumes from before Marco Polo's day bespangle a barefoot bride and groom at a Moslem wedding in Sumatra (above). Auspicious month, day, and hour are important in making the marriage contract and to the ceremony itself.

Indonesians rarely fast during Ramadan. Yet the 115 million Moslems in this largest of Islamic nations take the rest of their faith seriously. Students memorize the Koran; the devout pack the mosques for Friday prayers. Though far from the holy land of Arabia, Indonesia sends thousands by government-chartered ships on the pilgrimage to Mecca.

*F*rom the highest minarets of Mecca pealed the call to morning prayer, swelling across the rooftops and echoing from the surrounding hills.

Allah is most great. Allah is most great....

To me, a mere drop in the human flood below, the lofty summons came as comfort, a ritual of Islam's familiar fabric, as unerring and timeless as the desert stars yet blazing in the pre-dawn sky.

There is no god but God, Mohammed is the messenger of God....

The gathering crowds swept me through the narrow streets and covered markets that led to the great Haram Mosque in the center of the holy city. Under the twin spires that flank the Gate of the King I slipped off my sandals and pressed my way into the galleries, already jammed with the faithful.

Come to prayer. Come to salvation. Prayer is better than sleep....

I hurried on to join the overflow crowds filling a nearby rooftop and gazed down, breathless, on the sacred courtyard. At its center stood the Kaaba, Islam's holiest shrine, a stark cube-shaped granite house of God some fifty feet high, veiled by black silk lettered in gold. Moslems believe that the prophet Abraham and his son Ishmael built the original Kaaba where Adam had uttered man's first prayers to God. Chanting pilgrims circled the shrine like moths about a flame. Over the din of fervent prayers I heard the muezzin end his call:

...there is no god but God.

WHERE CARAVANS OF OLD CONVERGED, *flocks of the faithful, robed in pilgrims' white, pour into M*

The churning subsided. The congregation, half a million strong, formed up shoulder to shoulder in ever widening circles, their white costumes, the humble ihram prescribed for all who visit Mecca, reflecting the first morning light. Then the prayer began. Blacksmith, banker, Bedouin—prime minister or pauper—all bowed in unison, equal in the eyes of the Almighty.

"It is the dream of my lifetime fulfilled," said the white-bearded man next to me. He had come from a village in the Moroccan Sahara, more than 3,000 miles away. Walking much of the distance, working at odd jobs along the way, he had taken 16 months. He was bent with the hardships of this world, but his eyes, glazed with tears, were on the next. For to the Moslem the hajj, or pilgrimage to Mecca, is more meaningful than even birth or death. "And proclaim unto mankind the pilgrimage," it is written in the Koran. "They will come unto thee on foot and on every lean camel . . . from every deep ravine"—though today's pilgrims come by ship, bus, or jet plane more often than by camel.

I had traveled to Mecca with a group of Jordanian villagers by chartered bus, a big Ford scraped, bruised, and smooth-tired from years on desert roads. Mottoes from the Koran painted on it warded off harm. Boxes of spare parts piled on the roof offered further insurance. Beside them we lashed our baggage: trunks, cooking pots, water cans, mattresses, sacks of rice and flour. In a thousand miles of desert we would find few hotels—none not already filled.

he 12th month of the lunar year. Goal of every Moslem is to make this pilgrimage to the cradle of Islam.

THOMAS J. ABERCROMBIE, NATIONAL GEOGRAPHIC STAFF

A festive crowd surrounded the bus as we boarded. Children handed up bags of sweetmeats and oranges. Through the cloud of dust, wishes pursued us: "*Hajj mabruk! Hajj mabruk!* Blessed pilgrimage!"

Following the classic pilgrim route that leads south from Damascus, we bounced off the asphalt road into open desert near the rose-red ruins of Petra. The bone-jarring trail stretched endlessly across dusty gravel flats toward a horizon broken occasionally by black volcanic hills that seemed to float on quivering mirages. Each noon and at four o'clock the driver stopped, opening the hood to cool the engine while we passengers lined up beside the bus to pray. Whenever the going got rough, Abd al-Jalil, one of the village elders, recalled his first pilgrimage, nearly half a century before. "Eighty-six days we marched by camel from Jerusa-

CITY FOR A DAY *dissolves at dusk as the multitude streams from Arafat. Pilgrims experience their supre*

lem to Mecca," he told us. "Many of the old died along the way. And there was always the danger of Bedouin raiders. Allah be praised, we were spared." Today soldiers patrol the pilgrim highway. We even camped among the black tents of the Bedouin—quite safely, for desert laws of hospitality protect the guest. At Wadi Ramm a sheik slaughtered a young camel to feast us.

That night I walked across the soft silent sand under the blazing stars. It was no accident, I thought, that in the harsh and humbling desert the seeds of three great religions—Judaism, Christianity, and Islam—took root. Those early prophets, shared by all three faiths, must have sensed amid this vast landscape how infinitesimal man is compared to his maker. Life was cruel, but man could endure—with nothing between him and his God but the broad blue sky. The

urs on this plain, mindful that here Mohammed gave his farewell sermon and received a final revelation.

SAFOUH NAAMANI

wandering herdsmen had no need for priests nor room in their packs for idols. And Islam has veered little from the original credo that the prophet Mohammed received in the wilderness outside Mecca. No patriarchs or cardinals, no vicars or abbots need interpret the word. The message of the Koran our fellow passenger, the farmer Azzat, read in the original Arabic by the dying embers of our Bedouin campfire had survived the centuries unchanged. Here in the desert it had all begun. And here too, years ago, I had discovered and embraced Islam.

THOMAS J. ABERCROMBIE, NATIONAL GEOGRAPHIC STAFF

"THERE IS NO GOD BUT ALLAH," *chants a pilgrim amid the tents of Arafat during the afternoon-long rite of standing before God.*

At an oasis, Saudi Arabian officials stamped our pilgrim visas and waved us on. Small dust clouds far behind us told of other pilgrim buses following. Finally we reached asphalt again and sped south, skirting dunes and cutting through a sterile plain of black basalt boulders even the hardy Bedouin avoid.

North of Medina, a holy city of Islam, we stopped to wash and pray and don our pilgrim costumes, two lengths of white seamless cotton. One I wrapped around my waist, then Azzat showed me how to drape the other properly over my left shoulder. Sandals, a money belt, and a green umbrella completed my costume. From now on we must go bareheaded, even under the relentless sun. Late next day we reached Jidda, Mecca's port on the Red Sea.

Lateen-rigged dhows plied among anchored steamships waiting their turn at the quays. Bright red buses shuttled the joyous crowds from dockside to hotels and pensions throughout the city. "Pilgrim City," new blocks of transient accommodations, housed the overflow.

That same afternoon we joined fleets of taxis, buses, and open trucks on the four-lane highway to Mecca, 45 miles inland. At the last of three police checkpoints a warning was posted in Arabic and English: RESTRICTED AREA, MOSLEMS ONLY PERMITTED. Minutes later, passing army barracks and modern villas on the sandy outskirts of forbidden Mecca, we rounded the foot of the last hill. The holy city burst into view.

"*Labbayka Allahumma labbayka!*" At the sight, Azzat, Abd al-Jalil, and I shouted the pilgrims' cry. "Here I am, at your service, O God!"

266   The highway cut through an ancient labyrinth of pastel-colored houses that

crowded the narrow Mecca valley and climbed the steep black hillsides. Modern shops and hotels lined the square in front of the gleaming mosque. "Allah be praised!" exclaimed old Abd al-Jalil. "How God's house has grown! I can hardly believe it!" Fifteen acres of marble now enclose the original eighth-century mosque. Seven new minarets soar 300 feet. Before entering we washed hands, mouths and nostrils, finally our feet.

Pilgrims thronged in and out of the mosque's twenty gates, each group rallying around a banner carried high by their *mutawwif*, or pilgrim guide. From the Gate of Salvation we followed our guide seven times around the Kaaba barefoot, repeating after him in Arabic the prescribed phrases of devotion: "O mighty Allah. This mosque is your mosque. This peace is your peace. This slave is your slave."

We tried to reach the sacred Black Stone set in silver on the eastern corner, an object of worship since the days of Abraham or before. But we could only raise our hands in ritual salute each time we passed. Old women, children, soldiers, Bedouin, babes in arms, bearded savants—we all churned together. Bearers carrying the sick and the lame jostled us with their wooden litters. A thousand toenails tore my heels and calves. Azzat and I slowed our pace to keep with Abd al-Jalil. Tears of ecstasy bathed his face.

After our *tawaf*, or circumambulations, we marched briskly, as custom commands, seven times back and forth between the hills of Safa and Marwa, now enclosed by the half mile of arcades that forms the eastern wall of the mosque. Our guide explained the meaning of the ceremony: "Abraham once left Hagar here in the desert with their infant son Ishmael. Frantically she ran back and forth between Safa and Marwa searching for water for her child. Finally the angel Gabriel appeared and led her to a spring."

A spring still feeds the Well of Zamzam. Here, Azzat and I washed our faces in its holy waters while Abd al-Jalil doused himself with bucketfuls. In the markets around the mosque, merchants and pilgrims haggled over bolts of Damascus brocade, prayer beads, and Korans. Abd al-Jalil bought a small morocco-bound edition and took care, I noticed, to argue about the price of the binding only. "The holy pages themselves are priceless," he explained, "and always free."

*N*ext day, on the ninth day of the lunar month of Dhu al-Hijjah, the focus of the pilgrimage shifted to the plain of Arafat, 14 miles east of Mecca. Azzat and I climbed the small hill where the Prophet addressed his followers on his "farewell pilgrimage" shortly before his death. I could see a city of white tents stretching to the horizon. An empty desert only a few days before, Arafat now bloomed with a population the size of Washington, D. C.

All afternoon the multitude stood praying until the white-hot sun slowly quenched itself in the caldron of haze beyond Mecca. Sunset signaled the climax of the pilgrimage. Supplications of a million souls rose to a crescendo.

Our Lord, to thee we approach, dismounted in thy open place. . . . Accept this pilgrimage and forgive our sins.

A cannon boomed. The hillsides burst into life as the white landslide poured into the valleys and streamed west across the holy plain. The hundreds of

STONING SATAN, *pilgrims jam the village of Mina during Id al-Adha, feast of the sacrifice (upper left). Following Allah's command revealed in a dream, the prophet Abraham prepared to sacrifice his son Ishmael (not, Moslems believe, the younger Isaac, as in the Old Testament). Thrice Satan tempted Ishmael to flee. Each time the son stoned him. (Three pillars mark the sites.) After testing Abraham, Allah substituted a ram for the sacrifice.*

The pilgrim, alone or in a group, puts an animal to the knife (opposite), recalling Abraham's steadfast faith. Then he bares his head to a curbside barber in a final ritual, and pays another visit to the Kaaba in nearby Mecca, eager to touch or to kiss once more the Black Stone (left) framed in silver. Moslem tradition maintains that the rock, probably meteoritic, was borne to earth by the angel Gabriel.

thousands on foot moved faster than those on wheels through the tangle that stretched into the dusk toward the village of Mina and the Devil's pillars.

The rush season in Mina lasts just three days. The rest of the year the village is practically deserted. That explained the high hotel rate: $100 a bed, four and five to a room. I was lucky at that. Most pilgrims camped in the bleak hills or curled up on their small prayer rugs in the dust of the streets.

But the rigors of the journey were forgotten in the three-day celebration of a successful pilgrimage. I went with Abd al-Jalil to help him cope with the crowds milling around the Devil's pillars in Mina's main street. The three columns mark where Moslems believe the Devil attempted to lure Ishmael away from his father Abraham, who meant to sacrifice him to the Lord. Ishmael stoned the Devil, showing a contempt still felt by pilgrims. Azzat gritted his teeth as he hurled his stones, pebbles gathered in the night enroute from Arafat. Once, I was told, a soldier emptied his revolver into one of the pillars.

Commemorating Abraham's sacrifice of a ram substituted by Allah, pilgrims offer up thousands of sheep—and sometimes cows and camels—outside the village. Stripped and dried in the sun, much of the meat is distributed to the poor. Completion of the stoning rites and the sacrifice entitles the pilgrim to trim his hair, as Mohammed is believed to have done here. One of the army of curbside barbers shaved Abd al-Jalil bald. Azzat and I, as is permitted, had only a few symbolic locks cut. Then we changed back to our regular clothes.

Once a uniform white, the crowds now blazed with costumes from many lands: green calicos from Nigeria, indigo caftans from Yemen slung with silver daggers, the red headcloths of Jordan, striped Moroccan galabias, sarongs from Indonesia. Each pilgrim carefully folds his precious ihram to carry home with him. He will wear it once more—when he is lowered into his grave.

*F*ew return home without visiting Medina, 250 miles north. Here Mohammed spent the last ten years of his life after his Hegira from Mecca in A.D. 622. With his own hands he helped build a sanctuary of sun-dried bricks and palm trunks. The centuries have enlarged and enriched it. And here under its giant green dome Azzat, Abd al-Jalil, and I paid our respects before his tomb. "O Allah, blessings upon our prince. Grant him dignity and favor. . . ."

From Jidda jet planes would soon speed us on our separate ways. Old Abd al-Jalil studied his ticket, shaking his head. The desert that had once cost him 86 days on camelback he would conquer tomorrow in two hours.

The 20th century is reshaping Arabia. Mecca broadcasts the Koran on television and nearly everywhere loudspeakers have dislodged the muezzin from his minaret. But the word endures, the message of Mohammed, as pure, as overpowering, as eternal as the harsh and holy land from which it sprang.

MOSQUE OF THE PROPHET *in Medina enshrines Mohammed's tomb. From this oasis his successors, fired by the new faith, rode forth to carve out an empire vaster than Rome's at its zenith, spreading Islam from Morocco to Mongolia. Now each year throngs from the far-flung Moslem world come to pay homage at the wellsprings of their faith.*

THOMAS J. ABERCROMBIE, NATIONAL GEOGRAPHIC STAFF

Sacred Writings of the West

"T̲ake thee a roll of a book, and write," God commanded Jeremiah. "What thou seest, write," said a voice to the author of Revelation. "In the name of thy Lord . . . recite!" spoke Allah to Mohammed. Each obeyed, swelling scriptures sacred to half mankind, scriptures that tap the wisdom of millenniums and undergird societies of the West.

Mother of both Christianity and Islam, Judaism for generations passed along orally the traditions of its heroes — Abraham who taught his clan of Yahweh 3,700 years ago; Moses who gave Hebrews the Law five centuries later. In time sacred lore became sacred writ, and sages divided the scriptural books into the Law, the Prophets, and the histories, psalms, and lessons called the Writings.

This was the Bible Jesus knew; texts of it survive in the Dead Sea Scrolls. Less than a century later a Christian corpus sprouted, nourished almost from the beginning by the letters of Paul. As it grew, fathers of the second and third centuries, from whose era the oldest New Testament manuscripts survive, winnowed — now accepting Revelation, now rejecting Shepherd of Hermas, now sifting a welter of gospels. In St. Jerome's fourth-century Vulgate Bible the New Testament took the shape Christians revere in scores of translations.

Many men transmitted the Bible. But from the mouth of Mohammed alone sprang the Koran, the holy writ of Islam. Through him, Moslems believe, God made known his word to man; the revelations were compiled, after Mohammed's death, in chapters called *suras*. The Arabic of these "courses of brick laid together side by side" is often called untranslatable; the powerful, rhythmic prose moves men to tears with emotive "guidance for those who act piously."

In each religion the centuries have produced men of spiritual genius whose works refined scriptural treasures and inspired the faithful with fresh insight.

273

Scriptural heroes like Daniel and prophets like Isaiah shape the faith — and art — of Western man. Detail from The Well of Moses," c. 1406, by Claus Sluter, at the monastery of Champmol, France; Eddy van der Veen

THE TORAH

The Shema

From verses of the Pentateuch comes Judaism's confession of faith, named for its first word. The heart of daily prayer, death cry of Jewish martyrs, it is encased in tefillin and in containers called mezuzahs *at observant homes, as this passage from Deuteronomy commands:*

ear, O Israel: the Lord our God, the Lord is one. And thou shalt love the Lord thy God with all thy heart, and with all thy soul, and with all thy might. And these words, which I command thee this day, shall be upon thy heart; and thou shalt teach them diligently unto thy children, and shalt talk of them when thou sittest in thy house, and when thou walkest by the way, and when thou liest down, and when thou risest up. And thou shalt bind them for a sign upon thy hand, and they shall be for frontlets between thine eyes. And thou shalt write them upon the doorposts of thy house, and upon thy gates.... that your days may be multiplied, and the days of your children, upon the land which the Lord swore unto your fathers to give them, as the days of the heavens above the earth. (6:4-9, 11:21)

Leviticus

Though much of Leviticus details rites relating to priests and Levites, its "Holiness Code," which includes the 19th chapter excerpted here, stresses the unity of ethics and religion:

And the Lord spoke unto Moses, saying: Speak unto all the congregation of the children of Israel, and say unto them: Ye shall be holy; for I the Lord your God am holy. Ye shall fear every man his mother, and his father, and ye shall keep My sabbaths: I am the Lord your God. Turn ye not unto the idols, nor make to yourselves molten gods: I am the Lord your God.... Ye shall not steal: neither shall ye deal falsely, nor lie one to another.... Thou shalt not oppress thy neighbor, nor rob him....

Thou shalt not curse the deaf, nor put a stumbling block before the blind.... Thou shalt not take vengeance, nor bear any grudge against the children of thy people, but thou shalt love thy neighbor as thyself: I am the Lord.... Thou shalt rise up before the hoary head, and honor the face of the old man, and thou shalt fear thy God: I am the Lord. And if a stranger sojourn with thee in your land, ye shall not do him wrong. The stranger that sojourneth with you shall be unto you as the homeborn among you ... for ye were strangers in the land of Egypt.... Ye shall do no unrighteousness in judgment... in weight, or in measure.... And ye shall observe all My statutes ... and do them: I am the Lord.

THE PROPHETS

Micah

When evil ways arose among the children of Israel, God spoke to them through prophets. In the eighth century B.C., *Micah foresaw disaster as the fruit of sin and oppression; his classic counsel stands unsurpassed in its simple ideal:*

"Wherewith shall I come before the Lord,
And bow myself before God on high?
Shall I come before Him with
    burnt-offerings,

With calves of a year old?
Will the Lord be pleased with thousands
  of rams,
With ten thousands of rivers of oil?
Shall I give my first-born for my transgression,
The fruit of my body for the sin of my soul?"
It hath been told thee, O man, what is good,
And what the Lord doth require of thee:
Only to do justly, and to love mercy, and
    to walk humbly with thy God. (6:6-8)

THE WRITINGS

Varying in tone and substance, the Writings chronicle history, the deeds of heroes, the drama of spiritual struggle. Here, also, superb poetry traces the ebb and flow of passion—the cool wisdom of Ecclesiastes and the throbbing sensuousness of the Song of Songs. Both books are traditionally associated with King Solomon:

To every thing there is a season, and a
   time to every purpose under the heaven:
A time to be born, and a time to die;
A time to plant, and a time to pluck up
   that which is planted;
A time to kill, and a time to heal;

Behold, thou art fair, my love; behold,
   thou art fair;
Thine eyes are as doves behind thy veil;
Thy hair is as a flock of goats,
That trail down from mount Gilead.
Thy teeth are like a flock of ewes all
   shaped alike,
Which are come up from the washing;
Whereof all are paired,
And none faileth among them.

Ecclesiastes

A time to break down, and a time
   to build up;
A time to weep, and a time to laugh;
A time to mourn, and a time to dance;
A time to cast away stones, and a time
   to gather stones together;
A time to embrace, and a time to refrain
   from embracing;
A time to seek, and a time to lose;
A time to keep, and a time to cast away;
A time to rend, and a time to sew;
A time to keep silence, and a time to speak;
A time to love, and a time to hate;
A time for war, and a time for peace. (3:1-8)

Song of Songs

Thy lips are like a thread of scarlet,
And thy mouth is comely;
Thy temples are like a pomegranate
   split open
Behind thy veil. . . .
Thy two breasts are like two fawns
That are twins of a gazelle,
Which feed among the lilies. . . .
Thou art all fair, my love;
And there is no spot in thee. (4:1-7)

THE TALMUD

After the Babylonian exile Jewish sages began guiding their people with oral teachings that later came to be collected in the Talmud. Still treasured, it offers scholarly tracts on the Bible, law, and science, along with gems like these:

abbi Tarfon was very rich, but did not give enough to charity. Rabbi Akiba asked him for a large sum to purchase a village, but when he received the money, he distributed it among the poor. When Rabbi Tarfon asked for the deed to the village, Rabbi Akiba opened the Psalter to 112:9, and read: " 'He hath scattered abroad; he hath given to the needy; his righteousness endureth forever.' This have I purchased for thee," added Rabbi Akiba, and Rabbi Tarfon embraced him.

When Rabbi Yochanan Ben Zakkai's son died, Rabbi Eliezer Ben Arak came to offer consolation. He said: "To whom may I liken you? To a man who has received for safekeeping a jewel from his king. As long as he has it . . . he is troubled with anxiety regarding it; when the king takes it back in the same good condition, the man rejoices. You, O Master, have received for safekeeping a dear soul. He . . . died without sin. You have returned it in perfection, and you should find comfort in the knowledge of this."

THE PRAYER BOOK

The Amidah

Daily companion of the devout, the prayer book mirrors the soul of a people in Bible and Talmud passages and the inspirations of holy men across the centuries. The solemn Amidah, said softly while standing, offers 19 benedictions of praise, petition, and thanksgiving:

Blessed art thou, O Lord our God and God of our fathers . . . who rememberest the pious deeds of the patriarchs, and in love wilt bring a redeemer. . . .

Cause us to return, O our Father, unto thy Torah; draw us near, O our King, unto thy service. . . . Heal us, O Lord, and we shall be healed; save us and we shall be saved, for thou art our praise. . . .

Sound the great horn for our freedom; raise the ensign to gather our exiles. . . . Blessed art thou, O Lord, who gatherest the dispersed of thy people. . . .

And for slanderers let there be no hope, and let all wickedness perish. . . . Blessed art thou, O Lord, who breakest the enemies and humblest the arrogant. . . .

Grant peace, welfare, blessing, grace, lovingkindness and mercy. . . . Bless us, O our Father, even all of us together, with the light of thy countenance. . . .

The Adoration

Dating from Temple times, the Adoration acknowledges Israel's duty to serve God, and looks to the day when all men will accept the divine yoke. It concludes all congregational services:

It is our duty to praise the Lord of all things, to ascribe greatness to him who formed the world in the beginning, since he hath not made us like the nations of other lands. . . . For we bend the knee before the supreme King of kings. . . . He is our God; there is none else. . . . We therefore hope . . . that we may speedily behold the glory of thy might. . . . Let all the inhabitants of the world perceive and know that unto thee every knee must bow. . . . For the kingdom is thine, and to all eternity thou wilt reign in glory. . . .

The Gospels

The Meaning of Jesus

The Gospel of John seeks to explain the enigma of Jesus, a man yet more than man. John refers to him as "the Word," Logos, meaning "God in action," and describes his eternal nature, his divine role, and his mission on earth:

In the beginning was the Word, and the Word was with God, and the Word was God. He was in the beginning with God; all things were made through him. . . . In him was life, and the life was the light of men. The light shines in the darkness and the darkness has not overcome it. There was a man sent from God, whose name was John. He came for testimony to bear witness to the light, that all might believe through him. He was not the light, but came to bear witness to the light.

The true light that enlightens every man was coming into the world. He was in the world, and the world was made through him, yet the world knew him not. He came to his own home, and his own people received him not. But to all who received him, who believed in his name, he gave power to become children of God; who were born, not of blood nor of the will of the flesh nor of the will of man, but of God.

And the Word became flesh and dwelt among us, full of grace and truth; we have beheld his glory, glory as of the only Son from the Father. (1:1-14)

The Sermon on the Mount

Matthew's gospel focuses on Jesus' teachings. Most famous of his discourses is the Sermon on the Mount. In its Beatitudes passage, Jesus *promises God's reward for those who live by his lessons; other sections urge rejection of worldly standards and condemn hypocrisy:*

lessed are the poor in spirit, for theirs is the kingdom of heaven.
"Blessed are those who mourn, for they shall be comforted.
"Blessed are the meek, for they shall inherit the earth.
"Blessed are those who hunger and thirst for righteousness, for they shall be satisfied.
"Blessed are the merciful, for they shall obtain mercy.
"Blessed are the pure in heart, for they shall see God.
"Blessed are the peacemakers, for they shall be called sons of God.
"Blessed are those who are persecuted for righteousness' sake, for theirs is the kingdom of heaven.

"Blessed are you when men revile you and persecute you and utter all kinds of evil against you falsely on my account. Rejoice and be glad, for your reward is great in heaven, for so men persecuted the prophets who were before you." (5:3-12)

"Therefore I tell you, do not be anxious about your life, what you shall eat or what you shall drink, nor about your body, what you shall put on. Is not life more than food, and the body more than clothing? Look at the birds of the air: they neither sow nor reap nor gather into barns, and yet your heavenly Father feeds them. Are you not of more value than they? And which of you by being anxious can add one cubit to his span of life?... Consider the lilies of the field, how they grow; they neither toil nor spin; yet I tell you, even Solomon in all his glory was not arrayed like one of these. But if God so clothes the grass of the field, which today is alive and tomorrow is thrown into the oven, will he not much more clothe you, O men of little faith? Therefore do not be anxious, saying, 'What shall we eat?' or 'What shall we drink' or 'What shall we wear?' For... your heavenly Father knows that you need them all. But seek first his kingdom and his righteousness, and all these things shall be yours as well." (6:25-33)

"Judge not, that you be not judged. For with the judgment you pronounce you will be judged, and the measure you give will be the measure you get. Why do you see the speck... in your brother's eye, but do not notice the log... in your own eye? Or how can you say to your brother, 'Let me take the speck out of your eye,' when there is the log in your own eye? You hypocrite, first take the log out of your own eye, and then you will see clearly to take the speck out of your brother's eye." (7:1-5)

The New Commandment

At the Last Supper Jesus prepares his disciples for his coming death and eternal life. In this *passage from the Gospel of John, he sets forth a guiding principle to bind his followers:*

"This is my commandment, that you love one another as I have loved you. Greater love has no man than this, that a man lay down his life for his friends. You are my friends if you do what I command you. No longer do I call you servants, for the servant does not know what his master is doing; but I have called you friends, for all that I have heard from my Father I have made known to you. You did not choose me, but I chose you and appointed you that you should go and bear fruit and that your fruit should abide; so that whatever you ask the Father in my name, he may give it to you. This I command you, to love one another." (15:12-17)

PAUL

First Letter to the Corinthians

Paul's work established the Christian church at Corinth; his letters helped it mold a concept of Christian life. In this passage he hymns the quality that must inspire such a life:

 f I speak in the tongues of men and of angels, but have not love, I am a noisy gong or a clanging cymbal. And if I have prophetic powers, and understand all mysteries ... and if I have all faith, so as to remove mountains, but have not love, I am nothing. If I give away all I have, and if I deliver my body to be burned, but have not love, I gain nothing. Love is patient and kind; love is not jealous or boastful; it is not arrogant or rude.... Love bears all things, believes all things, hopes all things, endures all things.

Love never ends; as for prophecy, it will pass away; as for tongues, they will cease; as for knowledge, it will pass away. For our knowledge is imperfect and our prophecy is imperfect; but when the perfect comes, the imperfect will pass away. When I was a child, I spoke like a child, I thought like a child, I reasoned like a child; when I became a man, I gave up childish ways. For now we see in a mirror dimly, but then face to face. Now I know in part; then I shall understand fully, even as I have been fully understood. So faith, hope, love abide, these three; but the greatest of these is love. (13:1-13)

THE LIVING WORD

The Two Cities

Greatest of Christian theologians, Augustine wrote The City of God *to refute pagans who blamed Christianity for Rome's fall. In it he sees the diversity of human cultures as essentially two opposed societies, sacred and profane:*

God, desiring not only that the human race might be able by their similarity of nature to associate with one another, but also that they might be bound together in harmony and peace by the ties of relationship, was pleased to derive all men from one individual, and created man with such a nature that the members of the race should not have died, had not the two first (of whom the one was created out of nothing, and the other out of him) merited this by their disobedience; for by them was so great a sin committed that by it human nature was altered for the worse, liable to sin and subject to death.... The deserved penalty of sin would have hurled all headlong even into the second death, of which there is no end, had not the undeserved grace of God saved some therefrom. And thus it has come to pass that though there are very many and great nations ... yet there are no more than two kinds of human society, which we may justly call two cities.... The one consists of those who wish to live after the flesh, the other of those who wish to live after the spirit.

Salvation by Faith

Martin Luther challenged Christendom with a concept radical for his time: Faith alone — not good works — makes man acceptable to God. In his 1520 treatise on Christian liberty, Luther hammered out his creed:

When you begin to believe, you learn at the same time that all that is in you is utterly guilty, sinful, and damnable, according to that saying, "All have sinned, and come short of the glory of God" (Romans 3:23).... When you have learned this, you will know that Christ is necessary for you, since he has suffered and risen again for you, that, believing on him, you might by this faith become another man, all your sins being remitted, and you being justified by the merits of another, namely Christ alone.

Since then this faith can reign only in the inward man... and since it alone justifies, it is evident that by no outward work or labor can the inward man be at all justified, made free, and saved; and that no works whatever have any relation to him.... Therefore the first care of every Christian ought to be to lay aside all reliance on works, and strengthen his faith alone... and by it grow in the knowledge, not of works, but of Christ Jesus.

Pacem in Terris

In his 1963 encyclical Pacem in Terris, *"Peace on Earth," Pope John XXIII laid down* *the rights and duties of nations, then pointed out the vital role of Christian love:*

Every believer in this world of ours must be a spark of light, a center of love, a vivifying leaven amidst his fellowmen: and he will be this all the more perfectly the more closely he lives in communion with God and in the intimacy of his own soul. In fact, there can be no peace between men unless there is peace within each one of them, unless, that is, each one builds up within himself the order wished by God.

God commands in the Koran—and Moslems obey, viewing their religion as a community that reaps positive value from a joyous response. These suras offer guidance on the essence of faith, God's oneness, the vitality of the Koran, the role of Mohammed and the prophets, and true piety:

raise belongs to God, the Lord of all Being, the All-merciful, the All-compassionate, the Master of the Day of Doom. Thee only we serve; to thee alone we pray for succor. Guide us in the straight path, the path of those whom Thou hast blessed, not of those against whom Thou art wrathful, nor of those who are astray. (Sura I)

... He is God, One, God, the Everlasting Refuge, who has not begotten, and has not been begotten, and equal to Him is not any one. (Sura CXII)

That is the Book, wherein is no doubt, a guidance to the godfearing who believe in the Unseen, and perform the prayer, and expend of that We have provided them; who believe in what has been sent down to thee [Mohammed] and what has been sent down before thee, and have faith in the Hereafter; those are upon guidance from their Lord, those are the ones who prosper. (Sura II, 1-4)

Say you: "We believe in God, and in that which has been sent down on us and sent down on Abraham, Ishmael, Isaac, and Jacob, and the Tribes, and that which was given to Moses and Jesus and the Prophets, of their Lord; we make no division between any of them, and to Him we surrender." (Sura II, 130)

It is not piety, that you turn your faces to the East and to the West. True piety is this: to believe in God, and the Last Day, the angels, the Book, and the Prophets; to give of one's substance, however cherished, to kinsmen, and orphans, the needy, the traveller, beggars and to ransom the slave; to perform the prayer; to pay the alms. And they who fulfil their covenant... and endure with fortitude misfortune, hardship, and peril, these are they who are true in their faith, these are the truly godfearing. (Sura II, 172, 173)

The Way of Righteousness

Mingling religion and ethical precept, Islam's holy writ makes moral conduct a service to God:

Surely this Koran guides to the way that is the straightest and gives good tidings to the believers who do deeds of righteousness.... Thy Lord has decreed you shall not serve any but Him, and to be good to parents.... And give the kinsman his right ... and never squander.... And keep not thy hand chained to thy neck, nor outspread it widespread altogether, or thou wilt sit reproached and denuded.... And approach not fornication; surely it is an indecency, and evil as a way. And slay not the soul God has forbidden.... And fill up the measure when you measure, and weigh with the straight balance.... And walk not in the earth exultantly; certainly thou wilt never tear the earth open, nor attain the mountains in height. (Sura XVII, 9, 23-37)

Judgment Day

Soaring passages tell of a day of doom and of fates governed by records in the books of life:

When the sun shall be darkened,
when the stars shall be thrown down,
when the mountains shall be set moving,
when the pregnant camels shall be
  neglected,
when the savage beasts shall be mustered,
when the seas shall be set boiling ...
when Hell shall be set blazing,
when Paradise shall be brought nigh,
then shall a soul know what it has
  produced. (Sura LXXXI, 1-14)

On that day you shall be exposed, not one
  secret of yours concealed.
Then as for him who is given his book in
  his right hand.... he shall be in a
  pleasing life in a lofty Garden, its
  clusters nigh to gather....
But as for him who is given his book in his
  left hand, he shall say "Would that I ...
  had not known my reckoning!" ...
Take him, and fetter him, and then roast
  him in Hell....
He never believed in God the All-mighty ...
  therefore he today has not here
  one loyal friend. (Sura LXIX, 18-37)

The Hadith

Incidents in Mohammed's life, tales of his likes and dislikes, his maxims — such is the fare of the Hadith (Story), the collection of traditions that augments the Koran in guiding Moslems:

aid the Messenger of God: "While a man was walking on the road, his thirst grew strong and he found a well and descended into it and drank and was leaving, when he saw a dog hanging out its tongue and licking the ground from thirst, and the man said, 'This dog's thirst is like the thirst I had,' and he went into the well again, filled his shoe with water ... and gave the dog to drink. And God approved of his act, and pardoned his sins." They said, "What, Messenger of God, shall we be rewarded for what we do for animals?" He replied, "Yes, there is a reward on every living creature."

A man's true wealth hereafter is the good he does in this world to his fellowmen. When he dies people will ask what property has he left behind him, but the angels who examine him ... will ask what good deeds hath thou sent before thee?

Work for this world as if you live in it forever; and work for the other world for you will die tomorrow.

280

CHRISTIANITY

"I AM THE RESURRECTION AND THE LIFE"

W. D. Davies

The world was bathed in gold, heaven and earth merging in the Galilean sunset that greeted my arrival at Safad, "a city that is set on an hill." Amid such luminosity how natural seemed the vision in the first chapter of the Gospel of John: "Hereafter ye shall see heaven open, and the angels of God ascending and descending upon the Son of man."

Is there a connection between geography and religious intensity in this small corner of our world; mere accident that Jesus appeared in luminous Galilee?

I often wondered about this as I came to know the radiant face of that land and gazed upon the Sea of Galilee—now a sheet of bright pewter, now a plate of blue china rimmed with gold. But I could not forget the dark side of the Galilee of 2,000 years ago—the misery and the violence, for the centuries-old conflict between Hellenism and Judaism was coming to a climax in blood.

The Hellenistic ideal stemmed from Alexander the Great's attempt to unite the diverse peoples of his empire. Embodied in the Roman Empire, it set aside ethnic and national distinctions in the interest of a common culture. In Palestine it collided with the Hebrew belief that the One God had chosen the Jews to make his revelation known to all mankind, and commanded them to live by his law uncontaminated by alien cultures. Having known the yoke of Assyria, Babylonia, Persia, Greece, and Rome, the Jews and their cherished land were harrowed to be the seedbed for deep things. Faithful to the God who had delivered them out of bondage in Egypt, the people yearned to be delivered again. Many centered their hopes on a future savior whom they called the Messiah.

285

"*And she brought forth her firstborn son, and wrapped him in swaddling clothes, and laid him in a manger; because there was no room for them in the inn. And there were . . . shepherds abiding in the field. . . . And, lo, the angel of the Lord . . . said unto them . . . I bring you good tidings of great joy. . . . For unto you is born this day . . . a Savior . . . Christ the Lord. . . . And they came with haste, and found Mary, and Joseph, and the babe lying in a manger*" (Luke 2:7-16).

This story of Jesus' birth in Bethlehem took form, perhaps in Corinth, around the year 80. Attributed to Luke, companion of Paul, it evangelized the Gentiles.

Matthew may have written his narrative about the same time, but for Jewish converts, stressing Jesus' descent from Abraham and David. Jesus, Greek for the Hebrew Joshua, means "Jehovah is salvation."

Like Luke, Matthew hailed Mary as a virgin and dated the Nativity in Herod's reign. This king of Judaea died in 4 B.C., bench mark for scholars, who place Jesus' birth between 8 and 4 B.C. and his crucifixion in the year 30 or 31.

Matthew and Luke drew from Mark, who may have heard Peter reminisce on Jesus and addressed his gospel to Christians in Nero's Rome.

John's gospel ("good news") looks beyond the facts of Jesus' life to their inner meaning: "For God so loved the world, that he gave his only begotten Son, that whosoever believeth in him should not perish, but have everlasting life" (3:16).

Jesus thus came to a land prepared for him, among a suffering, believing, hoping people who ascribed authority to a book, and who were challenged in their loyalty to their God and in their identity as a nation.

From the first, those who identified Jesus as the Christ, or Messiah, looked upon his life as the fulfillment of Jewish expectations revealed in their scriptures. Our earliest formulation of Christian belief comes from Paul, a Jew who persecuted the infant church, then became its greatest missionary following his conversion on the road to Damascus. Writing to a congregation at Corinth about A.D. 50—some 20 years after Jesus' crucifixion—Paul hammers home these central points: ". . . that Christ died for our sins according to the scriptures; And that he was buried, and that he rose again the third day according to the scriptures: And that he was seen of Cephas [Peter], then of the twelve" (I Corinthians 15:3-5).

Faith in the resurrected Christ would influence the course of Western civilization. Men would die for that faith, crusade for it, carry its message to the ends of

the earth. It would inspire cathedrals, sublime art, music—and the disharmony of theological controversy, religious war, and the proliferation of antagonistic sects. Today, across two millenniums, Christ's message shapes the ideals and societies of 950 million adherents of the world's largest faith.

Although millions upon millions have felt the impact of Jesus' personality and message, few facts about his life are known. Even the gospels of Matthew, Mark, Luke, and John were not primarily concerned with biographical detail. Writing in the *koinē*, the common Greek understood almost everywhere, the evangelists held up the example of Jesus' life to guide his followers as they spread out and established communities of believers in the Greco-Roman world.

Only Matthew and Luke narrate Jesus' birth in Bethlehem, and they say little about his growing to manhood in Nazareth; yet all four gospels yield much information indirectly. We can see the strong influence of the Galilean landscape on his thought when Jesus speaks of wheat and tares, laborers in the vineyard,

TED SPIEGEL, RAPHO GUILLUMETTE

"City of David" spread above terraced, sheep-nibbled slopes, Bethlehem made room for pilgrims soon after the birth of Jesus. Birthplace too of the oldest complete Bible extant, Bethlehem in the fourth century sheltered St. Jerome as he translated Hebrew texts for the Latin Vulgate in a monastery beside the Nativity grotto. Above it the church of the Nativity, oldest active church in Christendom, raises its squarish bell tower in center background.

289

Ancient land of the Jews, outpost of the Roman Empire — this was the Palestine Jesus of Nazareth knew. Dan to Beersheba, it spanned but 150 miles, a week's walk. Its hub, Jerusalem (beyond the Mount of Olives at right), spans the ages and three faiths.

TED SPIEGEL, RAPHO GUILLUMETTE

lilies of the field, and birds of the air. He likens God's word to seed sown on good ground, and asks whether men gather grapes from thorns or figs from thistles. He weaves parables — challenging lessons — around sowing and reaping, the felling of unfruitful trees, the finding of lost sheep. Our knowledge of the social and religious background also indicates other influences on him.

"Galilee of the Gentiles," as the scriptures called it, had a mixed population — "mongrel" in Jerusalem's scornful eyes. Jewish families had settled here during the heady patriotic Maccabean uprising against the Seleucids that preceded the Roman take-over in 63 B.C. They mingled with Syrian shepherds, Greek merchants, and Roman soldiers in cosmopolitan Tiberias and Capernaum. Even in humble Nazareth, Jesus may have played with Greek children, heard the Latin of the soldiers. He spoke Aramaic, the Semitic language common in Palestine.

Jesus grew up as the son of a carpenter among artisans and small farmers, who bore a double burden of Roman and Temple taxes. A member of a pious family, he doubtless was schooled in his people's age-long encounter with their God, the demands God placed upon them, the exhortations and consolations of the prophets God sent to them, the wisdom of their sages, the visions of their dreamers — all preserved in the Hebrew scriptures which Christians refer to as the Old Testament. How well he learned is attested by Luke's story that when Jesus was only 12 he astonished teachers in the Temple at Jerusalem with his questions and answers. Enshrined in those scriptures he would find expression of hopes particularly alive in Galilee, where nationalists fiercely opposed to foreign rule sought to raise the land in revolt.

N ow out of the wilderness a new voice sounded. Repent! Prepare the way of the Lord! In John the Baptist's cry the voice of prophecy, silent for centuries, sounded again. It struck deep into the troubled nation's consciousness: "And there went out unto him all the land of Judaea . . . and were all baptized of him in the river of Jordan" (Mark 1:5). Among the crowds was Jesus of Nazareth, probably in his early thirties.

Standing by the Jordan, I was overcome by how commonplace that river seemed — narrow, shallow, muddy. Only extraordinary events could have transformed such a scene and such a stream into symbols of such power in the life of men. As pilgrims bustled between Hijlah Ford and the Monastery of St. John the Baptist, I tried to imagine the press of the populace, the commanding figure of John clad in camel's hair, the electric moment when he recognized Jesus' uniqueness. In the rumble of trucks on the Israeli frontier I heard echoes of Joshua leading the Israelites against the Canaanites to claim the Promised Land. Men of Jesus' day yearned for a new Joshua to lead the people out of the wilderness of their suffering into the promised kingdom of God.

Jesus' baptism marked a turning point in his life — and in history. There in the waters of the Jordan, Jesus underwent an experience of singular intensity that confirmed he was now set apart in a special way for the service of God. But how should he fulfill his new vocation? In the story of the temptations, the gospels symbolically give us a glimpse of the dilemmas with which Jesus wrestled as he

0   20
STATUTE MILES

MAP BY NANCY SCHWEICKART
GEOGRAPHIC ART DIVISION

• *Sidon*

And Jesus went out, and his
disciples, into the towns of
Caesarea Philippi.... And Peter
saith unto him, Thou art
the Christ. (Mark 8:27, 29)

*Then Jesus went thence, and
departed into the coasts of
Tyre and Sidon. (Matthew 15:21)*

• *Tyre*

Caesarea Philippi •
Dan •

*Then he arose, and rebuked
the winds and the sea;
and there was a great calm.
(Matthew 8:26)*

MEDITERRANEAN

SEA

*So Jesus came again
into Cana of Galilee,
where he made the
water wine. (John 4:46)*

Chorazin •
Capernaum
Tabgha •   *Bethsaida* •
GALILEE   *Magdala* •
Cana •   *Tiberias* •

SEA OF
GALILEE

*...they returned into Galilee,
to their own city Nazareth.
And the child grew, and waxed
strong in spirit, filled with
wisdom: and the grace of God
was upon him. (Luke 2:39-40)*

Nazareth •   MOUNT
+ TABOR

• *Nain*

• *Megiddo*

• *Caesarea*

*...Jesus taketh with him Peter,
and James, and John, and leadeth
them up into an high mountain
...and he was transfigured
before them. (Mark 9:2)*

JORDAN
RIVER

*There cometh a woman of Samaria
to draw water.... The woman saith
unto him, I know that Messias cometh,
which is called Christ.... Jesus saith
unto her, I that speak unto thee am he.
(John 4:7, 25-26)*

SAMARIA

• *Jaffa*
• *Arimathaea*

*Then was Jesus led up of the
Spirit into the wilderness to be
tempted of the devil. (Matthew 4:1)*

*Then cometh Jesus
from Galilee to
Jordan unto John,
to be baptized of him.
(Matthew 3:13)*

•
avneh

*Behold, we go up to Jerusalem;
and the Son of man shall be betrayed
...and they shall condemn him
to death. (Matthew 20:18)*

Jericho •

*Hijlah
Ford*

Bethany
Jerusalem • •
JUDAEA

Qumran •

MOUNT
NEBO +

• *Bethlehem*

*For unto you is born this day in
the city of David a Saviour, which
is Christ the Lord. (Luke 2:11)*

DEAD
SEA

MOAB

Masada •

• *Beersheba*

*Coming up out of the water, he saw the heavens opened, and the Spirit like a dove
descending upon him" (Mark 1:10). Baptized by John in the Jordan, Jesus fasted "forty days"
in the wilderness, then began the brief ministry that would change the world.*

accepted and persisted in that service. The Devil posed dazzling alternatives: command the stones to become bread; cast yourself down from the pinnacle of the Temple, to be saved at the last moment by angels; seize "all the kingdoms of this world, and the glory of them" (Matthew 4:8). We might think of these as offering salvation through economic well-being, using supernatural powers for vainglorious exhibitionism, or seizing political power. These temptations Jesus rejected, whether in the Judaean wilderness or in the fastness of his mind. He returned to Galilee a servant of God and man.

Soon after the start of his public ministry, Jesus went into the synagogue at Capernaum to teach. Challenged by a man with "an unclean spirit," he cast out the spirit. In performing this exorcism Jesus revealed that he was more than a follower of the Baptist. John placed less emphasis on the good that the kingdom of God might bring than on the wrath and the winnowing that would accompany it. Jesus stressed forgiveness and compassion. The troubled mind, the twisted limb should be ministered to now. Thus the great healer introduced a startlingly new variation on an ancient theme: "If I cast out devils by the Spirit of God, then the kingdom of God is come unto you" (Matthew 12:28).

The kingdom of God has already begun to manifest itself, here and now, in the midst of men, Jesus teaches, though the older order has not completely passed away. A time of decision is at hand, and men must face its challenges.

Around him Jesus drew disciples who "forsook all, and followed him." Their number symbolizes the twelve tribes of Israel; their vocations reflect the everyday life of Galilee's bustling towns. Matthew was called from the customhouse at Capernaum, astride the caravan route from Damascus to Egypt. The two pairs of brothers—"Simon called Peter" and Andrew, James and John—made their living by fishing in the lake known as the Sea of Galilee.

Watching a fisherman tend a double-ended skiff near Capernaum where warm springs still draw fish toward the shore, I recalled Simon Peter's skepticism when Jesus said, "Simon, launch out into the deep and let down your nets."

Simon replied, "Master, we have toiled all the night, and have taken nothing." Then under Jesus' gaze: "Nevertheless at thy word I will let down the net."

Luke goes on to relate that Simon Peter had to call his partners to come and help, so great was the catch. Astonished, he fell down at Jesus' knees, saying, "Depart from me; for I am a sinful man, O Lord."

Simon Peter became the leader of the disciples, chosen to help Jesus spread the gospel that God's kingdom is present and at work. On them Jesus placed demands of comprehension and obedience that were to test them to the uttermost. In the end they would prove all too human.

Significantly, it was to those on the edges of society that Jesus reached out. To the "lost sheep of the house of Israel" he brought the good news of God's mercy. He ate with "publicans and sinners," did not condemn a woman taken in adultery, nor spurn Zacchaeus, a Jewish collaborator who gathered taxes for the hated Romans. To sufferers of ailments which society might view as the result of sin, Jesus brought healing and redemption. Comforting the afflicted and bringing the

293

strayed back into the fold were both manifestations of the grace which emanated from Jesus like the father's love for the returned prodigal son.

John the Baptist, imprisoned by Herod Antipas, tetrarch of Galilee, sent followers to appraise the new prophet. They asked Jesus, "Art thou he that should come, or do we look for another?" Jesus told them to tell John what they saw and heard: "The blind receive their sight, and the lame walk, the lepers are cleansed, and . . . the dead are raised up. . . . And blessed is he, whosoever shall not be offended in me" (Matthew 11:3-6).

But some were offended. Pharisees coming from Jerusalem to check on Jesus' "signs and wonders" were outraged. By what authority did this Nazarene upstart act? His claim to be able to forgive sin usurped the prerogative of the divinely ordained sacrificial system and priesthood. He must be possessed by Beelzebub, the scribes agreed, "and by the prince of devils casteth he out devils" (Mark 3:22). Furthermore, he violated sacred law when he ate with the "unclean," and his disciples picked grain on a holy day. Jesus' reply was sacrilege to their ears: "The

Dawn discovers men of Galilee tending nets as their forebears did. To such men Jesus turned, bidding Simon (called Peter) and Andrew, his brother, follow him and become "fishers of men." Symbol of Christ, fish in Greek (ichthys) forms an acronym for "Jesus Christ Son of God Savior." Christ means Messiah in Greek.

ANGELS DRAWING NETS GATHER SOULS TO SALVATION IN A FOURTH-CENTURY ROMAN
MOSAIC IN THE BASILICA OF AQUILEIA, ITALY. RIGHT: TED SPIEGEL, RAPHO GUILLUMETTE

sabbath was made for man, and not man for the sabbath: Therefore the Son of man is Lord also of the sabbath" (Mark 2:27-28).

Equally startling was the moral teaching of Jesus, presented in large part in the Sermon on the Mount, which tradition places near Tabgha overlooking the lake. With the gentle beatitudes presented in the fifth chapter of Matthew ("Blessed are the meek: for they shall inherit the earth") stand these stern injunctions:

"Ye have heard that it was said . . . Thou shalt not kill. . . . But I say unto you, That whosoever is angry with his brother . . . shall be in danger of the judgment . . . whosoever shall say, Thou fool, shall be in danger of hell fire."

"Ye have heard that it was said . . . Thou shalt not commit adultery: But I say unto you, That whosoever looketh on a woman to lust after her hath committed adultery with her already in his heart."

"Ye have heard that it hath been said, An eye for an eye, and a tooth for a tooth: But I say unto you, That . . . whosoever shall smite thee on thy right cheek, turn to him the other also."

"And Jesus went about all Galilee, teaching . . . and healing all manner of sickness" (Matthew 4:23). But the ministry was only prelude. Scandalized by his teachings, Pharisees watched with concern as Jesus set out on his fateful journey to Jerusalem.

"CHRIST HEALING THE SICK," ETCHING BY REMBRANDT VAN RIJN, C. 1645; RIJKSMUSEUM, AMSTERDAM

Jesus asked obedience to a new law of love: Those who receive grace should show grace. So demanding a doctrine inevitably came into conflict with the world of men. Though his following increased, he grew aware that much of this popularity rested on a false understanding of his intention.

I pushed my car into low gear as I climbed into the hills at the northern end of the Sea of Galilee. Israeli Army jeeps ground up the grades with me. Not long ago, these highlands were under bombardment from Syrians across the Jordan Valley. My eyes scanned the rises and gullies where, in an earlier day of war fever, Jesus may have walked on his way to a fateful rendezvous.

All four gospels refer to a vast crowd of about five thousand following Jesus to a solitary place. He had sought refuge to rest, but took compassion on them, feeding them, we are told, through a miraculous multiplication of loaves and fishes. In solidarity with his followers he anticipated—by the breaking and blessing of bread—his relation to them as the giver of life.

But they did not comprehend. They hungered not so much for spiritual sustenance as for political freedom. An army without a general, they sought to push Jesus into the role of their champion. This miracle worker would deliver them from grinding burdens of taxation and the tyranny of foreign rule.

John relates that Jesus, perceiving "that they would come and take him by force, to make him a king" (6:15), withdrew into the hills alone. Their hopes dashed, many of his followers "went back, and walked no more with him."

Jesus must have sensed that his Galilean ministry was over. Even Nazareth had rejected him, evoking his comment, "A prophet is not without honor, save in his own country, and in his own house" (Matthew 13:57). He felt it imperative to re-examine his mission and deepen the understanding of the few who remained.

"For which of you, intending to build a tower, sitteth not down first, and counteth the cost, whether he have sufficient to finish it?" (Luke 14:28). The carpenter's son doubtless had long pondered the cost of his commitment. Now, withdrawing northward with his disciples to Caesarea Philippi, Jesus proceeded to teach them that "the Son of man must suffer many things, and be rejected of the elders, and of the chief priests, and scribes, and be killed, and after three days rise again" (Mark 8:31). Peter objected: The Messiah could not possibly suffer. But Jesus rebuked him and concentrated henceforth on preparing himself and them for their confrontation with Jerusalem, and for derision, defeat, and death.

Word had come that Herod Antipas sought Jesus to kill him. But Jesus determined to take his message to the center of the nation's religious life—to a city that had rejected Jeremiah, Ezekiel, and Micah—because "it is unthinkable for a prophet to meet his death anywhere but in Jerusalem" (Luke 13:33).

Jesus entered Jerusalem at the festival of Passover when pilgrims streamed into the city to commemorate Israel's deliverance from Egypt. Mark tells us that when Jesus approached by way of Jericho, a beggar hailed him as Son of David. His procession became a multitude, crying "Hosanna; Blessed is he that cometh in the name of the Lord: Blessed be the kingdom of our father David, that cometh . . . Hosanna in the highest" (11:9-10).

*G*o ye into the city, and there shall meet you a man bearing a pitcher of water:
follow him" (Mark 14:13). Thus in Jerusalem (opposite) did the disciples find their way
to a "large upper room" set for the Passover meal. Breaking bread with them for the
last time, Jesus said he would be betrayed by one who "dippeth with me in the dish."

EARLY 13TH-CENTURY FRESCO OF THE LAST SUPPER; STUDENICA MONASTERY, YUGOSLAVIA. OPPOSITE: TIBOR HIRSCH, PHOTO RESEARCHERS

Those cries must have ignited nationalist fervor in the teeming city. If the Son of David was on the way, deliverance was at hand. But Jesus responded with two symbolic acts. He rode in, not on a spirited charger as the warrior son of David, but on a donkey as the king of gentleness prophesied by Zechariah: ". . . behold, thy King cometh unto thee: he is just, and having salvation; lowly, and riding upon an ass . . . and he shall speak peace . . . and his dominion shall be . . . even to the ends of the earth" (9:9-10). And Jesus cleansed the Temple, confirming that his challenge was religious, not political.

Mark makes it clear that the cleansing was calculated—not a sudden burst of indignation. On entering the city, Jesus went in and looked around the Temple, as a general surveys a field of coming battle. Next day he returned to drive out traders and money changers who clogged the great outer Court of the Gentiles. Here pilgrims bought sacrificial sheep and birds, and changed their money into acceptable currency to pay the half-shekel Temple tax. In restoring the Temple's area for Gentiles, Jesus evoked Isaiah 56:7: ". . . mine house shall be called an house of prayer for all people." He had prophesied that "many shall come from the east and west, and shall sit down with Abraham, and Isaac, and Jacob, in the kingdom of heaven" (Matthew 8:11), heralding the day when Jew and Gentile would worship the One God.

In the Temple he healed the blind and lame, and taught the multitude. According to Matthew 23:24, he castigated scribes and Pharisees who "strain at a gnat, and swallow a camel," who cloaked iniquity under a show of righteousness. They tried to trick him into a seditious statement by asking if it was lawful to give tribute to the emperor, but he replied: "Render to Caesar the things that are Caesar's, and to God the things that are God's" (Mark 12:17). He praised

"Father, forgive them; for they know not what they do." The cry of compassion from the cross in Luke 23:34 resounds through the ages.

Seized in the Garden of Gethsemane after Judas' betrayal, charged with blasphemy by the chief priests, Jesus was condemned to death by Pontius Pilate, Rome's procurator in Judaea. Roman soldiers scourged him, mocked him, took him to Golgotha, *"place of the skull."* There, between two criminals, they crucified him.

The Latin initials INRI signal the charge of sedition: Iesus Nazarenus Rex Iudaeorum, *"Jesus of Nazareth, King of the Jews."* Soldiers cast lots for his clothing while three Marys—Jesus' mother, her sister Mary, and Mary Magdalene— and the apostle John mourn at left.

"Now in the place where he was crucified there was . . . a new sepulchre, wherein was never man yet laid" (John 19:41).

Constantine, Rome's first Christian emperor, in 335 raised a shrine which Crusaders magnified into the church of the Holy Sepulcher. In it pilgrims caress the Stone of Unction, comforted in their belief that women going to Jesus' tomb at first light after the Sabbath found it empty: Christ is risen!

CHARLES HARBUTT, MAGNUM. OVERLEAF: "THE CRUCIFIXION" BY ANDREA MANTEGNA, 1459; THE LOUVRE, P

the poor widow's offering of two mites above the abundant gifts of rich men. Indeed, he had said "it is easier for a camel to go through the eye of a needle, than for a rich man to enter into the kingdom of God" (Matthew 19:24). Now he shocked his hearers by predicting the Temple's destruction: "There shall not be left one stone upon another, that shall not be thrown down" (Mark 13:2).

The "establishment" in Judaism clearly saw that Jesus had laid an axe to the root of their tree. He threatened their law, their way of life, the very existence of their nation. His revolutionary activities could well bring down the wrath of Rome upon the Jews. According to John, Caiaphas the high priest had counseled that it was expedient that one man should die rather than the Jewish people. The priests in council moved to arrest Jesus.

Aware of their intent, Jesus held a last supper in Jerusalem with his disciples. Later those who shared in it came to think of it as a new Passover in which Jesus bound them to himself as a community of a new Exodus. For "Jesus took bread, and blessed, and brake it, and gave to them, and said, Take, eat: this is my body.

And he took the cup, and . . . said unto them, This is my blood" (Mark 14:22-24).

Betrayed by one who had shared that sacramental meal, Jesus faced the ultimate test of obedience in a garden at the foot of the Mount of Olives. In his
agony he prayed: "Abba, Father, all things are possible unto thee; take away this
cup from me: nevertheless not what I will, but what thou wilt" (Mark 14:36).
A company of armed men arrived with the traitor Judas, and at his signal, a kiss,
took Jesus into custody. All the disciples ignominiously fled.

Recently I entered that Garden of Gethsemane, a haven of peace apart from
the tensions of Jerusalem. The gnarled olive trees appeared twisted with bitter
memories; the cock's second crow—by which time Peter had thrice denied Jesus
—seemed still to hang in the air. I pondered Jesus' noncommittal reply to Pilate's
query, "Art thou the King of the Jews?" A political question implying an attempt
to overthrow the government. And the ultimate question from the high priest,
"Art thou the Christ, the Son of the Blessed?"

According to Mark, Jesus answered, "I am." The other gospels are less explicit.   303

Yet I had only to recall Jesus' prayer in this very garden: "Abba, Father. . . ." In all Jewish literature nothing parallels this use of *Abba,* without a suffix, as an address to God. The equivalent in human endearment to "Dad," it indicates the intimacy the evangelists perceived between Jesus and God, son and father. Clearly, Jesus shunned the title of Messiah in his ministry because to affirm it would have been to court misunderstanding. Many would have foisted on him their concept of a Messianic warrior come "to slay their foes and lift them high." Of that Messiah Jesus wanted no part, so he had to avoid their term. He was to be a suffering Messiah, a compassionate Christ who would "give his life as ransom for many." He might have used to his contemporaries the words of William Blake: "The Vision of Christ that thou dost see, Is my vision's greatest enemy. . . ."

Condemned for blasphemy by his priestly opponents, Jesus was taken before Pontius Pilate; the Roman governor had to review any case involving the death penalty. He found Jesus guiltless. But the mob cried, "Crucify him!" When Pilate offered to release Jesus under the traditional Passover amnesty, the mob instead demanded Barabbas, one of three insurrectionists awaiting execution. Faced by tumult, Pilate freed Barabbas. He "washed his hands" of Jesus' blood and "delivered him to be crucified" (Matthew 27:24, 26). To be nailed to the cross—a slow, agonizing death reserved for slaves and non-Roman criminals.

In the gospels Jesus goes to the cross sinless, solitary, sovereign. They report "darkness over all the land" at the hour of his death—a symbol of God's judgment on a sinful world that had rejected his son. And they assert that the veil before the Temple's holy of holies was "rent in twain from the top to the bottom." This suggests that through the death of Jesus the veil separating man from God has been sundered. His body, as Jewish law required, was removed before the Sabbath began at sunset. He was buried hastily but decently through the good offices of a sympathizer, whose name is given as Joseph of Arimathaea.

As I left the garden and walked back toward the walled city, I reflected on the fact that the story might have ended there, had Jesus "merely" died on the cross. Anatole France's portrayal of an aging Pontius Pilate, the governor, failing to recall anyone by the name of Jesus of Nazareth is plausible.

But death did not vanquish him. The gospels assert that on the Sunday morning after the Friday of the Crucifixion the tomb was found empty and that Jesus "rose again from the dead." He appeared to Peter, to James, to all the apostles (including Thomas who at first doubted), and then to more than "five hundred brethren." The impact of their encounters with Jesus after his death drew his scattered, disillusioned, discredited followers together to launch a community into the world—an enduring community of the forgiven, sustained by his living, dynamic presence. It was the conviction that Jesus had returned to renew his fellowship with those who had failed him that created the Christian church.

Easter had followed the Crucifixion and turned Black Friday into Good Friday because Jesus had risen. "I am the resurrection, and the life: he that believeth in me, though he were dead, yet shall he live; And whosoever liveth and believeth in me shall never die" (John 11:25, 26).

David F. Robinson

Where the Fathers Preached and Martyrs Bled

"*O* Son of God, who didst rise from the dead; save us who sing unto thee: Alleluia."

Black-robed choristers chant in Greek a liturgy 15 centuries old. In splendid crown and vestments the archbishop of Crete murmurs a prayer. A jingling censer weaves a garland of incense. Under a soaring dome stand the folk of Heraklion, hands arcing in the sign of the cross of Christ.

"*Kyrie eleison,*" sing the choristers ranged on both sides of the altar. "Lord, have mercy."

To my Western ear their Greek scale and quavering quarter tones sound minor, mournful. Yet the divine liturgy unfolding here in the cathedral of St. Minas is a joyous drama, a celebration of Jesus' covenant with his church, expressed in the bread and wine of the Eucharist.

His Eminence holds high the Precious Gifts. The words he speaks are the words of Jesus, repeated by the faithful since the dawntime of Christianity: "This is my body.... This is my blood."

In this shrine of the Eastern Orthodox church— popularly, the Greek Orthodox—I begin a trek that will take me through Greece and Asia Minor, listening for echoes from distant days when apostles scattered the gospel afar. Days when Rome and paganism all but drowned the infant faith, when its fathers shaped it and martyrs died for it, when heretics splintered it and councils tried to bind the wounds, when its patriarchs stood at last with emperors to rule the church-state called the Byzantine Empire.

LIPS PURSED *in adoration bless a holy relic, an age-old gesture of faith. Cradled in silver, decked with blooms, a bit of bone draws Greek Orthodox Christians of Crete to the cathedral at Heraklion in homage to St. Minas, protector of the city.*

Christians have venerated relics since the first century; in the fourth the practice boomed when Emperor Constantine's mother dug from Jerusalem bits of wood said to be Jesus' cross.

THOMAS NEBBIA

POMP AND PIETY *mingle in the Feast of St. Minas in Heraklion. White-robed Archbishop Eugenios of Crete leads his bishops in divine liturgy, then marches with canopied reliquary and garlanded icon. Loaves baked with the saint's image (bottom, foreground) will gladden tables of the devout.*

Those days seem as yesterday in the timelessness of Orthodoxy. Its basic theology has not changed since the eighth century. Its worshipers have intoned the Nicene Creed since the fourth. The "Alleluia" that fills its domed cathedrals comes straight from pre-Christian Hebrew, an untranslated cry of joy.

Close to noon the service ends. Anyone can join the procession that follows on this feast day of St. Minas, a fourth-century martyr. So I link arms with a leathery farmer and parade the crowded streets of Heraklion.

In the tiny old church of St. Minas at the cathedral's elbow I catch my breath, rest my feet, and feed my soul on icons. Candleglow gilds the silver halos on saints' portraits dark with age. From the frames hang little metal tags embossed with an arm, a stomach, a car, a baby, a crutch. Each tag bears a prayer; in ancient belief a bit of a saint's power to heal or intercede with God lives in his icons and relics. With a wet smack a tot on tiptoe kisses each icon she can reach; the old belief will endure at least another generation.

That afternoon Archbishop Eugenios and his priests tell me of their saint. They speak of the Easter of 1826 when he was seen spurring his white horse around the church of St. Minas to save worshipers inside by turning away Turkish soldiers bent on massacre. "Even now he waits close by," a layman assures me; "my grandmother has heard the horse's hoofbeats by night."

Of the historical Minas, the archbishop can tell me little. For Minas left no writings, wrought no miracles in a life snuffed out by a Roman executioner. As we speak I begin to see Minas at a watershed. Behind him marched the grim age of martyrs; ahead loomed the formative age of the great church fathers, when sages freed from persecution would wrestle instead with dissent.

And now I must meet these martyrs, these fathers. With a whiskery kiss on each of my cheeks His Eminence bids me go with God.

*B*y plane, boat, donkey cart, and *dolmuş*—a kind of Turkish group taxi—I take up my quest. Ghosts aplenty wait to greet me: philosophers of Athens lending a tolerant ear to Paul's new religion . . . the idolmakers of Ephesus shouting him down lest he preach them out of business . . . an exile named John, in a cave on the isle of Patmos, writing to persecuted brethren a message of hope that Christians still revere as the Book of Revelation . . . Emperor Constantine striding into Nicaea to meet with church leaders in the first of the great churchwide councils. Everywhere the old sites evoke them. But how ironic that so little remains of the city where fathers and martyrs forged so much of the church's early history: "Antioch the Golden," third greatest city of the Roman Empire.

I pull myself from an overcrowded dolmuş and look about at pleasant little Antakya in southern Turkey. She hides her past well; who would guess that on her manicured fields sat booming Antioch in the heyday of the Roman world? From Antioch caravan routes linked Palestine and Asia Minor, Mesopotamia and the Mediterranean. Goods from Persia, India, even China thudded onto stone wharves to be barged down the Orontes to the sea. By Jesus' time, East and West had mingled here for three centuries. Down colonnaded boulevards swaggered Roman soldiers loyal to the Persian god Mithras. Greeks revering

the gods of Olympus jostled Jews who worshiped the God of Abraham. Tolerant Romans who made Antioch the capital of Syria in 64 B.C. asked of other religions only that they make room for Rome's.

In Antioch the apostle Paul—who as Saul the Pharisee had fought the new belief—began his epic trek to sainthood. But here the great sower of churches found one already thriving, perhaps less than a decade after the Crucifixion. Missionaries from Palestine had arrived before him in the Jewish quarter with a wondrous story: The Son of God had lived, died, and risen in glory!

On a hillside above Antioch I blink in the dim light of a shallow cave long revered as the "Grotto of St. Peter." At the ancient spring in a corner I can sense the big fisherman beside me, preaching that "baptism doth also now save us. . . ." After study and fasting, his converts would gather at the Orontes for the triple immersion that washed away old sins and bound them to the new faith. Now they could join in the *agape*, or lovefeast, and witness the Eucharist that climaxed the ritual meal.

Some, reared in paganism's lusty rites, may have overdone the kiss of peace or the dinner wine, for soon bishops would separate feast from Eucharist

ITALY
† Rome
† Puteoli

BLACK SEA

Constantinople
† Philippi
Thessalonica † † Apollonia   • Nicaea
MT. ATHOS † Troas †   ASIA MINOR   CAPPADOCIA
GREECE   Pergamum † Thyatira †   • Caesarea
Nicopolis †   † Sardis   † Pisidian Antioch   Edessa †
          Smyrna † † Philadelphia
          † Hierapolis   † Iconium
Patras †   Ephesus † † † † Colossae
          Miletus † Laodicea † † Derbe † Tarsus
Corinth   Athens †   Tralles Perga Lystra   † Antioch
          PATMOS †   Magnesia   SYRIA

                    † Salamis
          CRETE   Heraklion •   Paphos † CYPRUS
                              Sidon † † Damascus
MEDITERRANEAN SEA   † Tyre
                    Ptolemais (Acre) †
                    Caesarea † † Pella
                    Joppa † † Samaria
                    Lydda † † Jerusalem •
          • Cyrene

                    Alexandria †

AFRICA   EGYPT

† Christian Churches by A.D. 100

SUN GREETS SEAMEN *in
Alexandria, second city of the
Roman world at Christianity's
dawn. Their forebears rendered
unto Caesars Egyptian grain to
dole to Roman mobs—and sowed
seeds of change when ships bore
Paul, tentmaker and apostle,
down sea-lanes of destiny.
Like Paul, some missionaries
worked a trade part time; others
drew pay from home churches
as they spread their news from
city to city along trade routes,
dotting their world with the cross
as the first century unfolded.*

*No one knows who bore the
faith to many sites—Tyre, Sidon,
even Rome whose church, wrote
Paul a scant three decades after
the Passion, "is spoken of
throughout the whole world."*

to keep the latter holy. Perhaps after one such feast
an Antiochene coined in scorn a name the faithful
would wear in pride: "Oh, those Christians!"

In the synagogue of Antioch the early missionaries
had found eager listeners—Jews yearning for a
Messiah, Gentiles weary of earthy pagan gods. Fertile ground, but they would have to till carefully,
for the cries of Stephen still rang in their ears. To
Jews of Jerusalem Stephen had preached the fall
of the Temple, the changing of the Law, the second
coming of the carpenter they had sent to the cross
a few years before. Enraged by such blasphemy, a
mob dragged Stephen to the city wall and opened
the age of martyrs in a shower of stones. Persecution
followed, and many of the faithful fled.

The event changed history. What had been a
small local sect scattered from Jerusalem to seed the
Roman world with churches of the Jewish Christ.
Swelled by Gentile converts, Antioch's church soon

GEORG GERSTER

FOR ONLY MINUTES *a day, the sun at its zenith lights the scriptures for priests beneath a ceiling hole in the underground chapel of Dabra Abuna Aaron in Ethiopia (opposite). To these highlands in the fourth century came Frumentius, a Syrian from Tyre, to root a church that lives today amid neighbors long won to Islam. It owns a third of Ethiopia's land; one man in six serves as deacon, monk, or priest.*

A deacon (above) cradles a Christ of wood. His church, like Egypt's Coptic, clings to a monophysite, or "single nature," creed that denies Christ's humanity and calls him totally divine.

outshone Jerusalem's. It was Antioch that sent Paul on his great missionary journeys.

Yet did these converts become Jews? They cherished the Jewish scriptures but added writings of their own: Paul's epistles to his churches, the letters of other apostles, the emerging gospels. Worship focused not on the Jewish Sabbath but on Sunday, the day of the Resurrection. Paul persuaded Peter, the new faith's leader, to drop circumcision and food taboos of the Jews. Christianity's locus shifted from Jerusalem as Peter's mantle fell to Linus of Rome about A.D. 67; a few years later the emperor Titus razed Jerusalem. The infant church veered from its mother's side — and collided with Imperial Rome.

Since the time of Augustus, emperor worship had helped hold the motley Roman realm together. But when Domitian donned the purple in A.D. 81 he inherited an empire dotted with churches that obeyed him as ruler but rejected him as god. Indeed, they scorned *all* the old gods. For this Christians were called atheists, and haters of mankind as well, since they angered gods of grain and wine, love and war, birth, death, and all between.

Nero had already found it convenient to blame the burning of Rome in A.D. 64 on such misanthropes, to light a garden party with burning Christians, perhaps to put Paul to the sword and Peter on a cross, head down. Under Domitian the first systematic persecution began, and John on Patmos wrote of his searing vision of Rome, the harlot "drunken . . . with the blood of the martyrs."

No one knows how many thousands died by cross, sword, pyre, lion, and a grisly array of refinements. Others survived torture, afterwards glorying in the empty eye socket, the missing tongue, the limp that earned them honor as "confessors" of their faith. Some fled to live as hermits. Others paid bribes or token homage and went free.

But St. Ignatius, bishop of Antioch as Christianity's first century ended, fairly begged for martyrdom. "Do nothing to stop me," he asked all the churches as soldiers took him off to Rome to die in the arena. "God's wheat am I and I shall be ground by the teeth of the beasts, that I may become

the pure bread of Christ." If the beasts were not hungry, he vowed, he would "coax them to consume me." For his writings on the role of bishops and the continuity of the Old Testament and new scriptures, Ignatius lives as a father of the church.

"In all things am I an offering for you, I and my chains," wrote Ignatius to his friend Polycarp, bishop of Smyrna. Some 50 years later old Polycarp joined him in martyrdom and sainthood.

"Say 'Away with the atheists,'" ordered a Roman official as Polycarp stood in Smyrna's arena. Polycarp obeyed with a sweep of his hand—not at his fellow Christians but at his pagan tormentors.

"I have beasts," warned the proconsul.

"Bring them in," Polycarp retorted. "Why delay?"

To pagans howling for blood, such readiness to lose it seemed madness. Not to Christians. Martyrdom was better than baptism, for it washed away sin

MOUNTAIN MIST *masks Antakya (left) as time hides its ancestor, "Antioch the Golden." Clearer air unveils the Turkish town (above), golden in sunset, beneath heights where sumptuous villas once housed pleasuring plutocrats. Street lights held back night for half a million citizens whose fountains, temples, arenas, and homes packed the vale of the Orontes to its ridges.*

To this city—third greatest in Rome's world and hub of trade routes—came Paul to preach. Here East and West had mingled for three centuries; three more and a citizen could still dub Greek-speaking, Greek-founded Antioch "fair crown of the Orient." Scoffing Antiochenes were first to call Paul's converts "Christians."

314

at the moment when a man could sin no more. Steeled by the prospect of instant sainthood, the martyrs endured their agonies, often with a bravery that moved jaded pagans to embrace such a compelling faith.

The account of Polycarp's death, written by an aide, is our oldest eyewitness report of a martyrdom; but the idea of feast days and veneration of relics had already begun. From Polycarp's funeral pyre followers snatched "his bones, being of more value than precious stones." Each year they hailed "with great gladness and joy the birthday of his martyrdom," perhaps celebrating the Eucharist over his tomb, as was the custom with later martyrs. Thus our altars look like tombs; some churches seal martyrs' relics into them. Into altar cloths Orthodox churches sew a chip of bone, a wisp of hair, some tangible link to a martyr.

Persecution rose to a crescendo under Diocletian at the end of the third century. Torturers labored to break a Christian's faith, slaying him if they failed; to his accuser often went the dead man's property. Priceless Christian writings went up in flames as Diocletian's edicts emptied church libraries. Daring bishops hid their scriptures and damned those who let the soldiers rampage.

Among the spectators of the bloodshed stood young Constantine, soon to rule the Western provinces and war his way to the throne. As he braced for battle with

his last rival in 312, Constantine the pagan saw a cross of light in the sun. Stirred by the vision, he emblazoned his troops with a symbol of Christ, the intertwined Greek letters *chi* and *rho* (✻), and led them to victory. Incredibly, the empire that had hounded Christians for three centuries found a Christian sympathizer on the throne. The faithful numbered perhaps one in ten; in the next 50 years the church so prospered that not even pagan emperor Julian could shake it.

Dubbing himself "God's man," Constantine raised Christian churches, freed clergy from civic duties, made Sunday a holiday, put the chi-rho in standards of the empire. Byzantium blossomed as Constantinople, his new capital; soon its bishops ranked with patriarchs of Rome, Alexandria, Antioch, and Jerusalem. But if Constantine expected the church to cement the empire, he was disappointed. As no other major faith, Christianity had been splintered by dissent since its birth. Paul chided preachers of "another gospel" as he taught of the Son of God. And was Jesus fully divine, fully human, both — or neither?

Second-century Docetists called him divine, his body and agony only illusion. To third-century Adoptionists he was man; God had "adopted" him at baptism. Fifth-century Nestorians echoed that belief and railed at the cult of Mary as *Theotokos*, bearer of God; visions of God in diapers appalled them. Christianity honors among its fathers the great theologians who wrestled with the welter of beliefs, for in attacking what the faith was not, they helped define what it was.

*E*arly in the fourth century the Alexandrian priest Arius launched a doctrine that would sunder the church. God's son cannot be God, he reasoned, but only a sublime creation. From the same city rose Athanasius in reply: Christ had two natures, one human and one divine, else how could he intercede between eternal God and temporal man?

Bishop Gregory of Nazianzus joined the fray; his preachings against the Arians won him the title "the Theologian." From Antioch rang the eloquence of John Chrysostom, the "Golden-mouthed"; applause punctuated his anti-Arian sermons. As the great fathers defined the Son of God they laid firm footings for the coming definition of the third in the Trinity, the Holy Spirit.

"O . . . what a wound did my ears receive," sighed Constantine over the Arian "squabbles." Calling the heresy "unworthy of men of sense," he ordered bishops to Nicaea in 325; when they damned Arianism, he put teeth in the verdict by exiling its leaders. But his successor recalled them and banished their foes. As the battle seesawed, Athanasius trudged into five exiles totaling nearly 20 years. Though Arianism had died in the East by the end of the fourth century, it lingered into the seventh among Germanic tribes as the faith spread westward.

Thus exiling replaced mere shunning of heretics. Then in 386 the Spanish heretic Priscillian was executed; this ominous precedent would echo in horrors

DROPLET OF CHRISTIANITY *in a sea of Islam, Sarilar in southern Turkey schools her youth (far left) in Orthodoxy, reads prayers (lower) in Arabic — once the script of Turkey — and answers to patriarchs in Damascus. These prelates reigned of old in Antioch, where pilgrims still pray in a cave (upper right) that may have heard Peter fishing for men.*

MONKS IN A MOONSCAPE *kept Christianity alive in Cappadocia, ancient province of central Turkey. Here nature shaped spires of stone and holy men burrowed into them to live, pray, labor, and die. To the surrealistic Goreme Valley (opposite) St. Basil of Caesarea led his followers: "Let there, then, be a place such as ours, separate from intercourse with men, that the tenor of our exercises be not interrupted from without."*

In strode hermits of the fourth century to chisel new dens or to hole up in ones dating back perhaps to the Hittites of 1600 B.C. Some perched on spires, aping St. Simeon (above) who lived nearly 40 years on a pillar in Syria and inspired generations of "stylites." Next came monks to carve citadels towering to ten stories, with cells, tombs, and chapels set aglow by the artist's hand. At last whole Christian families moved in; a few lived here as late as 1922. Now some cones serve as dovecotes, and from others come farmers in a daily exodus to sandy fields made fruitful by the guano.

such as inquisitions and internecine wars. Indeed, Christians down through the ages slew more Christians than ever the Romans had martyred.

Now church and state were wed. Emperors helped shape theology, prelates dabbled in statecraft. Basilicas dazzled, their coffers bulged—and deserts began to fill with anchorites, "withdrawers," seeking alone the purer faith of old.

St. Anthony of Egypt had sought solitude in the hills near the Nile in the third century—in vain, for many followed him. At length he organized them in a loose community of hermits. St. Pachomius, a fellow Egyptian, expanded the concept and launched the first Christian monastery. The idea spread—but so did the ideal of the pious hermit, battling as had Jesus and Anthony the demons in the desert.

"The solitary life has only one goal, the service of its own interests," wrote St. Basil from central Asia Minor nearly a century after Anthony. "That clearly is opposed to the law of love...." Drawn to his ideal of charity and work and his sensible rules for communal life, many hermits quit their caves.

With martyrdom now eclipsed, what could the zealot do? Some monks mortified themselves with chains that made them hobble, cells that made them stoop, fasts that made them faint. A young Syrian

319

ELLIOTT ERWITT, MAGNUM. OPPOSITE: DETAIL FROM A 12TH-CENTURY MOSAIC IN THE CAPPELLA PALATINA, PALERMO; SKIRA

monk named Simeon buried himself to his chin for months, then bound his waist so tightly the flesh rotted. Finally Simeon raised piety to a new high.

In the Syrian hills near Antioch I climb a holy height and enter the magnificent shell of St. Simeon's Basilica. Where its four arms focus, I find only a scarred boulder. In the fifth century this humble stump soared some 60 feet into the sun, rain, and cold. And on its top for his last 37 years stood Simeon — like St. Anthony, "a daily martyr in conscience."

Stood, literally, claimed a disciple. On his tiny roofless platform Simeon Stylites, the "pillar man," couldn't lie and wouldn't sit. Held on by a railing, fed by ladder, crawling with lice, he preached twice daily to emperor and commoner below. Pillars sprouted everywhere as imitators vied in endurance; one stylite stood for 53 years, then lay for 14 more when his feet failed him. Simeon's feat sent stylites up their columns into the 12th century. But the solid sense of Basil

ROBED IN BLACK *but canopied
in color, monks of richly frescoed
Dionysiou Monastery share plain fare
and a life of work and worship on
Mount Athos in Greece, where no
woman has trod for a thousand years.
Their regimen traces to highborn
St. Basil (above), fourth-century monk
whose grandmother, parents, sister,
and two brothers rose to sainthood.
Disciples often clustered around
holy men; to such loose communities
St. Basil's* Asceticon *gave rules
basic to monastic life ever since.*

still inspires the monks of Greece. His rule is a potent force in the 20 monasteries that ring Mount Athos, a great jut of rock on a 30-mile-long peninsula in the north Aegean. In this thousand-year-old theocracy I end my trek with a glimpse of a life-style that is almost pure Byzantine, a time capsule of the great church-state that survived ancient Rome by a millennium.

An aged monk grins through a steel-wool beard, and I follow him to the guest house of the monastery of Iviron. No sound but ours quickens this fortress of faith, walled from the world and turned inward to the church in its court. Laundry, all of it black, flaps from a high window. Other windows light empty cells, for where hundreds once worked and worshiped, only a handful carry on.

An oil lamp glimmers as the guestmaster brings bean soup and olives. When I finish, the monks are already in bed. At midnight they rise for church services. At dawn the day's work begins: fishing, tilling, tending (Continued on page 324)   321

The Orthodox Church: Bastion of the East

Proudly professing their faith, Christians the world over recite the Nicene Creed, first formulated in 325 when Emperor Constantine called together the church's bishops at Nicaea. Down the centuries the words resound: "I believe in one God, the Father Almighty.... And ...in one Lord, Jesus Christ.... And I believe in the Holy Spirit, the Lord and Giver of life...." But there the chorus divides. Eastern Orthodox Christians say "who proceeds from the Father"; Christians of the West say "who proceeds from the Father and the Son."

The three added words of the Western version (known as the *filioque* clause) rang theologically false in the East. So did the mounting claims to primacy by the bishop of Rome, the pope. For Constantinople — no longer Rome — was the center of the Roman Empire, which would endure in the Greek-speaking East for a thousand years after the Latin West fell apart under barbarian attack.

Patriarchs of this Eastern Roman (or Byzantine) Empire, infuriated by Rome's proselytizing in the Balkans, denounced such "heresies" as the filioque clause, the Latin belief in purgatory, the insistence on priestly celibacy, and the use of unleavened bread in the Eucharist.

The controversy reached its climax in July 1054 when three papal legates stormed into Hagia Sophia church in Constantinople as afternoon services began and thrust a document upon the altar. Censuring the Byzantine clergy for *not* including the filioque clause and for using leavened bread, and erroneously accusing them of failing to baptize women in labor or to grant communion to clean-shaven men, the bull excommunicated the patriarch "and his followers . . . along with all heretics, together with the devil and his angels." The patriarch retaliated by excommunicating the papal legates. Hope of healing the schism died in flame, blood, and desecration 150 years later when Crusaders sacked Constantinople.

Eastern Orthodoxy survived centuries of "Ottoman captivity," flourished in Slavic lands, gloried in onion-dome churches enriched by Russian tsars. Despite Soviet harassment, it stands as the world's third largest Christian faith (chart, page 380).

Orthodox churches (from Greek *orthos* and *doxa*, "true belief") differ in language and name — Greek, Russian, Syrian, Coptic — but not in theology or liturgy. Under mosaic-encrusted vaults, richly robed priests and deacons wreathed in clouds of incense chant the service to a congregation standing before the iconostasis, a screen adorned with sacred images that separates nave from sanctuary. The traditional church is squarish, in the form of a Greek rather than Latin cross.

Partly because of their ancient quarrel with the pope, some Orthodox churches have not accepted the modern calendar (introduced by Pope Gregory XIII in 1582); none accept the doctrine of the Immaculate Conception (promulgated by Pius IX in 1854). Yet in 1964 in Jerusalem, Pope Paul VI met and embraced Athenagoras I, Ecumenical Patriarch of Constantinople. In a healing gesture both rescinded the excommunications that sundered the "one, holy, Catholic, and Apostolic Church" nine centuries ago.

Robed in red, Constantine sits by a throne for the unseen Christ at the Council of Nicaea (now Iznik in northwest Turkey). Below squirms Arius, denounced by the bishops for seeing Jesus as less than God. Rome recognizes 21 such councils, Orthodoxy only the first seven.

ICON BY MICHAEL DAMASKINOS, 1591, IN THE CHURCH OF ST. KATHERINE, HERAKLION

vineyards, cutting wood. At intervals they assemble for brief services. Except for special holy days, each day is like every other.

"Think much and talk little." The monks at most of the Holy Mountain's monasteries heed Basil's dictum when I try to converse. Then at Koutloumousiou I meet Father Erasimos, and we talk of the masterpieces inside his church. "Maria. Christos." He gently strokes the figures of an intricately carved altar-piece. "Ibrahim. Isak." The figures are in shallow relief, for in 787 bishops in council condemned church sculpture in the round as smacking of pagan idolatry; a nose that could be grasped between thumb and finger went too far.

By the sleeve Erasimos leads me to headier fare, a narthex frescoed floor to ceiling with scenes of martyrdom. With extravagant theatricals he pantomimes the horrors: nails hammered into heads, limbs severed, lions gnawing fiercely. I lose myself in reflection. Then I look for Erasimos, but he has vanished like a black shadow into his Byzantine world, a holy haven from history, a remnant of the realm that rose from the ashes of Rome. On its banners shone the cross of the risen Christ. On its brow sat the crown of empire. Today that crown is gone, but the church endures. To men of every nation it speaks the words of the early fathers. And the blood of the martyrs still courses its veins.

"SOLOMON, I HAVE VANQUISHED YOU!"
*cried Emperor Justinian (below right) as
artisans raised a new Hagia Sophia, church
of the Holy Wisdom (right), in sixth-century
Constantinople. Constantine had chosen the
city as capital of the empire he made safe
for Christianity; there rose his son's Hagia
Sophia, later to burn. With Justinian's
priests intoning prayers, masons built holy
relics into the new dome — hub of Orthodoxy
"suspended from the heavens by a golden
chain," said a witness. It saw patriarchs
crown Byzantine emperors amid pomp.
Moslem invaders made the church a mosque,
plastered over images their faith forbids, hung
instead roundels naming saints in Arabic,
added minarets that spike the sky of modern
Istanbul (below). Moslem headstones — plain
for women, ornate for men — watch dawn gild
the Golden Horn. Haze dims Hagia Sophia,
survivor of clashing creeds and 1,000 quakes.*

DETAIL FROM A 10TH-CENTURY MOSAIC IN HAGIA SOPHIA MUSEUM, ISTANBUL. LEFT:
WINFIELD PARKS, NATIONAL GEOGRAPHIC PHOTOGRAPHER. TOP: ERICH LESSING, MAGNUM

"*S*ing unto the Lord a new song.... For ...he will beautify the meek with salvation."
Rapturous words of the 149th Psalm, seeming to swell from marble-throated choristers,
portend the tide of Christian faith that would sweep the Western world.

CHOIR GALLERY CARVING BY LUCA DELLA ROBBIA, C. 1435, IN THE MUSEO DELL' OPERA DEL DUOMO, FLORENCE; GIANNI TORTOLI

THE FORGING OF CHRISTENDOM

John P. Whalen

*I*n August of the year 386 a young man, 32 years of age, suffered an agonizing
soul-searching in the garden of his home in Milan. For some years he had lived
immorally. He had prayed, " 'Give me chastity, but not yet' . . . for I was afraid
lest Thou shouldest hear me too soon, and heal me of the disease which I rather
wished to have satisfied than extinguished."

Born in North Africa, the child of a pagan Roman official and a Christian
mother, he was schooled in the classics and in the dissolute ways of Carthage,
greatest seaport in the western Mediterranean and a crossroads of religious
currents. Swept up by Manichaeism—belief that spiritual forces of good are
locked in eternal combat with material forces of evil—he became disillusioned
and journeyed to Rome and Milan to seek his fortune teaching rhetoric. He embraced Neoplatonic philosophy, listened with growing respect to the sermons of
St. Ambrose, bishop of Milan. Still he could not escape the torment in his soul.

On this August day, overwhelmed by self-contempt, the young scholar threw
himself down in his garden and wept. Thinking he heard a child say, "*Tolle, lege*—
Take up and read," he rose and opened the epistles of Paul to the vivid words:
". . . not in reveling and drunkenness, not in debauchery and licentiousness,
not in quarreling and jealousy. But put on the Lord Jesus Christ, and make
no provision for the flesh, to gratify its desires" (Romans 13:13-14).

Suddenly "all the darkness of doubt vanished." Calmed, now clear in purpose,
he prepared for baptism by Ambrose, entered a life of monastic austerity, and
began to pour out a torrent of writings that blueprinted the age of faith.

He was Augustine of Hippo—St. Augustine.

Augustine stepped into history at a pivotal period; in 392 Emperor Theodosius
made Christianity the Roman state religion. Augustine flung himself into the
crusade to suppress mystery cults and heresy. For 34 years as bishop of Hippo

327

(now Bône, Algeria) he thundered against heresy, shaping doctrines from which Catholic *and* Protestant thought flows to this day. He died in 430 while the Vandals pounded at Hippo's gates. Yet out of the shambles of empire he conveyed Rome's classical spirit to the medieval world. Cicero and Christ, Paul and Plato, Athens and Jerusalem met in his mind — and lived in his treatises, his sermons heard down the centuries, his *Confessions* still read after 1,600 years.

His masterwork, *The City of God*, rose out of the shock of Rome's fall to the Visigoths in 410. Setting out "to challenge the view of those who hold the Christian religion responsible for . . . the recent barbarian sack of the city of Rome," he ended up 13 years later creating a world view for the Middle Ages. Augustine saw all history as a struggle between love of God and love of self — between the *Civitas Dei* (heavenly City of God) and the *Civitas Terrena* (terrestrial City of Man). In his own struggles between religion and earthly desires, religion prevailed. In universal history the same must hold true. Both cities might coexist; but if conflict comes, the heavenly city so vital to salvation must prevail.

*T*his theme runs through the rise of the Christian West. Christendom was not systematically achieved. It grew out of church efforts to sanctify the world and, in the process, to civilize it. For more than 1,100 years, from Augustine to the Reformation, church and state in the West sometimes succeeded, and more often failed, in maintaining the delicate balance between priesthood and kingship, between the *sacerdotium* and the *imperium,* that resulted in that unique amalgam, the *Imperium Christianum* we call medieval Christendom.

Through the sacramental system, men lived in close association with the church from cradle to grave. They came to share a faith that united them even when fighting one another. This oneness of belief, despite conflicting feudal loyalties and national differences, culminated in the 13th century in a single all-embracing Christian society — the City of God on earth. Membership in the church meant submission to the Christian prince; adherence to the prince implied membership in the church. Dissenters from the established order were at once traitors and heretics. Tried by the church's inquisitors, apostates who refused to recant and do penance were handed over to the state's magistrates for punishment — in Augustine's analogy, saving the body by amputating the rotten limb.

*T*onsured giant who bridged
the ancient and medieval worlds,
St. Augustine of Hippo set
men's eyes on the City of God.
Bishops of Rome, the popes,
claimed the keys to this kingdom
as successors to Peter, to whom
Christ had entrusted his church;
"and whatever you bind on earth shall
be bound in heaven" (Matthew 16:19).
Dome of St. Peter's Basilica (left)
rises above the traditional site of the
martyred apostle's grave in Rome.

329

Classical and Christian mingle in Rome's church of St. Costanza, originally a tomb for the daughter of Constantine, whose Edict of Milan in 313 gave toleration to despised and persecuted Christians. Their catacombs extend near this rotunda, with its mosaic vines, birds, and other secular scenes.

The sack of Rome in 410 by Alaric's Visigoths heralded doom for the empire that had gloried under the Caesars. "Sobs choke my words," lamented St. Jerome from his monastery in Bethlehem. "That great city, which once captured the whole world, has herself been seized!"

As the gloom of barbarism settled over Europe, one light continued to shine: the church. It toiled to bring tribal chieftains within the fold, to substitute saints for pagan deities, to Christianize heathen rites, myths, festivals. It converted a midsummer orgy into the Feast of St. John and consecrated as Christmas December 25 — the winter solstice celebrated by ancients as the birthday of Mithraism's sun god.

The church even established our chronology. The custom of dating events B.C. *(before Christ) and* A.D. (anno Domini, *in the year of our Lord) was introduced about 525 by Dionysius Exiguus, a Roman abbot and astronomer who set Christ's birth 753 years after the founding of Rome.*

BRIAN BRAKE, RAPHO GUILLUMETTE

"Peregrinations for Christ," epic evangelizing efforts such as St. Patrick's fifth-century conversion of Ireland, won most of pagan Europe to the cross by 800. Wherever they went, missionary monks established monasteries, self-sustaining outposts of faith and learning. Through them Christianity, the Greco-Roman heritage, and Germanic culture fused to create the medieval foundations of Western civilization. A brother at Ligugé (above), oldest monastery in France, founded about 360 by St. Martin of Tours, keeps enameling skills alive.

Just as Augustine laid the classical and theological foundations for Christendom, Gregory the Great bequeathed the Roman genius for organization and administration to the medieval church.

Born in Rome around 540, the son of a wealthy family of senatorial rank, Gregory grew up amid the ravages of Justinian's wars against the Ostrogoths. At 33 he rose to the rank of prefect, highest civil official in Rome. For generations no emperor had lived there. Overseeing officials, finances, grain distribution, aqueducts, sewers, and defenses, Gregory became, in effect, the imperium. But, torn between service to the City of Man and the desire to turn from it to the City of God, he founded seven monasteries with his patrimony—one in his own home —and renounced the purple toga for a monk's coarse robe. Called from seclusion to serve seven years as papal emissary to the imperial court in Constantinople, he returned to his monastery only to be elected pope in 590—against his wishes. Now, in a sense, he was the sacerdotium.

As Pope Gregory I, he strengthened a church organization patterned on Roman civil government—just as Rome's seven principal churches (basilicas) on the seven hills mirrored lawcourts of the emperor *(basileus),* with altars replacing judges' thrones. He disciplined the clergy, extended the church in Visigothic Spain, Vandal Africa, and Anglo-Saxon England, and wrote the *Cura Pastoralis,* which set pastoral practice for the Middle Ages. The sacramentary, a book detailing liturgical form, and the chants sung even today are both called Gregorian.

Columbanus carried Celtic Christianity to the Continent in the late 6th century, founding monasteries at Luxeuil and Bobbio.

PICTS

Iona COLUMBA AIDAN

SCOTS

Donegal

Bangor Lindisfarne

IRISH

Whitby

ENGLISH

COLUMBANUS

WELSH

WILLIBRORD FRISIANS

London Utrecht BONIFACE SAXONS

Canterbury

Fritzlar

Fulda

Paris

Chartres Clairvaux

FRANKS Luxeuil

Tours COLUMBANUS

Ligugé St. Gallen

AUGUSTINE Cluny

Venice

Pola

Bobbio

Arles To the Holy Land

Assisi

Nursia

Rome

Monte Cassino

Santiago de Compostela

Patrick, born a Christian in Britain, was enslaved at 16 by Irish marauders. Escaping to Gaul, he became a monk, returning in 432 to convert all Ireland. A century later, Columba founded a Celtic center on the island of Iona and evangelized northern Scotland. In 635 Aidan built a monastery at Lindisfarne as Celtic Christianity spread southward. In England, conflicting Celtic and Roman ways, especially for calculating Easter, were resolved in favor of Rome at the Synod of Whitby in 663.

Knight and peasant, saint and sinner thronged to three main pilgrims' goals— crossing the Pyrenees to the shrine of St. James at Santiago de Compostela, threading the Alps to St. Peter's in Rome, taking ship at Venice for Jerusalem, center of the medieval universe.

Founded in 910, the abbey of Cluny rose as a leader in monastic reform; by 1100, its network of hundreds of daughter abbeys made it a powerful religious force in Europe. As Cluniac zeal waned in the 12th century, Cistercian fervor grew. Led by Bernard of Clairvaux, the white-robed monks of Cîteaux sought to recover Benedict's ideals of asceticism and poverty. In contrast to the cloistered monks, mendicant friars of the Franciscan and Dominican orders went out into the world preaching and teaching. They and the Jesuits helped carry Catholicism to the New World.

Augustine of Canterbury, a Benedictine monk sent by Pope Gregory I, evangelized southeastern England in 597. English monk Willibrord carried the gospel to the Frisians and established his see at Utrecht around 700. Boniface continued the work in Germany. His abbey at Fulda, founded in 747, became a center of learning.

Hippo

Carthage

Augustine of Hippo was one of three great leaders Roman Africa gave to Latin Christianity. The others: Tertullian ("The blood of martyrs is the seed of the church") and Cyprian ("There is no salvation outside the church"), both of third-century Carthage. Dwelling in the monastery he founded in 395, Augustine preached from a bishop's throne and through his voluminous writings. He formulated doctrines of the Trinity, original sin, the sacraments, salvation by God's grace—also predestination and justification by faith. Christian belief is assured by the church's authority, he maintained; this in turn is assured by the apostolic succession—the handing down of the apostles' power from bishop to bishop.

Benedict of Nursia established his Monte Cassino abbey about 529. Stern, yet tempered with moderation, his rule for monastic life, with its vows of obedience, chastity, and poverty, was adopted by abbeys all over northwestern Europe.

Exceptionally experienced as statesman and churchman, he took over civil, military, and ecclesiastical governance of Rome. When the emperor wouldn't defend the city against Lombard invaders, Gregory did. When famine stalked it, he fed the populace from vast church estates. He asserted Rome's primacy, making his the court of appeal for controversies of other sees. When Moslem conquests later swept away the patriarchates of Jerusalem, Antioch, and Alexandria, all 250 bishoprics of Africa, and those of Spain, only the patriarch of Constantinople remained to rival the bishop of Rome.

The evangelization of England was close to Gregory's heart. Legend tells that one day in the Roman marketplace he saw several youths for sale as slaves. He asked who they might be, who were so fair, and was told they were Angles from England. Well-named, he said, for their faces were like the angels in heaven. Sad that "such handsome folk are still in the grasp of the Author of darkness," Gregory himself had wanted to head a mission to England. In 596 he sent one of his own monks, Augustine, who became the first archbishop of Canterbury.

Human understanding illumines letters written by Gregory, self-styled "servant of the servants of God." He instructs Augustine "to destroy the idols, but the temples themselves are to be sanctified with holy water, altars set up, and relics enclosed in them. In this way, we hope the people, seeing that its temples are not destroyed, may abandon idolatry and resort to these places as before, and may come to know and adore the true God. . . . They are no longer to sacrifice beasts to the Devil, but they may kill them for feasting to the praise of God. . . . If the people are allowed some worldly pleasures in this way, they will more readily come to desire the joys of the spirit. For it is certainly impossible to eradicate all errors from obstinate minds at one stroke. . . ."

The monastic historian Bede relates that the spring goddess Eostre gave her name to Easter (eggs and Easter bunnies recall her fertility rites). And he describes a council in 627 at which King Edwin of Northumbria decided to abandon the old gods. One of his advisers compared man's fleeting life to the winter flight of a sparrow through the king's banqueting hall. Flying in one door and out another, the sparrow is warm and safe for a few moments, then vanishes into the stormy darkness whence it came. "Similarly," the adviser said, "man appears on earth for a little while, but we know nothing of what went before this life, and what follows. Therefore if this new teaching can reveal any more certain knowledge, it seems only right that we should follow it."

A century after Edwin's conversion, Boniface, an English monk, carried the "new teaching" into the German wilderness. He proved Teutonic gods powerless by chopping down the sacred oak near Fritzlar and building a chapel of its wood. In its place he dedicated to the Holy Child the fir, symbol of survival through the death of winter — thus giving us our Christmas tree. After 35 years welding the Germanic peoples into Christian unity, Boniface longed for the peace of his monastery at Fulda. But a call for help from his flock in Frisia sent the 80-year-old "Apostle of Germany" north once more — to martyrdom.

Fulda and other monasteries and convents founded by Boniface followed the rule St. Benedict had devised at Monte Cassino in sixth-century Italy. Benedictine monks led communal lives of prayer, study, and work in strict obedience to

*P*iety, pain, and pleasure
abound in a Spanish romería,
a festive pilgrimage that exalts
the memory of a saint. In the
Galician village of Ribarteme
a procession of coffins bears
grateful survivors of serious
illness; the groans of penitents
shuffling on bloodied knees
recall the religious fervor
of medieval times.

The pageant honors St. Martha,
sister of Lazarus, who is said
to have interceded with Christ
for her brother's life. Celebrants
in the July festival parade the
saint's image—garlanded with
bank-note offerings—through
streets resounding with song and
dance. Some wear shroud-like
mortajas to represent the
"living dead" miraculously cured.

an abbot (father), who was exhorted to correct them with prudence, "lest being too zealous in removing the rust he break the vessel." Benedictine monasticism prevailed over the more rigorous Celtic monasticism from Ireland and northern Britain and became a major force in civilizing barbarian Europe.

Monks sowed the Christian faith, nurtured and organized in Greco-Roman cities, among pagans (*pagani,* country dwellers) and heathens (dwellers of the heath). Monks made wastelands bloom, taught settlers advanced ways to drain swamps, plow fields, fertilize, and rotate crops. They offered haven for the oppressed, received travelers as they would Christ. Copyists in the cloister passed on Latin classics to posterity. Centers of colonization and sanctity, monasteries sent forth reformers, scholars, lawyers, administrators to mold the ways of man.

When Charlemagne in 800 built his Germanic kingdom into a restored Roman Empire in the West, the pendulum swung the other way. Grandson of Charles Martel, who stemmed the Moslem invasion of France near Tours in 732; son of Pepin the Short, whom the pope had anointed king of the Franks; defender of the pope against the Lombards, Charlemagne ruled as "the representative of God who has to protect and govern all the members of God."

His biographer Einhard describes Charlemagne as "tall but not ungainly," with a nose "rather larger than is usual," and a "brisk and cheerful" expression. When he wasn't pacifying a realm that reached from the Pyrenees to the Elbe,

or converting Saxons with the sword, he liked to have "the great deeds of men of old" read to him at meals. "He took delight also in the books of St. Augustine, and especially in . . . *The City of God*."

He left little untouched in his reforming fervor. Laymen were not to work on Sunday. Landowners must pay tithes—a tenth part of their produce—to support churches. He forbade clergy to go to taverns, carry arms, hunt, keep concubines. They should open free schools. He defined the duties and authority of metropolitan bishops, even summoned and presided over synods that ruled in doctrinal controversies—interventions that would have made Gregory the Great, had he been alive, want to bloody the emperor's "rather larger than usual" nose.

But if the emperor delved into church affairs, the clergy also had a hand in his government. Royal chaplains formed his chancery. Bishops and abbots played important civil roles. To check on local affairs, Charlemagne sent royal inspectors in pairs—a layman and an ecclesiastic. Throughout the Middle Ages, key personnel in church and state were often the same.

With the breakup of the Carolingian Empire into a patchwork of fiefs torn by war and Viking raids, grave abuses arose. Clergy treated church lands like hereditary domains; princes endowed relatives and favorites with ecclesiastical benefices.

"I cry, I cry, and I cry again," wrote Pope Gregory VII. "The religion of Christ, the true faith, has fallen so low that it is an object of scorn not only to the Devil but to Jews and Saracens and pagans. . . . These keep their law, as they believe it,

but we, intoxicated with the love of the world, have deserted our law." With the
aid of reformers from Cluny and other monasteries and the newly constituted
college of cardinals, Gregory struggled to stamp out simony (buying and selling
of church offices) and to establish clerical celibacy (to cut family and worldly
concerns, thereby bringing priests back into true marriage with the church). To
achieve these reforms, the church needed the power to select its bishops.

There the reform movement collided with the Holy Roman Empire. Bishops
were landed magnates, and land spelled power. The emperor, Henry IV,
insisted on putting his man into any vacant bishopric. The investiture controversy waxed so bitter that Henry demanded Gregory be deposed. Gregory
excommunicated Henry, releasing his subjects from allegiance to him.

Faced by anarchy in this world, his soul condemned to everlasting damnation
in the next, Henry crossed the Alps in the dead of winter in 1077 and came to
Canossa, where the pope was staying. For three days he stood at the castle gate,
barefoot and in penitential garb, before Gregory absolved him.

In 1095, Pope Urban II diverted Europe's energies eastward, launching the
first of the Crusades that for two hundred years pitted Christian against Saracen
in a seesaw struggle for the Holy Land.

The pinnacle of papal power was reached with Innocent III, whose Lateran
Council of 1215 put the capstone on Gregory's reforms. Now calling himself
Vicar of Christ, the pope was supreme arbiter of all Christendom. "Below God

and above man," he judged between king and king, between ruler and rebellious subject. He encouraged the great mendicant orders founded by St. Francis of Assisi and St. Dominic. Franciscans, wed to Lady Poverty, brought a revival of popular piety. Dominicans, devoted to learning, spurred the growth of universities. Among their ranks towered St. Thomas Aquinas, who "baptized" Aristotle to bring classical logic and divine revelation into a monumental synthesis.

I particularly like one of many stories about Thomas. One day while concentrating on a difficult scriptural passage, he suddenly became aware that the other monks were at Vespers and he was late. The rule insisted that one be punctual. It also demanded silence, except for prayer. As Thomas hurried along the corridor toward the chapel, a statue of the Blessed Virgin came to life and said, "Thomas, you are late." He stopped, looked up startled at Mary, and without speaking, pointed to a sign behind her. She turned and read: *Silentium.*

Medieval people felt familiar with their saints. If God seemed too awesome and remote, the Virgin was always there to lend a sympathetic ear. Conceiving the heavenly realm in terms of the feudal hierarchy, they would pray to saints to intercede for them with God—just as a peasant would petition his manor court, not the king.

The church embraced virtually every aspect of their lives. It cared for the sick, the orphan, and the widow, educated the young, protected the weak, and tamed the strong through traditions of chivalry that guided the knight's conduct. Center of help in times of distress, the church was the center of entertainment as well, with its miracle plays and guild pageants, its minstrels and its fairs. It inspired the people with sublime architecture, art, and music. The great liturgical celebrations on feast days were as close to heaven as they could imagine.

There were endless complaints about oppression by bishops and clergy, but very few ever conceived that churchmen were not necessary. With the growth of canon law and a supranational organization for justice and administration, the church gave men a far wider citizenship than any feudal state. Out of a chaotic milieu it created a single society under God.

We still stand in awe at some of the accomplishments of that seemingly remote age. In a sense, that which was best in medieval Christendom persists; that which was worst led to its inevitable dissolution and the transformation of Christianity.

343

The Seven Sacraments

Millions of Christians throughout the world believe that the key to salvation lies in the sacraments instituted by Christ. St. Augustine of Hippo called such rites "a visible form of an invisible grace." Through them man encounters God.

Down the centuries, celebration of the sacraments has involved holy water, bread and wine, oil, incense, and salt, as well as certain symbolic words and gestures. These visible elements, called "effective signs," are believed to act as channels through which God bestows grace on man.

The Roman Catholic church defined the nature of the seven sacraments at the second Council of Lyons in 1274. Most Protestant denominations limit the number to two—baptism and the Eucharist.

Also called Holy Communion, Breaking of the Bread, Lord's Supper, or Mass, the Eucharist commemorates Jesus' last supper and his sacrifice for mankind. A priest consecrates bread and wine with Christ's words: "This is my body.... this is my blood." Roman Catholics, Orthodox Christians, Anglicans, and some Protestants believe these become, actually as well as symbolically, Christ's body and blood.

Before most Christians receive the Eucharist, they must be baptized—a custom that stems from ancient Jewish practice, especially among the Essene sect, and before that to pagan rites of purification. Originally adult baptism was the custom—and then only after a period of probation and instruction called the catechumenate. Immersion, pouring, or sprinkling signified the washing away of sin and spiritual rebirth. Clothed in white to symbolize purity

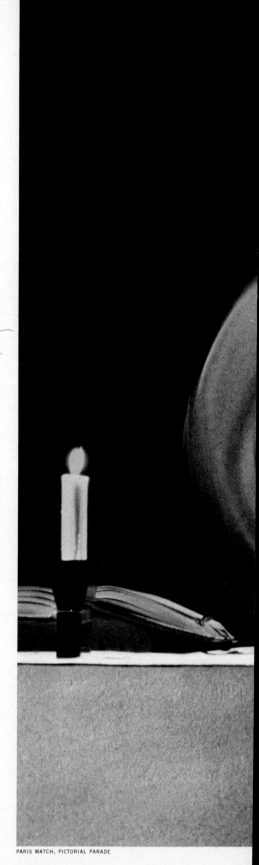

"Let us pray." Timeless commandment of a priest summons Catholic faithful to worship at Mass.

and bearing a lighted candle to signal enlightenment by God's grace, the initiate was anointed with "oil of instruction" and given milk and honey—he had symbolically entered the Promised Land.

Bestowal of a "Christian" name grew common in the third century. Baptism of infants finally prevailed and was formalized in the 12th century.

Today a Roman Catholic priest generally pours water over the infant's forehead three times in the form of a cross while reciting the words of baptism. The water is blessed on Holy Saturday—a vestige of the early practice of baptizing only during Easter season and at Pentecost.

Confirmation—closely associated with baptism, especially in the early church—confers the gift of the Holy Spirit and signifies a strengthening into Christian maturity. It is now generally administered to children 10 to 12 years old. Both it and baptism call for sponsors who undertake to instruct the child properly in Christian ways. Celebrated as a distinct sacrament

"Take this, all of you, and eat it; this is my body which will be given up for you." After these consecrating words of Christ, the priest elevates a wafer for adoration by the congregation during Mass, noblest of the sacraments. On the altar (which in Catholic churches contains a martyr's relic, according to custom predating the fourth century) the priest next consecrates and elevates wine in a gold chalice—the blood of Christ. Partaking of the Eucharist, the faithful receive eternal sustenance.

The priest's red chasuble derives from cloaks of antiquity; he wears it at Masses during Pentecost or to celebrate feast days of apostles or martyrs.

Bible readings (below) were universally given in Latin until 1963, when the Vatican approved use of the vernacular.

*Milestones of faith, sacraments
span the measure of a Catholic's
life. Baptism (below) restores
divine grace lost by Adam's fall
from innocence. Having blessed
the baby's mouth with salt,
its breast and back with oil
(to impart wisdom and fortitude),
the priest pours baptismal water
on its forehead with the words
"I baptize you in the name
of the Father and of the Son
and of the Holy Spirit."*

*Confirmation (opposite, upper)
marks attainment of Christian
maturity. Here a bishop anoints
the candidate and "lays on hands"
to bestow gift of the Holy Spirit.*

*Seeking God's mercy through
penance (right), kneeling petitioner
confesses his sins to a priest
(foreground) who exhorts him to
do better and grants absolution.*

*At life's ebb, anointing of
the sick (opposite, lower) brings
comfort and a pure soul. A priest
hears confession and blesses
the stricken with consecrated oil.*

WILLIAM J. GAGE

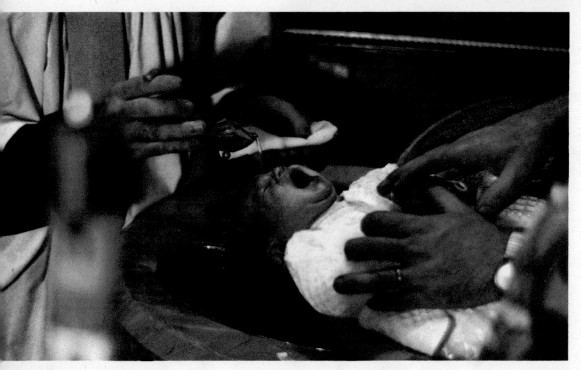

as early as the third century, confirmation in the Catholic church must always be administered by a bishop.

The sacrament of penance is based on the risen Christ's words to his disciples: "If you forgive the sins of any, they are forgiven; if you retain the sins of any, they are retained" (John 20:23). Penance was introduced to restore baptismal innocence to those who had committed serious (mortal) sins after baptism.

In the early church, committing such a sin after baptism often resulted in excommunication, or banishment, from the Christian community. Before the sinner could be reinstated, he had to undergo lengthy and arduous public penance. This led many to delay baptism until late in life, sometimes till their deathbeds. Gradually penance became easier. Private confession was introduced in the Middle Ages and priests were permitted to grant absolution

349

"*As the Father sent me,*" the risen Christ told his disciples, "*so I send you.*" Heeding the Lord's command to perpetuate his teaching, and committed to a life of celibacy, a candidate for priesthood kneels, hands clasped in prayer, to receive holy orders. Reading from a text held by an altar boy, a bishop (in miter) prepares to anoint the young cleric's palms with holy oil. Laying on of hands, signifying the transmission of priestly power to confer sacraments on others, will climax the ordination.

Solemnizing the union of man and woman, matrimony (below) sanctifies human love and the procreation of children. The Catholic church holds that, by its sacramental nature, a properly consecrated marriage cannot be broken by human authority.

Nuptial rites, sometimes followed by a Mass, consist simply of exchanging vows before clerical and other witnesses. Readings, giving of rings, and blessing, while symbolic, are not essential to the ceremony.

WILLIAM J. GAGE. UPPER: JAMES BLACK

before, rather than after, a supplicant had completed his penitential acts.

Anointing the sick (extreme unction) is meant to comfort and heal the elderly or seriously ill or to prepare them to meet God without blemish of sin. In this rite the endangered person's five senses are anointed with "oil of the sick."

Matrimony and holy orders are sacraments pertaining more directly to man's social life. Matrimony gives grace to the unique relationship between a man and a woman who have vowed a permanent life together. The elevation of marriage to a sacrament reflects Catholic belief that, through matrimony, a man and woman ex-

emplify Christ's own union with his church. Unlike other sacraments, matrimony has as its ministers the couple being married. They perform the sacrament mutually. All others serve as witnesses for the church.

As with matrimony, the church considers holy orders permanent. A young man must undertake eight years of intense studies beyond high school. (Since the Council of Trent, 1545-63, this instruction has centered in seminaries.) Ordained by a bishop, the priest is given the power to consecrate Christ's body and blood.

By the seven sacraments, given at life's crucial moments, millions of Christians receive God's sustenance and comfort.

Tapers flicker and white-robed priests chant before the altar in Mexico City's cathedral. Ranks of the faithful respond in the Roman litany as golden adornment draws eyes and thoughts upward.

In suburban Villa Madero, Aztec dancers in feather headdresses stamp to drumbeats. They pay homage to their Indian Madonna outside the Basilica of Our Lady of Guadalupe, built on the site of a shrine to the Aztec goddess Tonantzin.

This Latin-American coexistence of Christian worship and pagan survivals reaches back 450 years to a collision of cultures. Columbus had opened the door to the New World for Spain in 1492. Through it poured conquistadors, clergy, and colonists. But unlike Protestant settlers in the North American wilderness a century later, these crusading Catholics came up against civilizations practicing complex religions of their own—Hernán Cortés against the Aztecs in Mexico, Pizarro against the Incas in Peru.

Cortés and his followers recoiled from human sacrifices of the Aztecs and what seemed like satanic parodies of Christianity: eating pastry images of Huitzilopochtli, a god born of a virgin; venerating crosslike symbols of wind and rain gods; confessing sins; undergoing a kind of baptismal washing, with a prayer to ward off evil.

When the Spaniards pulled down temples and built churches, destroyed idols and substituted saints, many Indians took their religion underground; they hid their idols in the hills. Friars sought to win Indian souls by adapting the native love of dancing, music, drama, and costume to church holy days, and by catechizing in the Aztec tongue. They struggled to rescue Indian bodies from enslavement to new masters, to protect them from abuses by colonists and officials.

Catholicism was the very bone and marrow of the emerging Mexican nation—for the whites and the *mestizos* (of mixed Spanish and Indian blood) and in a special way

Where Conquistadors Planted the Cross

Zeal for God, gold, and glory drove Spaniards to conquer the Aztec empire. Hernán Cortés, depicted above with sword and cross by an Indian artist-reporter, landed near Veracruz (True Cross) in 1519. Hearing of the treasure at Tenochtitlán, the Aztec capital, he spread word that his men suffered from a sickness only gold would heal. The emperor Montezuma sought to cure them by gifts of gold. But Cortés feverishly pressed on to take the capital. On its site rose Mexico City. The cathedral (opposite) stands where Aztecs made human sacrifice to the sun. 353

HECTOR TORRES

Transfixed Guadalajarans welcome their patroness, Our Lady of Zapopan, on a circuit of city churches. She displays a general's sash and baton honoring her intercession when Mexico won independence from Spain.

for the Indians. Yet, in many parts of the country idols persisted behind altars, in spirit if not in wood or stone. An idol found behind an altar in one church was removed and put in a museum. The Indians stopped coming to that shrine. Even today the native gods refuse to stay dead. In a remote village church, men in tunics and sandals kneel on the earthen floor before carved wooden images of Christian *santos*, then stand in the doorway to invoke ancestral gods. As in parts of Spain, santos who do not answer prayers for rain or crops risk being taken out and beaten.

Pagan pageantry lives on in fiestas. In Guadalajara's October Festival honoring the Virgin of Zapopan, celebrants parade in masks like those of gods and animals Aztecs wore to gain strength and cunning.

Mexico's Holy Week ushers in a fervent spectacle, the Passion Play. Villagers reportedly once carried realism to the extreme of nailing a living Christ to the cross.

355

Pontius Pilate washes his hands of the blood of Christ in the Passion Play at Ixtapalapa, near Mexico City. From the village church Jesus takes up the cross and, as soldiers scourge him, climbs to Calvary through a throng of thousands. Tearful women minister to him along the way, then await the end in anguish at his feet atop El Cerro de la Estrella, Hill of the Star. Here ancestors of the villagers performed the ceremony of New Fire, marking the turn of an Aztec "century," every 52 years. Fires throughout the Valley of Mexico were put out, then rekindled after one was relighted on this hill by priests who sacrificed a slave.

In today's best known performance, at Ixtapalapa, Roman soldiers occasionally get carried away flogging Christ on the way to Golgotha. One man who portrayed Jesus said, "It was only after the ceremony that I realized my back was bleeding."

The Day of the Dead, another major religious festival in Mexico, falls on November 2, All Souls' Day. Children eat candy skulls and play with toy skeletons and coffins. Families visit cemeteries to honor their dead. Keeping an all-night vigil, an Indian in Michoacán kneels beside a grave, lights a candle, and burns copal incense. "*Salga, salga, salga*—Come out, come out, come out," he implores a departed soul. "Let the holy rosary break the chains that bind you." Fruit and pastry are spread in case the spirit arrives hungry.

In the New World the church once again revealed its resiliency in accommodating itself to local conditions and tenacious practices without yielding its central doctrines and rituals. In converting Latin America, it faced many of the obstacles it had had to overcome when Christianizing pagan Europe a thousand years earlier.

All Souls' Day. Strewing graves with marigold petals and lighting candles, they keep vigil with the dead.

THE REFORMING SPIRIT

Hans J. Hillerbrand

Scandalized by his evangelistic fervor, many of his fellow clergymen closed their churches to him. But George Whitefield, preaching outdoors where the breezes of reform swept unhindered through his sermons, drew multitudes wherever he went in 18th-century England and America. Stripping sinful souls naked before the vengeful gaze of God, he sent men and women quaking to their knees. He could bring tears to the eyes, it was said, merely by pronouncing "Mesopotamia"; Whitefield's eloquence made even thrifty Ben Franklin empty his pockets into the collection plate.

Calling for conversion, Whitefield cared little for denominational labels. In one sermon he presented this conversation: "Father Abraham, whom have you in heaven? Any Episcopalians?" "No!" "Any Presbyterians?" "No!" "Any Independents or Methodists?" "No, no, no!" "Whom have you then?" "We don't know those names here. All who are here are Christians!"

Whitefield's heaven may not have known such denominational names, but the New Jersey town where I live does, and I suspect my town is not unique in this respect. Out of some 35 churches, two are Catholic, the rest Protestant: Baptist, Christian Science, United Church of Christ, Episcopal, Evangelical Covenant, Lutheran, Methodist, Presbyterian, Reformed, Seventh-day Adventist, and on down the roster to the Trinity Temple Church of God in Christ. A bewildering diversity of denominations, yet a common bond unites them. All are related to that cataclysmic movement which shattered Christendom in the 16th century—the Protestant Reformation. To explore the roots of that complex of events which still affects us today, let me take you back to the land of my birth—Germany—where our story begins with a thunderbolt in July 1505.

Caught in a storm on his way back to the university, a 22-year-old student was hurled to the ground when lightning struck near him. He was Martin Luther, son of an ambitious miner of Eisleben, in Saxony, who reluctantly had followed his father's urgings to study law. A jovial fellow who liked to play the lute and sing with friends, he was also beset by anxiety about his eternal destiny. Terrified by the thunderbolt, he vowed, "Help me, St. Anne, and I will become a monk." The skies cleared—and he kept his promise, disappearing behind the walls of the Augustinian monastery at Erfurt.

But the deep comfort that monastic spirituality had given generations of the faithful eluded him. He felt that God asked him to marshal his moral resources. He was convinced that he did not possess any—and that God therefore condemned him to everlasting damnation. "I hated this God," Luther wrote, "who asked me to do the impossible." Then, like Augustine, agonized by his sense of hopeless sinfulness, Luther discovered the message of God's forgiveness in the epistles of Paul. Men are justified not by being good or doing good, he read, but by faith alone in God's mercy. To Luther, beginning a new life of redemption, it seemed as though "the gates of heaven opened before me."

Becoming a professor of theology at the University of Wittenberg, still a dutiful son of the church, he was excited by the revolutionary Greek and Latin edition of the New Testament published in 1516 by Erasmus of Rotterdam, leading humanist of the day. Where the church's authorized Vulgate text used the sacramental words "Do penance" for Jesus' call for repentance (Matthew 4:17), Erasmus asserted the original meant a sinner should "Be penitent"—contrition, but no scriptural sanction for any church-imposed penalty or indulgence.

Soon Luther's religious sensitivity received a rude challenge. In the summer of 1517 a Dominican friar named Johann Tetzel toured the neighboring province with great fanfare. For but a few gulden he would sell you an indulgence, a dispensation from the church remitting punishment for your sins or those of an ancestor in purgatory undergoing penalties imposed by God. "Don't you hear the weeping and wailing of your dead parents?" Tetzel implored. "They cry out in torment, and you, my hearers, could free them with a small alms."

Luther was shocked by the whole business. Archbishop Albrecht of Mainz, whose territory Tetzel worked, held not one but three high church offices. Since this pluralism was canonically illegal, and Albrecht was under the minimum age of 30 for episcopal rank, his fees to the papacy were high. Half of Tetzel's proceeds went to pay off the archbishop's debt to a banking house, the Fuggers of Augsburg; the other half went to Rome to help finance the reconstruction of St. Peter's, a project dear to the heart of Pope Leo X.

On All Saints' Eve, October 31, 1517, the scholarly young Luther posted "Ninety-five Theses Upon Indulgences" on the door of the Wittenberg castle church. An invitation to debate, the theses declared the pope had no jurisdiction over purgatory, nor was there any "treasure of the merits of the saints" from which he could transfer surplus credits to souls in need of salvation.

Luther had reached into a hornet's nest. The church probed his orthodoxy. Luther justified his position. A war of pamphlets broke out. Wittenberg's ruler, the Elector Frederick "the Wise" of Saxony, who prized his university and detested Rome's meddling in his state, chose to stand behind his embattled professor. Luther became hero to a motley group: priests eager for church reform, merchants, peasants, humanist scholars, German nationalists. Some misunderstood him; others felt his religiosity. Woodcuts appeared with a saint's halo or a dove signifying the holy spirit hovering over his head. Soon nine-tenths of the people reportedly would shout "Luther!" and the rest, "Death to the Roman court!"

Prophet of protest, Luther stands before fellow reformers: Erasmus of Rotterdam (fourth from right), who satirized the church but stayed Catholic; Philipp Melanchthon (far right), scribe of key Lutheran doctrines; Hans Lufft (far left), printer of Luther's Bible; and Wittenberg professors.

363

Snowy moon salutes Luther's statue in the old marketplace at Wittenberg, East Germany; behind it loom twin towers of the church where he often preached and where even today his portrait (opposite) oversees a wedding.

In June 1520, Leo X issued the papal bull *Exsurge Domine* — "Arise, O Lord. . . . A wild boar has invaded thy vineyard." It declared 41 propositions in Luther's writings "heretical" or "offensive to pious ears." Asked to recant, Luther, accompanied by students, marched outside Wittenberg's gates and cast the bull, together with a volume of the canon law, into a bonfire. The students rejoiced in the spree, but Luther trembled — the next fire might be his. In January 1521, he was excommunicated, in part because he defended some of the teachings of John Hus, Bohemian reformer burned at the stake a century earlier. Four months later, after Luther refused to recant at the Diet of Worms, Holy Roman Emperor Charles V declared Luther a political outlaw.

Spirited off to Duke Frederick's castle, the Wartburg, Luther wrestled with demons of self-doubt. Torments rose to haunt him: How could he claim he was right and all the faithful for 1,500 years in error? Was he that much wiser? He immersed himself in translating the New Testament into German, a masterpiece of popular style, and found scriptural sanction to dispel all doubt.

Like Erasmus, Luther wanted the plowman to be able to recite scripture in the field, the weaver at his loom. But unlike Erasmus, who sought to reform the church without raising tumult, Luther pressed on inexorably. "Printing is God's latest and best work," he said, and wielded it like a bludgeon. His tracts grew more strident, his views more rigid. The plea for reform within the church became a demand for existence without.

Monasteries closed down. Priests and nuns married. Luther himself, back at his professorship in Wittenberg, married a former nun. He rejected all but two of the seven sacraments — baptism and the Eucharist, modified so that communicants received both bread and wine. He preached that the faithful enjoyed

"City of God" to bearded John Calvin, Geneva thrusts its spires against the Alps in this 17th-century engraving. St. Peter's Cathedral, built in the 12th century when spirits and architecture soared, sheltered reform-minded citizens who voted in 1536 to abolish the Mass and to live under "sacred Gospel law and Word of God."

Surrounded by states still faithful to Rome, Geneva became a haven for Protestant refugees. Asked to teach, "that Frenchman" Calvin imposed an ecclesiastical constitution, spelled out his doctrine of predestination, and with unrelenting zeal transformed "merry and satirical" Geneva into "an amazing town where all was fire and prayer...labor and austerity."

YOUNG CALVIN BY AN UNKNOWN ARTIST, C. 1535; MUSÉE HISTORIQUE DE LA REFORMATION, GENEVA.
BELOW: ENGRAVING BY MATTHÄUS MERIAN, C. 1642; CHARLES GEORGE FOR PHOTO PIERRE, GENEVA

immediate access to God—"the priesthood of all believers." He extolled the Bible as the sole authority, not "man-made" church tradition, and maintained that salvation came through God's grace without any contribution of man. That was his pivotal concern. In 1529, Luther's supporters protested a decision by the Catholic majority of German rulers to prohibit Lutheran teaching—and promptly were labeled "Protestants."

Wars with France and the Turks kept the emperor, secular custodian of the church, from crushing this heresy. So Luther lived to see the sundering of Christendom. Grieved, he nonetheless believed the pope was "the Antichrist," that Rome had perverted true religion, and that the gospel had been restored. As for his role: "The Word did it all," he remarked. "Had I wished to do so, I could have started quite a conflagration. But while I sat quietly and drank Wittenberg beer with my friends, God through His Word dealt the papacy a mighty blow."

*B*ut God's Word was subject to manifold interpretation. As the fires of rebellion spread through Europe, the Reformation became not one movement but many. It was one thing to be against the Roman church, quite another to agree on what constituted the Christian religion. Feuds among Protestant factions grew hardly less intense than strife between Protestants and Catholics.

The last years of Ulrich Zwingli, Zurich patriot and reformer who died in 1531 in battle against the Catholics, were overshadowed by his controversy with Luther. Zwingli found it impossible to believe that the eucharistic bread and wine truly embodied the physical Christ; the Lord's Supper seemed to him to convey merely a spiritual presence. And whereas Luther composed chorales, prescribed a liturgy and catechisms, and retained vestments, Zwingli's followers considered hymns and traditional clerical garb unscriptural, stripped their churches of organs, images, and stained glass, and held the most austere of services.

Some Protestant radicals took issue with the reformers' acceptance of infant baptism, claiming there was Biblical mandate only for adult baptism upon confession of faith. So, in a peasant cottage or by a river they secretly received the rite, with baptismal water poured from a kitchen ladle by one of themselves. The authorities charged that theirs was a second baptism (after that in infancy), called them Anabaptists (*ana* means "again"), and persecuted them. Gentle, pious folk for the most part, who patterned their lives after the Sermon on the Mount and refused to swear oaths or take up arms, they ignited the wrath of Catholic prince and Protestant council alike. Ranks winnowed through the trial by fire and sword that marked their pilgrimage through Europe, Anabaptist followers of the Dutch reformer Menno Simons—the Mennonites—and the Tyrolean Jacob Hutter—the Hutterites—finally found haven in the New World to live by the Bible apart from worldly society.

The "New World" in America derived in no small degree from the principles of the "City of God" established at Geneva by John Calvin, the most famous reformer after Luther. The determination and rigidity that show in portraits of Calvin are mirrored in the tall-hatted, white-collared Puritans—grim and humorless, many of them, hard-working and frugal, dedicated to the proposition that anything enjoyable is sin. With zeal born of the conviction that they were an elect siding with God and fulfilling his purpose in the world, these Calvinists founded New England—and many an American fortune.

French by birth, lawyer-humanist by training, practical reformer in Geneva almost by accident, Calvin had come to Switzerland where he could safely publish his *Institutes of the Christian Religion.* A keystone of Protestant theology, it outlines with clarity what the reformers believed about God, man, and the world. He saw the book through press in Basel in 1536. Passing through Geneva later that year, the 27-year-old scholar was pressured into staying; the city had expelled its bishop, was in the process of reorganizing, and needed a Protestant teacher. Except for a three-year exile when he lost out in a clash with the city council, Calvin stayed on till his death in 1564, seeking to establish his vision of the apostolic church and a "community fit to worship God."

He preached the majesty and sovereignty of God—who had predestined those to be saved and those to be condemned. "To indulge oneself as little as possible" should be the Christian's goal, as well as "unflagging effort" to cut "all show of superfluous wealth, not to mention licentiousness." Calvin prevailed upon the council to set up a consistory to investigate offenses ranging from card playing, dancing, possessing a book of saints, to overcharges by physician or tailor. Wearing down, banishing his opponents—even getting the council to burn one, the anti-Trinitarian scholar Servetus—he persisted in molding Geneva into what John Knox, the dour disciple who took Calvin's message to Scotland, called "the most perfect school of Christ since the days of the apostles."

Yet, frail, nervous, constantly plagued by illness, Calvin shuddered at the calumnies and dangers he had endured. He confessed on his deathbed he was "naturally by no means bold." Only his conviction "that the Lord had truly blessed my labors" gave him his zeal and iron insistence he was right.

His legacy to Protestant mainstreams (chart, page 380) was immense. And he bequeathed a style of worship followed widely to this day: no elaborate liturgy, a simple gathering of the congregation for scriptural reading, prayer, singing, and sermon. Suspicious of harmony, he had his congregation sing in unison Psalms metrically matched to solemn tunes. The familiar doxology, "Praise God from whom all blessings flow," comes from Calvin's Geneva Psalter.

*H*ow different was England! Whenever I travel there I am impressed by the religious continuity. Whether in Canterbury Cathedral or in a Cambridgeshire parish church, the liturgy, the minister's vestments, the music remind me of the richness of Catholic Christendom. One might expect greater change, considering those turbulent 25 years in the 16th century when England broke with Rome, broke with Protestantism, and again broke with Rome.

The Reformation in England was related to "the King's Great Matter"—Henry VIII's attempt to get the pope to annul his marriage to Catherine of Aragon so he could marry Anne Boleyn. By 1532 Henry's patience ran out. The king (whom Pope Leo had dubbed Defender of the Faith for his essay against Luther) rejected papal authority, took the title Supreme Head of the Church in England,

Moravians bound for America in 1736 sing in the face of fear. Their simple faith and piety deeply influenced young, white-stockinged John Wesley, founder of Methodism. A candlelit blessing in restored Old Salem, North Carolina, recalls that piety.

wed his second queen, and enriched his gentry with monasteries of the realm.

In 1537, a year after English priest William Tyndale was strangled and burned as a heretic on the Continent, Henry authorized publication of a Bible translation, largely Tyndale's, printed in Catholic France. He ordered a copy put in each parish church and urged Englishmen to read it "as the very word of God and the spiritual food of man's soul." Like a hot wind, the new Bible spread

Protestant sparks ignited 150 years earlier when John Wyclif attacked church doctrine and privilege—influencing John Hus in Bohemia—and gave his countrymen their first Bible in English.

But Henry wanted an independent, not a heretical church. He soon prohibited the "common sort" from reading the Bible, and in 1539 his Parliament passed the Six Articles Act, which reasserted principal points of Catholic doctrine. Yet adamant Catholics were persecuted no less than Protestants. The willful monarch's executions provoked an observer's remark, "What country is this where they hang papists and anti-papists the same day?"

Henry's scholarly archbishop of Canterbury, Thomas Cranmer, swung with every regal breeze—even packing his wife off to her native Germany when the Six Articles restored clerical celibacy. (She reappeared after Henry's death.) Cranmer's religious genius shows, however, in the *Book of Common Prayer*. In this he created, from the Latin liturgical heritage, services in the vernacular whose cadences and beauty of language, like those of the King James Bible, have ennobled English worship for four centuries. In its 1559 edition it charted a middle course through burning theological issues. To transubstantiation it answered Yes, Christ is present in the bread and wine ("The Body of our Lord Jesus Christ which was given for thee, preserve thy body and soul unto everlasting life")—and No, we merely remember Christ in the Last Supper ("Take and eat this in remembrance that Christ died for thee, and feed on him in thy heart by faith with thanksgiving").

There was no compromise when Catherine's daughter Mary came to the throne in 1553, married Philip II of Spain, and forcibly reintroduced Catholicism in England. She committed a colossal blunder: she made martyrs. John Foxe, expanding on "Bloody Mary's" executions in grotesque detail in his *Book of*

Martyrs, convinced many that Englishmen should never again live under "popish oppressours." He told of heroic churchmen suffering "with greate rejoycing, as one going to a bridal." Not the last to go was Cranmer himself. At his trial Cranmer recanted. But on the day that he went to the stake, he astonished the assemblage by disavowing his recantations and lauding the Reformation. "And because this hand has sinned the most," he said, raising the hand that had signed the confessions, "it shall be the first burned."

The Church of England was firmly established during the long reign of Henry's other daughter Elizabeth. But for all its moderation, it continued to be buffeted by demands for change. First came the Puritans, bent on "purifying"

it of any popish taint. In time encompassing cranks and sages, apostles of instant utopia and brooders on the divine mysteries, the Puritans were terribly serious about religion. They tell us much about themselves in diaries filled with analyses of their thoughts and actions—moral account books listing spiritual credits and debits. Oliver Cromwell, Bible in one hand, sword in the other, would consider himself God's avenger and send a king to the executioner's block.

Scarcely had Elizabeth ascended the throne in 1558 when English exiles returned from Calvin's Geneva to complain that ministers should wear plain black gowns. Then they clamored for the governance of a local church by its lay elders (presbyters) rather than by a distant bishop—a presbyterian rather than an

episcopal organization. Later some even wanted to separate completely and set up independent congregations. Frustrated at Elizabeth's middle course, harried for nonconformity by King James, many Puritans sailed for the New World. They likened themselves to the Israelites setting out for the Promised Land. America had been kept hidden by God for a purpose, a Puritan divine noted. God had sent them on an "errand into the wilderness," where he would "create a new heaven and a new earth, new churches and a new commonwealth."

But even in this Congregationalist Eden dissension arose. Dissenters who had left Europe in search of religious freedom frequently denied this to others in their midst. It took a Roger Williams to remind Puritan elders that "forced worship stinks in God's nostrils." Banished from Massachusetts Bay Colony, he named his Rhode Island settlement "in commemoration of God's Providence," drew up America's first document separating church and state, and founded America's first Baptist church.

On both sides of the Atlantic the role of the dissenter long remained hard. Take George Fox, founder of the Quakers: "The people fell upon me and with their fists, books, and without compassion or mercy beat me down in the steeple-house and almost smothered me...." Fiercely opposed by church and society in 17th-century England, Fox was unshakably convinced that God had called him to proclaim the message of repentance, of inward attitudes rather than out-ward rites. He insisted that the "light of Christ" glimmered in all men. Christians should not wage war nor swear oaths, should address everyone, whatever his title, as "friend," using the familiar "thee" instead of the formal "you." Jailed often, frequently trounced, the layman "with the leather breeches" journeyed about the British Isles, to the Continent, even to the American colonies, seeking followers. Known for the simplicity of their lives, their pacifism, their stress on

375

religious freedom, the Quakers worshiped without liturgy or clergy in plain steeple-less meetinghouses. Sitting thoughtfully, one might rise to speak from the heart or mind, then another, then all would listen to the inner voice. In 1681 the Quakers found a New World home in Penn's Woods—Pennsylvania—named for their patron William Penn, Fox's most illustrious disciple.

*J*ohn Wesley had a stormy crossing to America. The mainsail split. Seawater, he recorded in his diary, "covered the ship and poured in between the decks, as if the great deep had already swallowed us up. A terrible screaming began among the English. The Germans calmly sang on. I asked one of them afterward, 'Was you not afraid?' He answered, 'I thank God, no.'"

The "Germans" were Moravian Brethren—followers of the Count of Zinzendorf. Wesley, who with his brother had founded a prayer group at Oxford (a group so methodical in devotions they had been nicknamed "Methodist") was on his way to minister to Georgia colonists and Indians. After that shipboard experience he kept in touch with those fervent Pietists whose steadfast faith had so impressed him. And at a Moravian service back in England in 1738, listening to

Luther's *Preface to the Epistle to the Romans,* he felt his "heart strangely warmed." This proved to be the pivotal experience of his life. He now began a mission that would see him preaching in churches, on highways and byways, in streets and in market squares. He traveled some 250,000 miles, mostly on horseback, delivering more than 40,000 sermons, composing hundreds of hymns. Initially this activity took place within the Church of England; he sought no separation. But as the years passed, those moved by his message drew together and assumed a separate existence—the Methodist Church.

The Methodist Revival, brought by Wesley's preaching, was like the waves of religious fervor that periodically rolled over the American colonies. Doctrinal concerns were swept away in a flood of brotherhood while "hell trembles, heaven rejoyces." Jonathan Edwards, the New England theologian, helped spark the "Great Awakening" of the mid-1700's. In sermons that seethed with emotional power, he demanded that sinners repent: "You are ten thousand times more abominable in [God's] eyes than the most hateful venomous serpent is in ours."

To his side came Wesley's friend George Whitefield and other itinerant divines "to thrust the nail of terror into sleeping souls." Together they created

*P*innacles of the Mormon Temple in Salt Lake City, Utah, duel with distant peaks under the eye of Moroni, the angel who revealed the sacred Book of Mormon *to Joseph Smith in 1827. Forced by hostile neighbors to flee New York, their leader shot to death by a mob in Illinois, Latter-day Saints began their epic westward migrations in quest of a "new Zion" under Brigham Young in 1846. Thousands followed in ox-drawn wagons; some pulled handcarts. Buffalo provided food, even fuel. Family in foreground makes a fire with dry "buffalo chips."*

a revival that shook New England's valleys. Converted "new lights" left the old Puritan churches, many to become Baptist missionaries spreading the Great Awakening southward and westward. Seven times, from 1738 to 1770, Whitefield journeyed to America, preaching from Maine to Georgia. Thus evangelical Protestantism helped to shape American life and thought on the eve of our great push for national freedom and westward expansion.

How would the churches meet the needs of the hundreds of new communities that were springing up, first in Ohio and Indiana, and then across the prairies of Illinois and Missouri and onto the plains of Kansas? There were not enough ordained clergy. Lay preachers were the answer: "St. Peter was a fisherman, do you think he ever went to Yale College?" Denominations which had stressed the ministry of all believers found themselves well prepared to accompany the emigrants westward. From the Baptist ranks strode forth the farmer-preacher, planting and preaching in the fertile fields beyond the Alleghenies. From Methodism went out the circuit rider—a lonely figure tirelessly making the rounds from hamlet to hamlet, everywhere at home, and yet nowhere at home. The camp meetings, the soul-searing revivals—these characterized religion on the American frontier. And with the winning of the West, the Baptists, Methodists, and Disciples of Christ won an important role in the nation's life.

Negro churches emerged to add their special flavor to American Protestantism. To a people carried in bondage from Africa to work on the plantations, the Bible spoke with special poignancy of the plight of the children of Israel in Egypt, the search for the Promised Land, the sufferings of Jesus, the vision of the Kingdom to come. And so the spirituals rang forth, sad yet charged with faith and hope: "When Israel was in Egypt's land, let my people go"; "Swing low, sweet chariot, coming for to carry me home"; "Were you there when they crucified my Lord?"

*T*he American experience transformed the Protestant churches that reached these shores—even as the Protestant Reformation had transformed the church of its time. Certainly the reforming spirit is not a Protestant invention. The burning desire to instill new spiritual vigor into the church, to renew piety, to stress commitment is as old as Christianity. The Middle Ages were full of men who called for reform; some wound up as saints, others as heretics. In the Catholic tradition reform tends to express itself in a non-separatist way—in new organizations, such as monastic orders, within the church. For most Catholics, truth and church are synonyms. Protestants recognize no such identity; the reforming spirit among them tends to lead to new churches.

The reformers of the 16th century believed that they had scriptural mandate to restore apostolic Christianity and the gospel, even if it meant casting down the "man-made" structures of the universal church. The reformers' cry coincided with political, economic, and intellectual forces then in the wind. So their work prospered. During the last four centuries, the growth of Protestant churches has vitally affected Western man's ways of thinking, living, and believing. Yet no human embodiment of Christ's church is perfect. The church has been reformed but, as the ancient saying put it, "must ever be in a process of reformation."

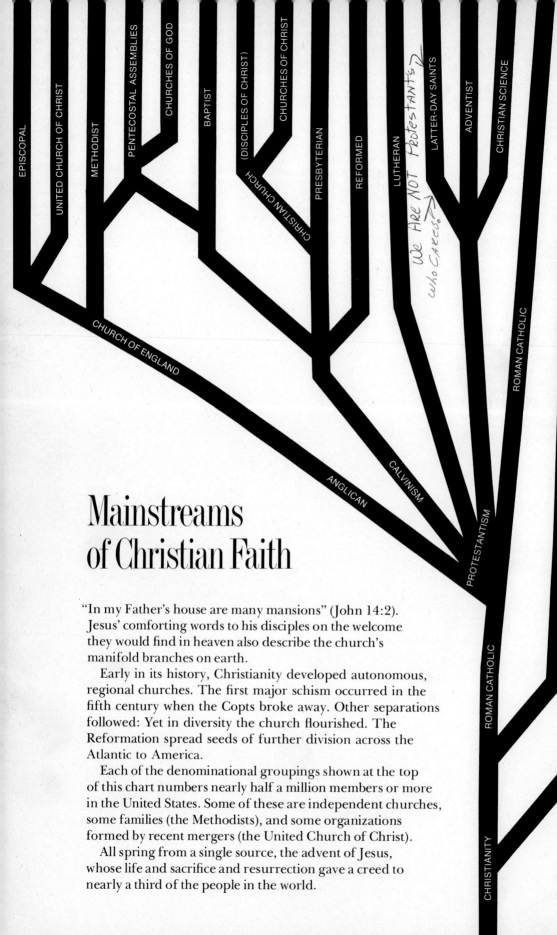

EPISCOPAL
UNITED CHURCH OF CHRIST
METHODIST
PENTECOSTAL ASSEMBLIES
CHURCHES OF GOD
BAPTIST
(DISCIPLES OF CHRIST)
CHRISTIAN CHURCH
CHURCHES OF CHRIST
PRESBYTERIAN
REFORMED
LUTHERAN
We Are NOT Protestants
who cares?
LATTER-DAY SAINTS
ADVENTIST
CHRISTIAN SCIENCE
ROMAN CATHOLIC
EASTERN ORTHODOX

CHURCH OF ENGLAND
ANGLICAN
CALVINISM
PROTESTANTISM
ROMAN CATHOLIC

Mainstreams of Christian Faith

"In my Father's house are many mansions" (John 14:2).
Jesus' comforting words to his disciples on the welcome
they would find in heaven also describe the church's
manifold branches on earth.

Early in its history, Christianity developed autonomous,
regional churches. The first major schism occurred in the
fifth century when the Copts broke away. Other separations
followed: Yet in diversity the church flourished. The
Reformation spread seeds of further division across the
Atlantic to America.

Each of the denominational groupings shown at the top
of this chart numbers nearly half a million members or more
in the United States. Some of these are independent churches,
some families (the Methodists), and some organizations
formed by recent mergers (the United Church of Christ).

All spring from a single source, the advent of Jesus,
whose life and sacrifice and resurrection gave a creed to
nearly a third of the people in the world.

CHRISTIANITY

ADVENTIST churches stem from the 19th-century preaching of William Miller: The second coming of Jesus is imminent, bringing destruction of evil on earth and the advent of a thousand-year reign of Christ with the resurrected faithful. The largest group, the Seventh-day Adventists, observe the Sabbath on Saturday, tithe their incomes, abstain from tobacco and alcohol. U. S. ½ million; world 2 million

BAPTIST churches share an ancient Christian conviction that infant baptism is unscriptural. Influenced by Anabaptists in Holland, John Smythe founded the first Baptist church in London in 1609, professing Christ's atonement for all believers (the Arminian doctrine) as against Calvin's doctrine of predestination. More strictly Calvinist were the Baptist church founded by Roger Williams in Providence in 1639 and many later American Baptist churches. Baptism by immersion, religious liberty, and staunch congregational autonomy stand as cardinal convictions. U. S. 27 million; world 31 million

CHRISTIAN CHURCH (DISCIPLES OF CHRIST) arose on the American frontier in the early 19th century. Led by evangelist Barton Stone and by Thomas and Alexander Campbell as a reform movement from Presbyterianism, it emphasized a simple faith in Christ as Lord, the Bible as the word of God, baptism by immersion, and weekly observances of the Lord's Supper. After a 1906 schism, the Disciples became the more progressive branch. Services allow instrumental music. U. S. 1½ million; world 1¾ million

CHURCHES OF CHRIST, the conservative branch of the Campbellite reform movement, trace their spiritual origins back to the apostolic church at Pentecost. They regard the New Testament as the sole, true, sufficient revelation of God; forbid musical instruments in services. Autonomous congregations cooperate in evangelism and missionary programs. U. S. 2½ million; world 3 million

CHURCH OF JESUS CHRIST OF LATTER-DAY SAINTS began in New York State amid the religious fervor of the 1830's; *The Book of Mormon*, translated by Joseph Smith, and the Bible gave hope to persecuted, westward-trekking Mormons, who set up a church state in Utah. Revelation continues today through the president of the church, which has a council of 12 apostles but no professional clergy. To spread its teachings, thousands of young Mormons go out in pairs each year. Unique to Mormons: baptizing for the dead and sealing in marriage for eternity. Plural marriage has been prohibited since 1890. U. S. 2 million; world 3 million

CHURCH OF CHRIST SCIENTIST — the name declares the faith: Christian in derivation from Christ the healer; scientific in its applicability to human ills and evils. Mary Baker Eddy, who founded the Christian Science church in 1879, made a theological distinction between the divine Mind (God, Life, Truth) and the mortal mind (sin, disease, error). Christian Scientists reject medical treatment; "practitioners" heal by prayer and reliance on divine law. Church bylaws forbid the publication of membership statistics.

EASTERN ORTHODOX churches, continuing original patriarchates of early Christianity, are now organized in 16 autonomous branches; most have American dioceses. Orthodox doctrine (defined on page 322) recognizes neither pope nor purgatory. Bishops must be celibate, priests may be married. After baptism infants or adults receive confirmation with holy oil. Ritualistic services re-enact the gospel; the faithful honor saints and the Virgin Mary, reverence icons and cross. U. S. 3½ million; world 125 million

LUTHERAN churches directly result from the reforms of Martin Luther, who rejected Rome and emphasized "justification by faith alone" but retained a formal liturgy. Doctrine, including belief in the real presence of Christ in the Communion bread and wine, is primarily based on Luther's Longer and Shorter Catechisms of 1529 and on Melanchthon's Augsburg Confession of 1530. Lutherans originally called themselves "Evangelicals." First synod established in America in 1748. U. S. 9 million; world 75 million

METHODIST churches, named for a religiously disciplined group of Oxford students organized by John and Charles Wesley in 1729, emphasized social consciousness and Christ-like conduct of life. In 1784 John Wesley ordained pastors for Methodist churches in America. Doctrinally the church is Arminian; preachers stress conversion and repentance. Bishops appoint pastors to churches annually. U. S. 12 million; world 19 million

PENTECOSTAL churches, most of whose original members were once Baptists or Methodists, now include many different revivalist groups. They emphasize a fundamentalist, or literal, interpretation of scripture and the working of the Holy Spirit — usually manifested in divine healing and "speaking in tongues" (ecstatic utterances). In the largest group, the Assemblies of God (organized in 1914), independent churches cooperate in mission work. The separate Church of God follows a similar pattern, and stresses the second coming of Christ. U. S. 1¾ million

PRESBYTERIAN churches drew inspiration from John Calvin's teachings and Europe's Reformed churches. Bishoprics were done away with, churches and communities ruled by elected elders (presbyters). The 1648 Westminster Confession of Faith stands as the Presbyterians' creed: They believe that God offers salvation to anyone who will accept it; baptism is necessary for church membership. First American presbyteries were organized in the early 1700's by Scotch-Irish colonists. U. S. 4½ million; world 20 million

REFORMED churches, adhering to a conservative Calvinism, trace roots back to conferences such as the 1611 Synod of Dort that arbitrated doctrines of Luther, Zwingli, and Calvin. Dutch colonists established the first Reformed church in America near Albany in 1614. Elders rule, as in Presbyterian churches, but under a bishop or synod. Congregations may follow the prescribed liturgy or worship in their own manner. U. S. ½ million

PROTESTANT EPISCOPAL CHURCH, the American branch of the Anglican Communion, chose this name after the Revolutionary War to designate itself as non-Roman. Yet Episcopalians state they belong to the "Holy Catholic Church," support orders of monks and nuns, and follow traditional church liturgy. Ministry comprises three ranks: bishops, who stand in the line of "apostolic succession"; priests, who may marry; and deacons. U. S. 3½ million; world (Anglican) 47 million

ROMAN CATHOLIC CHURCH honors Peter as leader of the apostles, recalling that he received "the keys of the kingdom" from Jesus. Peter's heir, the pope, heads a hierarchical organization that manages church affairs down to the smallest parish. Catholics observe seven sacraments (pages 344-51), hold that the eucharistic elements change into Christ's body and blood (transubstantiation). They make private confession, with penance set by the priest, and believe in purgatory (where souls are purged of sin before going to heaven). U. S. 50 million; world 575 million

UNITED CHURCH OF CHRIST was formed in 1961 by the merger of the Congregational church and the Christian church with the Evangelical and Reformed church (which had Calvinist roots). Seeking to found communities in which they might worship as they wished, many 17th-century Englishmen came to America, established Congregational churches (in the early 1800's some split off as Unitarian), set up free schools and town governments that helped give the U. S. its democratic base. Congregations are autonomous. U. S. 2 million

Geneva: The Healing Spirit

"There shall be one fold, and one shepherd." With this passage from John 10:16 as their theme, men of Christianity's many mansions meet at New Delhi, India, to seek common ground. In various ways—such as this assembly—the World Council of Churches from its headquarters at Geneva reaches healing hands round the oikoumene, the "whole inhabited earth" united in the council's aegis (below) with the ancient boat-and-cross symbol of Christ's church.

It looks like a modern research lab, its glassy rectangles rising from green lawns and shrubbery. In a way it is one, for to the Ecumenical Center in Geneva, Switzerland, the World Council of Churches draws dedicated men and women from around the globe to seek ways of making a dream come true: the unification of Christian churches everywhere.

Dr. W. A. Visser 't Hooft, retired general secretary of the council, has invested a long life in that dream—and has seen the council grow out of an assembly at Edinburgh in 1910 to become a focal point for the energies of some 230 denominations in 60 countries today.

"We cannot prophesy what the ultimate development will be," he explains; "we are in process. But nobody in the council stands for uniformity. The question is whether our differences need necessarily lead to separation, and our answer would be a loud 'No!'

"Some very good plans for church mergers have nearly succeeded and had to be given up; sometimes it's the theologians and sometimes the laymen who lack the imagination to see beyond their old ways. But in other cases denominations have realized that it matters little whether a local congregation conducts its services this way or that. Christ's unifying message is what counts.

"Much more difficult are the questions of church order. For example, must a church have bishops or not? In the course of history the denominations have become one-sided, each emphasizing its own type of order. Now the time has come to see whether we can't fuse the best elements

CHURCHMEN OF BURMA, UNITED STATES, INDIA LEAD PROCESSION AT WCC'S NEW DELHI ASSEMBLY, 1961; JOHN TAYLOR, WORLD COUNCIL OF CHURCHES

of the different traditions and bring the Christian brotherhood together.

"I recall how the Roman Catholic church in the early days not only stood outside the ecumenical movement but was very critical of it. But as the movement grew many Catholics began to ask, 'What about us? Have we not a role to play?' Pope John XXIII was the man who said, 'Yes, we have' —and we at the council are glad he did.

"The Roman Catholics still are not members of the council, but we now have a number of Catholic theologians working with us who have been sent here by the Vatican. And I have lived to see the day when Pope Paul VI visited the Ecumenical Center. That's an astounding development. Now when I hear people say the movement hasn't done very much, I say, 'You ought to have seen the situation 50 years ago!'"

More than a parliament of theologians, the council makes its member churches more effective in the things they do together. It offers massive aid to victims of war or catastrophe. Its young workers help underdeveloped peoples in programs like the Peace Corps. The council is linked to some 23 study centers worldwide.

A new section fosters dialogue with men of living faiths as well as those who follow such ideologies as Marxism. Its director, Dr. Stanley J. Samartha of India, envisions more than "just the so-called people of religion exchanging information about religion. In common human concerns— justice, peace, education, poverty—*all* men are involved. There are deep differences between us. But, we ask, what can we do together? For the future of man touches not just Christians. It touches us all."

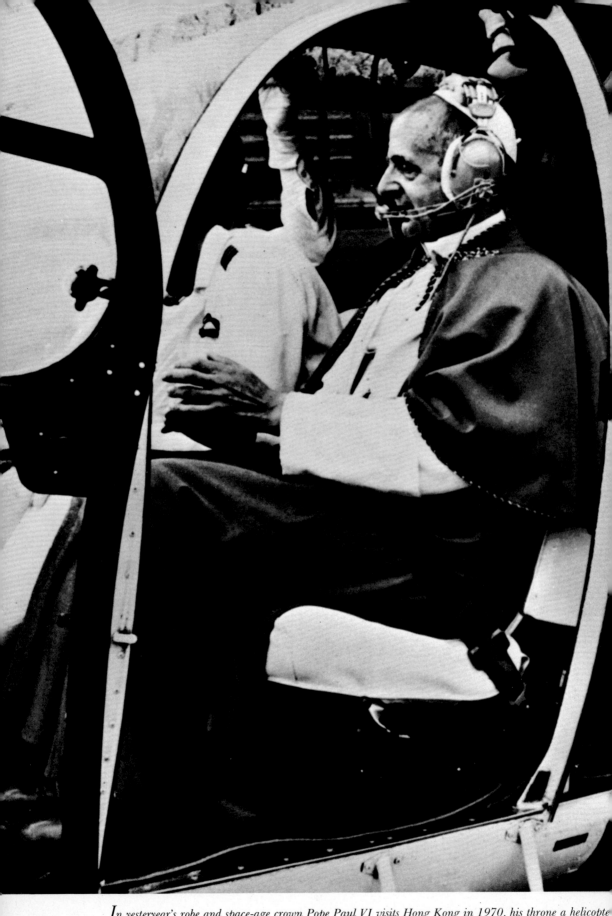

In yesteryear's robe and space-age crown Pope Paul VI visits Hong Kong in 1970, his throne a helicopter

Renewal in
Rome

In jet and helicopter he whirled from stadium to racecourse across the distance of Asia, speaking to vast crowds. But he dressed like a Renaissance prelate in vestments whose very names evoked a bygone era: *mozzetta, rochet, zucchetto.*

Successor to St. Peter, he drew his title pontiff (bridge builder) from pagan priests whose rites appeased the river Tiber's rage at being spanned. Now, having spanned seas and mountains, he took off his crackling earphones and in Hong Kong addressed "all the Chinese people, wherever they may be." He visited a dirt-floor shack in a Manila slum to extend the hand of charity to a poverty-wracked Filipino family. He chided Australians for discriminatory immigration rules and "the temptation to be satisfied" with prosperity. He watched sword dancers in Indonesia and was served a roast pig in Samoa.

Pope Paul VI on his journey to the Orient in December 1970 was a living symbol of the Roman Catholic hierarchy, a 2,000-year-old institution clothed with tradition, yet striving to present itself as a force fully relevant to the 1970's. Rome remains fixed as the central point of the Catholic church, but the Roman church is in renewal, from pope to parishioner, everywhere in the world.

The last great renewal of the church, the Counter-Reformation of the 1500's, was spearheaded by the Jesuit Order, founded by the Spanish knight Ignatius of Loyola. With dynamic art, intense mysticism, and a missionary spirit that reached India and Japan, the movement revitalized Catholicism. Then history forced the church to

s he adapts his venerable role to a modern world.

385

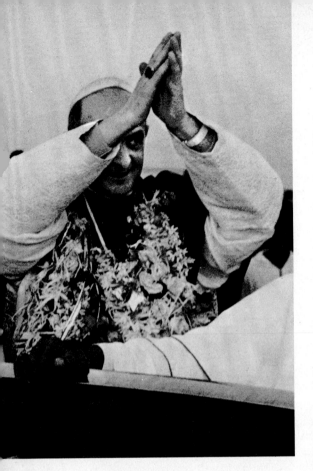

entrench: The French Revolution and its aftermath secularized much of Western life; the unification of Italy swept away the Papal States; in 1870 national forces captured Rome itself. The pope had just managed to convene the First Vatican Council before he became "prisoner of the Vatican." Yet in the face of diminished powers, that council proclaimed the doctrine of papal infallibility. And in 1910, in the face of scientific advances, Pius X condemned the secularizing spirit of the modern age.

"Hello Pope! Welcome Pope!" Faiths and voices mix as Hindu, Moslem, Buddhist, and Christian jam Bombay to greet Paul VI on his second long trip overseas. Many proffer rosaries (right) for blessing. His Holiness wins crowds at the city's airport with the traditional Indian gesture of greeting (above)—and later with a Hindu prayer and a plea for brotherhood under the fatherhood of God.

Dubbing himself "an apostle on the move," Paul in 1964 had journeyed to the Holy Land—first pontiff ever to make a pilgrimage to the home of Peter. His epochal trips coincided with the Second Vatican Council, one of whose pronouncements broke tradition by recognizing tenets found in other world religions.

Nine journeys in seven years— to Asia, Africa, the United Nations, to countries where few even knew who he was—bear out his pledge: "We will love those who are near and those far from us. . . . We will love Catholics, we will love the dissidents. . . . We will love the time in which we live: our culture, our science, our art, our sport, our world."

386

"The men of 1910 looked for a tight, logical, skeletal blueprint of the church . . . as an organization," wrote Gustave Weigel, the distinguished Jesuit theologian. "The bones came together but never lived. Since the . . . inner life of the church was scarcely touched, nothing was said about liturgy . . . prayer, and lay action."

But within that tightness rumblings began to be heard as the 20th century advanced. Spokesmen such as the French scientist-priest Teilhard de Chardin and the historian Henri de Lubac emphasized research, scholarship, vigor in meeting the world. Teilhard wrote: "Never again, I pray, may anyone dare to complain of Rome that it is afraid of anything that moves and thinks." At mid-century Pius XII permitted some use of native languages in the sacraments, and urged greater participation by the man in the pew.

Then in 1962 forces of renewal erupted and shook the whole Christian world as Pope John XXIII summoned 2,000

PARIS MATCH, PICTORIAL PARADE. OPPOSITE: REPORTERS ASSOCIÉS

Coronation of Pope Paul VI focuses eyes of the world on St. Peter's in Rome in June 1963. Stressing the need for self-knowledge, reform, and ecumenical dialogue, Paul furthered the work of Vatican II, opened in a blaze of glory eight months before under John XXIII. John had asked cardinals' support for the council in 1959; their silence stung but did not sway him. His council inaugurated a new era of Christian understanding.

cardinals and bishops to the Second Vatican Council. "The church," declared his convening letter, "must engage in a dialogue with the world in which she lives."

In its first enactment the council looked within the church and called for reform of the liturgy; priests in churches around the world now face their congregations and say the Mass and deliver sermons in the local tongue. By the last of four annual

MONDADORI PRESS, PICTORIAL PARADE

sessions the council had turned its gaze outward to offer itself as servant to all men everywhere. John was remembered as he had knelt in prayer; Paul was lauded as he went forth to cultivate vineyards of the world. At the United Nations in 1965, he cried out with the force of a global leader: "War, war—never again!"

Less dramatically, Paul stressed renewal within the church. From distant lands more bishops, priests, and laymen now come to Rome, and more and more the pope's curia —his top aides—listens to what they have to say. In 1961 four non-Italians held high Vatican posts; by 1970 they numbered 17 —and outnumbered the 11 Italians. Cardinals must retire from the curia at 80 and offer to at 75. Pope John had a word for this entire process: *aggiornamento,* or updating.

Dr. Emily Binns of Catholic University

Crowned at 78 under a name no pope had chosen since 1316, "good Pope John" awed many who expected only a caretaker pontiff. Though his reign ended in its fifth year, shortest since the 20 months of Pius VIII in the 1820's, his spirit still lives in Rome's continuing renewal — in wider contacts with Jews and with Protestants (page 383), and in a broadened power base at the Vatican.

The council that John called created the Synod of Bishops to advise popes on the future direction of the Catholic church. Every other year since 1967, colorfully capped and gowned bishops of the far-flung church have met in Rome (below). Relying more and more on their collegial advice if not on their consent, the pope is coming to stand with his bishops as the first among equals.

John's fame and form endure in memorable images: in bronze relief on a Vatican door (opposite) and in the words of Francis Cardinal Spellman who, on seeing non-Catholics mourn him in 1963, wrote, "He was their pope too."

in Washington, D. C., says, "The First Vatican Council 100 years ago stood for uniformity; the Second Vatican Council emphasized personal freedom. The changes were made gradually — for some, far too slowly, for others much too quickly. Today we find women in religious orders increasingly directing their own affairs without help from priests or bishops; priests expressing opinions on the possibility of a married priesthood and on the idea of having elected rather than appointed bishops; laymen speaking out concerning Catholic schools and parish organizations. On more difficult questions — population control and conscientious objection to war — the laity and religious alike, in increasing numbers, view papal instructions as but one of the many important components in arriving at personal decisions."

Theologian Karl Rahner, taking a backward look at the council he helped plan, commented, "Vatican II was only the beginning of the beginning."

Church Today

Robert McAfee Brown

*E*leven o'clock Sunday morning in America. Millions of people are sleeping, millions are reading the paper, millions are starting the marathon in front of television sets. But other millions—surprisingly in an era when God is rumored to be dead—are in church. The bells stop ringing, the organ prelude ends, the choir takes its place. The minister mounts the pulpit.

For the next hour a familiar scene unfolds. Comfortable people in uncomfortable pews are reminded that this is the Lord's day. They are led in prayer. They sing hymns with words drawn from another era. They confess their sins and ask forgiveness. They hear words of scripture. They listen to the choir. Sometimes there is a baptism, sometimes Communion. Nearly always there is a sermon, usually about God and usually lasting about twenty minutes. After the sermon there is an offertory (a muffled jingling of change, a loud crunching of bills), a prayer, a hymn, the benediction. Dependable as the Lord himself.

But a Sunday scene I have watched for some time in campus chapels across the land doesn't go that way at all. It's 9 a.m. and nobody is in the pews. Twenty-five to fifty students lounge in the chancel in slacks, blue jeans, bright skirts. Somebody begins to strum a guitar. Soon all are singing "Turn, Turn, Turn," or "Lord of the Dance," or even "Amazing Grace." The minister, his beard a little fuller than those of the rest, says that because this is the Lord's day be glad and rejoice! A youth in blue jeans reads from the prophets, Amos this time, indicting the people for letting "religion" be a cover-up for social irresponsibility, and ending with the words of the Lord: "I despise your feasts and take no delight in your

SINGING NEW SONGS UNTO THE LORD, *the church today gathers in joyous home services (below) and seeks fresh forms and symbols. Combining poetry and pop art (opposite), Corita Kent, a former nun, zestfully affirms God's presence in the world around us.*

GORDON W. GAHAN. OPPOSITE: SILK SCREEN PRINT, 1970

to believe in god
is to know
that all the rules
are fair
and that there will be
wonderful surprises
ugo betti
Corita

solemn assemblies . . . to the melody of your harps I will not listen. But let justice roll down like waters, and righteousness like an ever-flowing stream." Discussion: *Can* "justice roll down like waters" when bombs rain down like hail? Bread and wine are brought forward, a good big hunk of bread and a jug of wine. "Jeff, this is the body of Christ. Eat this so he can dwell inside you." Benediction: "The peace of our Lord Jesus Christ go with you." The chancel empties. The students go out to all kinds of callings: a group to support a farm workers' boycott, a committee to press for antiwar legislation, an organization to probe discrimination in housing and employment.

Just what *is* going on in the church in the United States today? Where is it heading? Not only have new ways of worship risen to shake time-honored patterns within the church. Teen-agers are witnessing for Christ in the streets or gathering in Christian communes about the nation, claiming, "The church is out, but Jesus is in." Others would redefine *church:* "The church is what happens when people leave the building. The church is found wherever teaching, caring, healing, reconciling, and challenging are going on in Christ's name—and sometimes where his name is never even mentioned."

TIME FOR TELLING IT LIKE IT IS: *The Reverend A. Cecil Williams packs Glide Memorial Methodist Church with San Franciscans tuned to his message that the church must be out in society working—not judging but joining. "The church has got to embrace* Shalom, *the peace that passeth understanding. Shalom: to receive all men in their fullest joy and sorrow." A decade ago this downtown church was dying. Today rock-jazz, light shows cast on whitewashed walls, counseling for young runaways, help for oldsters, forums on drugs and sex, task forces on urban problems mark its drive for relevance. A melodrama at its Intersection Theater (above) satirizes a fire-and-brimstone Bible thumper who revels in putting the fear of hell in a hippie.*

Not long ago you could describe the church in America with confidence. It was locatable, identifiable. You went into a village and there it was; or you drove into a town and there they were—such and such denominations on such and such streets. In a typical small city that we'll call Middleville you'd find Aldersgate Methodist Church at the corner of First and Main, its location indicating it was the first church in town. Red brick. Membership of 825. A choir, a missionary society, a thriving Sunday School, a sizable mortgage.

A couple of blocks back of Main Street you'd come to St. Clement's Roman Catholic Church, brownstone, imitation Gothic—its location indicating that St. Clement's came to Middleville later. Three priests living in the rectory, six masses per Sunday, from 6 a.m. Average of 1,750 communicants. Fourteen sisters assigned to the parochial school across the street. Bingo Wednesday evenings.

Continuing through town, you'd spot 16 other churches, from Greek Orthodox and Swedish Lutheran to African Methodist Episcopal and True-Seed-in-the-Spirit-Fire-on-the-Last-Day Pentecostal.

Returning today, you'd find most of the same buildings—but in some you wouldn't find the same things going on. Let's examine these changes by creating

IRA S. LERNER

a composite picture from many sources, many places, many experiences—a picture wholly imaginary, but in which every detail is real.

Listen to the choir director at Aldersgate Methodist: "We have trouble getting people out to a week-night rehearsal. Some of them have gotten hooked on ecology and spend their free time pressuring the city council to stop the pressed wood factory from dumping its wastes in the river."

Comments the factory manager: "I used to be active at Aldersgate Methodist, but that minister has half his congregation trying to put me out of business. He should preach the gospel instead of trying to mix religion and politics."

"That minister," the Reverend John Wesley Tipton, has his own problems: "One of our big givers pulled out because I said in a sermon that our zoning patterns discriminate against blacks. Before that a family left because they said I'd kept quiet too long about Viet Nam. You get it either way. And now our mortgage payments are eating into our medical missionary project in Uganda."

Father Murphy, aging senior pastor at St. Clement's, describes a different problem: "We used to have such a peaceful parish. We priests were the shepherds and the faithful were the sheep. But this new parish council—a group of laymen!—wants to make all the decisions. And young Father Francis, who helped organize the council, up and left the priesthood last month. He said the church was too slow in dealing with the 'issues of the day.' A good lad, but far too impetuous, far too impatient."

Reporting on the parochial school, Sister Theresa rues: "We just can't make expenses any more. We're going to have to phase out grades four through six and let the children go to public school. Too many of our people are hurling words like 'Catholic ghetto education' and taking their children out anyway."

One enthusiastic note comes from a young St. Clement's parishioner. "It was that ten o'clock rock mass that got me back. Finally, I said, this church is living in the 20th century. The traditional stuff leaves me cold."

PAUL BAILEY. OPPOSITE: RUSS BUSBY

A THOUSAND "DECISIONS FOR CHRIST" *were proclaimed each night when Billy Graham called for repentance in New York's vast Madison Square Garden. Echoing revivalists George Whitefield and Billy Sunday, the Baptist evangelist hammers home a simple message: America's battle is the battle for men's souls; the individual's choice is heaven or hell, society's is moral and spiritual renewal or anarchy and rebellion; there is no escape but conversion; "a divine computer" is busy recording even secret sins.*

Through mass media and the use of guest stars, Graham reaches more millions than any other preacher in the world. Like Oral Roberts, Tulsa's healing evangelist (right), he stands on the shore of an immense electronic Galilee.

"**I HAVE A DREAM.**" *Martin Luther King's vision of a nation uniting peacefully to break down racial barriers brought him a Nobel Prize —and martyrdom by an assassin.*

The young Baptist minister made a pilgrimage to the shrine in India honoring his hero Gandhi, apostle of nonviolent resistance. He cited Jesus' admonition to love one's enemies. To transform "dark yesterdays into bright tomorrows," he urged his people to "protest courageously, and yet with dignity and Christian love." Met by violence, he said, "I'm not going to use violence no matter who says so."

In 1965 he roused the nation's conscience with the civil-rights march from Selma to Montgomery, Alabama. White and black, clergy and laymen of many faiths surged forward by the thousands (below), singing "We Shall Overcome."

After a bullet struck him down, friends recalled Genesis 37:10, 20: "Behold, this dreamer cometh.... let us slay him ... and we shall see what will become of his dreams."

"How can you listen to God with all those guitars?" his uncle retorts. "We've got everything in church these days—long hair, noise, liturgy in English, social action—everything but reverence."

Rosalie McPhail, mother of six and a faithful communicant of St. Clement's for 30 years, can accept the new liturgy but is bitter about what's happening to the "unchanging" teachings of her church. "We were taught that birth control was a sin. So Don and I had six babies in the first seven years of our marriage. Then we were told things might change. So we waited. And when the pope finally and definitively said that birth control was *still* a sin, bishops in a lot of countries said Catholics could follow their consciences. What's the church coming to? Who's to know what's right?"

"We used to use 'Romanism' as a scare word in our sermons," the pastor of Aldersgate Methodist, Mr. Tipton, confesses to his dinner guest, Father Michael O'Reilly, assistant pastor at St. Clement's. "You remember—'Catholics are forbidden to read the Bible ... Don't let your daughter marry a Catholic.... They're just waiting until they get 51 percent of the vote to take over the country.' The Second Vatican Council cured all that."

The two men had conducted joint Lenten talks on the theme "The American Religious Experience." Speaking on alternate Wednesday nights in the other's parish hall, they agreed that in much of American history the Protestants got preferential treatment: The King James Version (Protestant) was compulsory in public school Bible readings; for too long few except Protestants were elected to high public office; Catholic immigrants had to live on "the wrong side of the tracks." The 1960 Presidential election marked a turning point. For the first time voters decided they could trust a Roman Catholic in the White House.

"The assumption that we are a Protestant nation can no longer be made," Mr. Tipton says, just a shade nostalgically, as if the idea of a Protestant nation had not been unattractive. Father O'Reilly agrees, just a shade eagerly. Both concur that we live in a pluralistic culture, with no one religious viewpoint dominant, and none likely to become so.

Already the two men are at work on the next ecumenical series, relating their churches' mission to a world in upheaval—a world their congregations may not be ready to face. Father O'Reilly notes Latin American bishops backing the peasant's call for land reform; Mr. Tipton sees the World Council of Churches defining the real split in today's world as not between East and West, Communist and non-Communist, but between Northern and Southern Hemispheres, rich and poor, white and colored. Their conclusion: The battle lines are no longer drawn between Catholic and Protestant churches but between those in them who accept the concept of widespread social change and those who don't.

"It's hard to find real areas of disagreement between us except the priesthood, the sacraments, and the papacy," comments Mr. Tipton. "That's still a lot," he

"COME OUT THE WILDERNESS,
*Leanin' on the Lord." Taking that
spiritual as a call to build new lives
amid New York's tenements, a team
of ministers and wives in the 1950's
moved in, opened storefront churches,
and worked with local leaders to
shape programs for inner-city needs:
narcotics clinic (Exodus House),
tutoring service, country retreat.*

*In the 1960's their East Harlem
Protestant Parish built a church,
aiding urban renewal that flanked
it with decent housing (opposite).
Involving youth with Jazz Vespers,
drama (From Beatnik to Bishop
portrays St. Augustine's struggles),
and other "happenings of God,"
the parish keeps pace with the 1970's,
refusing to let structures encase it.*

*In a parishioner's home (below)
plaid-shirted Hal Eads centers a
Bible study session on the rock opera*
Jesus Christ Superstar. *Members
of his Shalom Inc., a hive of learning
in an old delicatessen (left), spill into
streets for summer parades that note
the differences in his Puerto Rican,
Italian, and Negro flock, then break
bread together to signal its unity.*

hastens to add, "but while the theologians work on those problems, Mike and I make common cause on almost every other point.

"And who'd have thought I'd ever be calling a Roman Catholic priest by his first name!"

*B*ut not all is roses in the actual world beyond Middleville. Though the American church has survived this period of change; though mergers abound as regional Methodists pull themselves back into nationwide unity and Baptists try to bring North and South together; though the church has never shown more determination to work on inter-denominational problems, pain and confusion beset the land. These are birth pangs of hopeful beginnings, new directions that may demonstrate the continuing validity of the church in American culture. The abrupt shift from comfortingly familiar forms has upset many—just as the tenacity with which old forms have been retained disturbs others.

Men of good will differ as to how the ministry should confront our new age. Billy Graham, the well-known Protestant evangelist and unofficial chaplain to Presidents, stresses individual conversion to Christ as the cure for world problems; he feels that the minister's first priority is the gospel and that social and political involvement are secondary. On the other hand, such clerics as the Berrigan brothers, Roman Catholic priests, have gone to jail because they did get involved.

Norman Vincent Peale, minister of a large New York City church, holding unyielding optimism the keynote of the Christian life, is confident that one can successfully solve any problem if he takes it to God in prayer. Martin Luther King, Jr., minister of a smaller Atlanta church (until shot down at 39), told his followers that there is indeed power from

"NO CLOISTER BUT THE WARDS OF HOSPITALS," *ruled St. Vincent de Paul for the order he founded in 1633. Gone with the 1960's are winged bonnets and Normandy peasant garb Daughters of Charity wore 300 years; in simple drip-drys Sister Eugenia shares a smile in a Maryland children's home. Still conservative in dress (other orders have raised hems, even given up nuns' habits), this Catholic sisterhood holds to its call: "No monastery but the abode of the sick, no veil but holy modesty."*

404

God available to change things, but that it entails suffering and pain and the possibility of death.

Is there an image that might help us understand what is at the core of these divergent approaches? I believe there is: the image of the church as an institution that both *summons* and *sends*. The ritual people perform in church traditionally has been called "liturgy," a word whose original meaning was not religious at all. Rooted in the Greek words *laos* and *ergos*, it in ancient times literally meant "people's work"—public service. In this pristine sense, working for justice on a school board is liturgy just as much as singing a hymn or reciting a prayer.

The churches in America, however, often seem unclear which liturgy to stress—whether their role

CELEBRATING LIFE, *churches today often come out onto the sidewalks to invite all to rejoice. New York City's Washington Square Methodist Church hailed Christmas with a parade. After worship and a bread, wine, and cheese feast, celebrants donned costumes, lofted banners and balloons, and streamed through streets. They swelled their ranks in Greenwich Village (below), raised eyebrows in staider sections. "It's a sign of vitality," commented a minister. "We need continually to ask, 'Does the way we worship free us to express in the world of our day the love and joy which come to us in Jesus Christ?'"*

should be primarily that of *summoning* people into a special and somewhat exclusive relationship within the church, or of *sending* people to seek much broader relationships outside the church. Having been predominantly (though never completely) summoning communities in the past, they are presently being challenged to become (though never completely) sending communities in the future.

Encompassing both roles from the beginning, the church must find new ways to combine them in the context of our tumultuous age. Consider three propositions:

1. *The church is the summoning community.* It summons men to hear the message of Jesus, who embodied in a fully human life the presence of God on the human scene. It summons them to enter the community by baptism, signifying the washing away of the past and a new beginning. It binds them in fellowship through a ritual meal celebrating Jesus' sacrifice, his rising from the dead, and his presence amid those who gather around his table.

2. *The church is summoned for the purpose of being sent.* Committed to the brotherhood, Christians hope to be channels through whom God's love for them can be

poured out to others. The church is not just the place to which people come but the place from which they go to make what was true within true without.

3. *The church is sent to embody the love it has received.* If men learn about justice in church, they are to see justice done in the marketplace. If men discover that God does not differentiate between races around the Lord's table, then men must not differentiate between races around a restaurant table.

Here's a kaleidoscopic glimpse of ways in which groups today are reaching out and experimenting to strengthen both roles, summoning and sending:

Glide Memorial Church in San Francisco makes Sunday morning a rock-jazz and soul-music celebration, reasoning that if Christmas is true, it's time to rejoice; if Easter is true, there's nothing to fear; if Pentecost happened, there's power around. And Glide puts some of that power into bettering the world.

East Harlem Parish in New York City emphasizes three facets of membership: Sunday worship, Wednesday Bible study (keyed to a local problem), involvement in a community project. That turns an "only a Sunday Christian" into at least "a Sunday-Wednesday Christian," already a 100 percent improvement.

Four Kansas City churches run out of space. Instead of erecting four new buildings, they pool resources to put up one; St. Mark's houses Presbyterian, United Church of Christ, Catholic, and Episcopal worship and serves the black inner city with a Montessori preschool program. A growing new congregation in Burlington, Vermont, decides *not* to build a church, but to open a coffee house offering fellowship. In Anaheim, California, 50 young Christians join to man Hotline, a 24-hour phone service, and to visit those calling for help.

*I*n a world that is shaking every tradition, I recently found perspective in Jerusalem—spiritual home of American churches, for here Christianity began. On the hill of Tantur outside the city stands the new Ecumenical Institute for Advanced Theological Study. Scholars from all over the world come here to consider their divergent pasts and convergent futures—Americans, western Europeans, Japanese, Greeks, Russians, Indians. As they break bread together they can look out the dining room window and see Bethlehem—and an Arab refugee camp. Bethlehem, symbol of the coming of the Prince of Peace into the world. The refugee camp, symbol of continuing discord in that same world.

America too has its Bethlehems—places where hope and liberation and new possibilities shine through. But she also has her symbols of discord—the ghettos, the pockets of poverty, the ugly discrimination. The future of the church in America, as in the world, depends on the extent to which its people realize there is no real summoning to Bethlehem that does not go hand in hand with sending to the refugee camps. To be faithful to its origins and to its future, the church must not only comfort the afflicted but continue to spur the comfortable.

"GO FORTH INTO THE WORLD IN PEACE." *With a blessing for his departing flock, a pastor stands between sacred and secular worlds, confident that God unites both. As the 30,000 panes above him blend colors into a single cross, so men of faith raise earnest voices—distinct but increasingly in harmony—in the age-old dialogue with divinity.*

SECOND PRESBYTERIAN CHURCH IN FORT LAUDERDALE, FLORIDA; WAYNE MILLER, MAGNUM

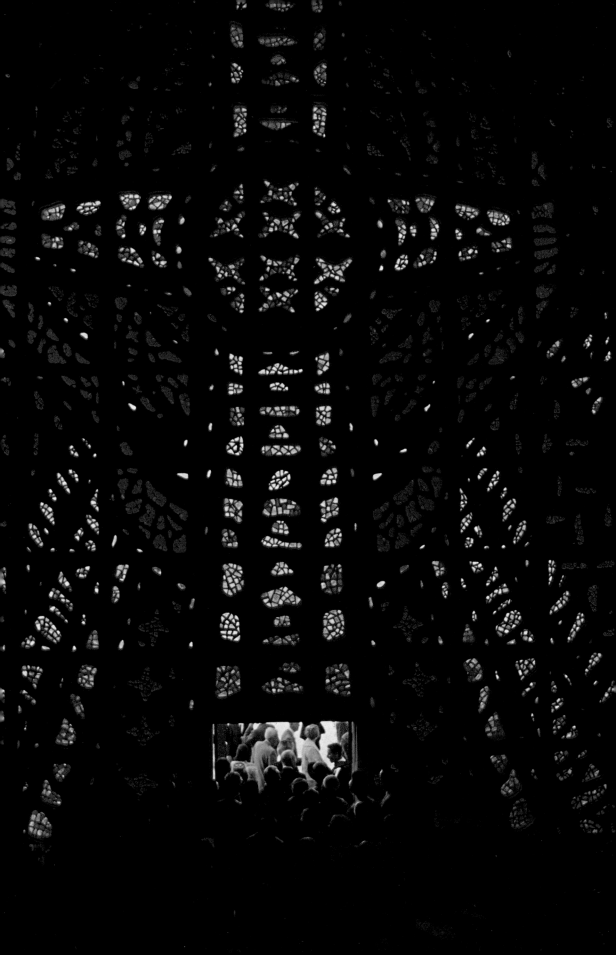

INDEX

Milestones of Faith
Across the Ages

Like an unrolling scroll, the chronicle of man's beliefs spans the horizons of history; some dates are approximations.

2500 B.C. Earliest roots of Hinduism: Aryan fire-sacrifice cult in Persia; Indus Valley culture at a peak

2000 Aryans begin migration to India

1750 Abraham leads his clan from Mesopotamia at Yahweh's bidding

1500-600 Vedas, holy writ of Hinduism, compiled from oral traditions

1240 Moses receives Ten Commandments

1000 David reigns in Jerusalem

950 Solomon builds the first Temple. At his death in 922 the kingdom splits into Israel (north) and Judah (south)

750-430 Hebrew prophets

600 Birth of Lao Tzu, traditional father of Taoism in China

587 Nebuchadnezzar razes Jerusalem; Jews exiled to Babylon until 538

563-483 Life of Buddha

551-479 Life of Confucius

540-468 Life of Mahavira, founder of Jainism in India

520 Jews rebuild Jerusalem's Temple

HINDUISM'S WARRIOR-GOD
Legendary Prince Rama, worshiped as an incarnation of the god Vishnu, battles a demon army at 12th-century Angkor in Cambodia. Unlike cathedrals built for worshipers, temples such as Angkor Wat served as symbolic abodes of the gods and as funerary temples for the ashes of kings.

SIGNS UNTO THE JEWS
Symbols of Judaism's ancient dialogue with Yahweh decorate a fourth-century gold-fused glass in Israel's National Museum. Found in Rome's Jewish catacombs, it shows six Torah scrolls between lions whose statues guarded synagogues. Below flicker two menorahs; such candelabra light rituals in Jewish homes.

275 B.C. Septuagint, first Bible in Greek, translated by Jews in Alexandria

246 Buddhism thrives in India under King Asoka and spreads into Ceylon

165 Maccabees rid Jews of Syrian rule

63 Roman rule imposed on Palestine

29 Theravada Buddhist writings compiled in Ceylon

6 B.C.-A.D. 31 Life of Jesus

A.D. 45 St. Paul spreads Christianity among the Gentiles

65 St. Mark writes the first gospel

70 Romans raze Jerusalem's Temple; dispersal of the Jews

100 Buddhism spreads into China

200 Mahayana Buddhist traditions take literary form in India

200 *Mahabharata* and *Ramayana*, once secular epics, now sacred Hindu texts

301 Armenia first Christian nation

313 Constantine legalizes Christianity

325 First Council of Nicaea rejects Arianism, formulates Nicene Creed

350-800 Golden age of Buddhism in China: 401 Kumarajiva translates Sanskrit texts into Chinese

405 St. Jerome completes translation of Vulgate Bible in Latin

410 Rome falls to Alaric; St. Augustine is inspired to write his *City of God*

450 Buddhism practiced in Burma, lower Thailand, Sumatra, and Java

496 Clovis baptized; Franks (dominant European tribe) converted to Christianity

A.D. 500 Buddhism begins to wane in India; learning centers survive into the 1100's

500 Jewish sages compile the Talmud

529 St. Benedict formulates his Rule

552 Buddhism reaches Japan

570-632 Life of Mohammed; Islamic era dates from his Hegira to Medina in 622

596 Pope Gregory I sends Augustine as missionary to England

632 Abu Bakr is first caliph; successors take Damascus, Jerusalem, Persia, Egypt

651 Moslem scholars compile the Koran

661 Muawiya begins Omayyad caliphate

680 Shiah Moslems break with Sunnites

711 Moslems invade India and Spain

731 Bede completes his *Ecclesiastical History of the English People*

THE PENITENT BUDDHA
A stone Buddha carved by unknown hands between the second and fourth centuries sits in perpetual fast in Pakistan's Lahore Museum. His body wasted from deprivation during an early, ascetic phase of his quest for holiness, Buddha eventually renounced such extremes, achieved enlightenment, and urged his followers to seek the Eightfold Path.

747 Tantric Buddhism reaches Tibet

750 Abbasids replace Omayyads; Moslem mystics launch Sufi movement

755 St. Boniface, "Apostle of Germany," slain by pagan mob in Frisia

786-809 Caliphate of Harun al-Rashid

800 Charlemagne crowned emperor by Pope Leo III

873-935 Life of al-Ashari, a leading defender of Moslem orthodoxy

414

CROSS OF CHRIST, ORB OF EMPIRE

Aglitter with gemstones and gold, this 12th-century German cross and orb in a Holy Roman Emperor's hand symbolized power. Artists showed Jesus holding such a device in token of his triumph over sin. This example of a favorite among Christianity's myriad symbols evokes bygone splendor for visitors to Vienna's Kunsthistorisches Museum.

A.D. 910   Fatimids establish a caliphate in North Africa, conquer Egypt in 969

1054   Christianity splits into Orthodox and Roman Catholic churches

1058-1111   Life of al-Ghazzali, who reconciled Sufism and orthodox Islam

1077   Emperor Henry IV bows to Pope Gregory VII's authority at Canossa

1095   Pope Urban II begins Crusades

1100-1300   Mahayana Buddhism flowers in Japan

1100-1400   Theravada Buddhism spreads over Southeast Asia from Ceylon

1135-1204   Life of Moses Maimonides, codifier of Jewish law

1209   St. Francis founds his Order

1215   Innocent III convenes Fourth Lateran Council; papal power at peak

1225-74   Life of St. Thomas Aquinas

1375   John Wyclif tries to reform the church; translates the Bible into English

1414-18   Council of Constance ends the church's Great Schism, which followed the "Babylonian Captivity" at Avignon

1415   John Hus, religious reformer, burned as heretic in Constance

1469-1538   Life of Nanak, founder of Sikhism, a blend of Hinduism and Islam

1492   Spanish Inquisition decrees baptism or exile for Jews

1517   Martin Luther posts his 95 Theses

1534   Henry VIII establishes the Church of England

1536   John Calvin publishes his *Institutes of the Christian Religion*

1540   Ignatius of Loyola founds the Society of Jesus—the Jesuits

1545-63   Council of Trent ushers in Catholic Counter-Reformation

1611   King James Bible

1620   Pilgrims land at Plymouth Rock

1692   Puritans in Salem, Massachusetts, hang 19 citizens as witches

1740   Religious revival sweeps America

1745   Reformer Mohammed Ibn Abd al-Wahhab founds Wahhabi sect

1750   Mystical Hasidic movement emphasizes joy in Jewish ritual

1772-1833   Life of Rammohun Roy, Hindu reformer

1791   U. S. Constitution guarantees freedom of religion for all

1810   First Reform synagogue founded in Seesen, Germany

1847   Mormons establish church state in American wilderness

1849-1905   Life of Mohammed 'Abduh, first of the Arab "modernists"

1850   Ramakrishna, Hindu mystic, preaches universal religion

1869-1948   Life of Mohandas Gandhi, Hindu champion of passive resistance

1870   First Vatican Council proclaims doctrine of papal infallibility on matters of faith and morals

1876-1938   Life of Mohammed Iqbal, Moslem poet and philosopher

ISLAM'S TOWER OF PRAYER

In Mohammed's day, Jews called believers to worship with the ram's horn, Christians used a bell or clapper. Hearing of these, Mohammed told an aide at Medina to call out from a rooftop. From that arose the minaret, a balconied tower like this over Cairo's al-Azhar Mosque.

1896   Theodor Herzl, founder of modern Zionism, writes *The Jewish State*

1897   Vivekananda, Ramakrishna's disciple, founds Hindu missions in the West

1947   Creation of Moslem Pakistan

1948   The State of Israel founded

1948   World Council of Churches formed

1950   World Fellowship of Buddhists

1962-5   Second Vatican Council

CLASH OF CREEDS: THE BLOODY CRUSADES

"God wills it!" Crusader cries seem to resound anew as Christian and Moslem duel in a 14th-century psalter in the British Museum. Knights *cruzada*, or "marked with the cross," sought for two centuries to take and hold Jerusalem's Holy Sepulcher, closed to pilgrims by Seljuk Turk warlords. Though the Crusading knights succeeded only briefly, West learned much from East; stonemasons' skills brought back to Europe found expression in great cathedrals.

Composition by National Geographic's Phototypographic Division,
JOHN E. McCONNELL, Manager.
Color separations by Beck Engraving Company, Philadelphia, Pa., Colorgraphics, Inc., Beltsville, Md., Graphic Color Plate, Inc., Stamford, Conn., The Lanman Company, Alexandria, Va., Lebanon Valley Offset, Inc., Cleona, Pa., Progressive Color Corporation, Rockville, Md., Stevenson Photo Color Company, Cincinnati, Ohio. Printed and bound by Fawcett Printing Corporation, Rockville, Md. Paper by Oxford Paper Company, New York.

ACKNOWLEDGMENTS
and REFERENCE GUIDE

The editors are grateful to the many individuals and religious organizations who assisted our authors and photographers in their field work in America, Europe, Africa, and Asia. In addition to the consultants listed on page 4, we benefited from the interreligious and interdenominational counsel of Dr. Mircea Eliade, University of Chicago; Finley P. Dunne, Jr., Temple of Understanding, Washington, D. C.; the Reverend Roger Ordmayer, National Council of Churches; the scholarship of Kay Bierwiler, New York State University; the Reverend John E. Lynch and Dr. Manoel da Silveira Cardozo, Catholic University; Andrew Y. Kuroda and Shojo Honda, Orientalia Division, Library of Congress; the translating of Harold Stewart, Kyoto, Japan, and of Marion Wiesel, who translated Elie Wiesel's essay on Judaism from the French; the editing of Wayne Barrett, calligraphy of Paul Breeden, and endsheets of Roger L. Schlaifer.

In shaping the volume's structure and themes, we found these works of general scope helpful: *The Religions of Man* by Huston Smith, *The Religious Experience of Mankind* by Ninian Smart, *Man's Religions* by John B. Noss, *Three Ways of Asian Wisdom* by Nancy Wilson Ross, and *Patterns in Comparative Religion* by Mircea Eliade. Well-thumbed reference works included *A Dictionary of Comparative Religion* edited by S. G. F. Brandon and *Dictionary of the Bible* by John L. McKenzie.

We gained insights into Hinduism and life along the sacred Ganges from *The Religion of the Hindus* by Kenneth W. Morgan, *The Wonder That Was India* by Arthur Llewellyn Basham, *The Spiritual Heritage of India* by Swami Prabhavananda, *The Hindu Pantheon* by Edward Moor, *The Dance of Shiva* by Ananda K. Coomaraswamy, *Hinduism* edited by Louis Renou, *A Source Book in Indian Philosophy* edited by Sarvepalli Radhakrishnan and Charles A. Moore, *Sources of Indian Tradition* compiled by William Theodore de Bary et al, *The Hymns of the Rigveda* by R. T. H. Griffith, *The Song of God: Bhagavad-Gita* translated by Swami Prabhavananda and Christopher Isherwood, and *Caste in India* by John H. Hutton. Useful sidelights came from *Island of Bali* by Miguel Covarrubias and *Trance in Bali* by Jane Belo.

For Buddhism we turned to *The Path of the Buddha* edited by Kenneth W. Morgan, *Buddhism: Its Essence and Development* by Edward Conze, *Buddhism* by Christmas Humphreys, *The Life and Times of Buddha* by Gabriele Mandel Sugana, *Buddha* by William MacQuitty, *The Buddhist Tradition* edited by William Theodore de Bary, and *Thai Buddhism, Its Rites and Activities* by Kenneth E. Wells. We consulted *Buddhism in Japan* by E. Dale Saunders, *History of Japanese Religion* by Masaharu Anesaki, *Shingon and Mt. Koya* (excerpt from *The Eastern Buddhist*, vol. V, no. 4) by Beatrice Lane Suzuki, *Essentials of Zen Buddhism* by Daisetz T. Suzuki, *The Way of Zen* by Alan Watts, and *Tibet* by Thubten Jigmi Norbu and Colin M. Turnbull. We learned more about Chinese religions in *The Way of Lao Tzu* by Wing-tsit Chan and *Confucius, the Man and Myth* by H. G. Creel.

We surveyed Judaism in *A History of the Jews* by Solomon Grayzel, *A History of the Jews* by Abba Eban, *Ancient Israel: Its Life and Institutions* by Roland de Vaux, *Between God and Man* from the writings of Abraham J. Heschel, edited by Fritz A. Rothschild, *The Standard Jewish Encyclopedia* edited by Cecil Roth, *The Jews* edited by Louis Finkelstein, *Eternal Faith, Eternal People* by Leo Trepp, *Great Ages and Ideas of the Jewish People* edited by Leo W. Schwarz, *A Book of Jewish Concepts* by Philip Birnbaum, *This Is My God* by Herman Wouk, *The Jewish Festivals* by Hayyim Schauss, *A Treasury of Jewish Holidays* by Hyman E. Goldin, *Our Living Bible* and *A History of the Holy Land* by Michael Avi-Yonah and others, *Portrait of Israel* by Moshe Brilliant, *Jerusalem* by Teddy Kollek and Moshe Pearlman, and *Kibbutz* by Melford E. Spiro. We quoted from *The Holy Scriptures according to the Masoretic Text*.

We traced the development of Islam in *History of the Arabs* by Philip K. Hitti, *History of the Islamic Peoples* by Carl Brockelmann, *Mohammedanism, An Historical Survey* by H. A. R. Gibb, *Cambridge History of Islam*, vols. I and II, edited by P. M. Holt, Ann K. S. Lambton and B. Lewis, *Islam — The Straight Path* edited by Kenneth W. Morgan, *The House of Islam* by Kenneth Cragg, *The Legacy of Islam* edited by Sir Thomas Arnold and Alfred Guillaume, *The World of Islam* by Xavier de Planhol, *Fez in the Age of the Marinides* by Roger Le Tourneau, *A History of Islamic Spain* by W. Montgomery Watt and Pierre Cachia, *Islam in Modern History* by Wilfred Cantwell Smith, and *Muhammadan Festivals* by Gustave E. von Grunebaum. Sir John Bagot Glubb provided a spirited military chronicle in his *Life and Times of Muhammad*, *The Great Arab Conquests*, *The Empire of the Arabs*, *The Course of Empire*, and *The Lost Centuries*. *The Sacred Journey* by Ahmad Kamal was our handbook for the hajj, and we compared passages in Koran translations by Mohammed M. Pickthall, Abdullah Yusuf Ali, and Arthur J. Arberry.

For the foundations of Christianity, we delved into *Invitation to the New Testament* by W. D. Davies, *The Founder of Christianity* by C. H. Dodd, *The Crucible of Christianity* edited by Arnold Toynbee, *Archaeology of the New Testament* by Jack Finegan, *Daily Life in the Time of Jesus* and *The Church of Apostles and Martyrs* by Henri Daniel-Rops, *The Interpreter's Bible*, *The Interpreter's Dictionary of the Bible*, *New Catholic Encyclopedia*, *History of Christianity* by Kenneth S. Latourette, *History of the Christian Church* by Williston Walker, *Church History* by Karl Bihlmeyer, *Patrology* by Johannes Quasten, *Butler's Lives of the Saints*, *Constantine and the Conversion of Europe* by A. H. M. Jones, *Antioch in the Age of Theodosius the Great* by Glanville Downey, *The Loom of History* by Herbert J. Muller, *A Treasury of Early Christianity* edited by Anne Fremantle, and *The Orthodox Church* by Timothy Ware.

Notable books on the rise of Christendom include *Augustine of Hippo* by Peter Brown, *Gregory the Great* by F. H. Dudden, *A History of the English Church and People* by Bede, translated by Leo Sherley-Price, *The Wandering Saints of the Early Middle Ages* by Eleanor Duckett, *The Birth of the Middle Ages 395-814* by H. St. L. B. Moss, *The Love of Learning and the Desire for God* by Jean Leclercq, *The Making of the Middle Ages* and *Western Society and the Church in the Middle Ages* by R. W. Southern, *Religion and the Rise of Western Culture* and *Medieval Essays* by Christopher Dawson, *A History of the Medieval Church 590-1500* by Margaret Deanesly, *Medieval Thought* by Gordon Leff, and *The Medieval Papacy* by Geoffrey Barraclough.

We reviewed the rise of Protestantism in *Here I Stand: A Life of Martin Luther*, *Erasmus of Christendom*, and *The Reformation of the Sixteenth Century* by Roland H. Bainton, *Christendom Divided* by Hans J. Hillerbrand, *The Reformation* by Owen Chadwick, *Renaissance and Reformation Movements* by Lewis Spitz, *The Christian Scholar in the Age of the Reformation* by E. Harris Harbison, *The English Reformation* by A. G. Dickens, *The Rise of Puritanism* by William Haller, *The Great Awakening in New England* by Edwin Scott Gaustad, *Revivalism and Separatism in New England, 1740-1800* by C. C. Goen, and *Righteous Empire: The Protestant Experience in America* by Martin E. Marty. Valuable in exploring special themes were *The Sacraments of Life and Worship* by John P. Schanz, *The Spiritual Conquest of Mexico* by Robert Ricard, *Apostle for Our Time* by John G. Clancy, *The Ecumenical Revolution* by Robert McAfee Brown, and *The Ancestry of Our English Bible* by Ira Maurice Price. We quoted from both the King James Version and the Revised Standard Version of the Bible.

Geographic staff members in many departments contributed to this book. See listing on next page. Many of the more than 940 issues of the GEOGRAPHIC portray lands where the great religions flourish. Consult the *National Geographic Index*.

The editors appreciate the advice of Dr. Robert C. Lester in selecting materials for this volume's scriptural portfolios and gratefully acknowledge permission to reprint excerpts from the following: *The Holy Scriptures according to the Masoretic Text*, copyright © 1955 by The Jewish Publication Society of America; *Revised Standard Version Bible*, copyright © 1946 and 1952 by Division of Christian Education, National Council of the Churches of Christ in the U.S.A.; *The Koran Interpreted*, translated by Arthur J. Arberry, published by The Macmillan Company, copyright © 1955 by George Allen & Unwin, Ltd.; *The Great Asian Religions* by Wing-tsit Chan et al, copyright © 1969 by The Macmillan Company; *Sources of Indian Tradition*, compiled by William Theodore de Bary et al, copyright © 1958 by Columbia University Press; *Sources of Chinese Tradition*, compiled by William Theodore de Bary et al, copyright © 1960 by Columbia University Press; and *The Hindu Tradition*, edited by Ainslie T. Embree, copyright © 1966 by Random House, Inc.